W9-ADI-448

BOOKS BY PAUL HEMPHILL

THE GOOD OLD BOYS

MAYOR: NOTES ON THE SIXTIES
  [IN COLLABORATION WITH IVAN ALLEN, JR., FORMER MAYOR
  OF ATLANTA]

THE NASHVILLE SOUND: BRIGHT LIGHTS AND COUNTRY MUSIC

THE
GOOD OLD BOYS

PAUL HEMPHILL

SIMON AND SCHUSTER · NEW YORK

SBN 671-21771-2
Library of Congress Catalog Card Number: 73-373
Designed by Eve Metz
Manufactured in the United States of America

1   2   3   4   5   6   7   8   9   10

*The author and publisher wish to extend their grateful acknowl-
edgment to the following for permission to reprint previously
published material:*

Cosmopolitan magazine, "The New Evangelism," November 1973.
Life magazine, "I Gotta Let the Kid Go," September 1, 1972.
New York Times Magazine, "Room at the Top," December 9, 1973.
"Motivatin' With Jabe," May 1973;
"Praise the Lord," December 1972.
Sport magazine, "A Football Factory Revisited," July 1973;
True magazine, "The Maddest Whirl of All," May 1972;
"What Ever Happened to Whatshername?" September 1972.

For my old man

CONTENTS

FOREWORD

One bright cold winter day in 1973 I landed at the airport in Charlotte, North Carolina, to give a talk at a women's school called Queens College. They had some sort of "Symposium on the South" going on that week, a favorite diversion on Southern campuses, and they had billed my lecture as "The Redneck Mystique." Lecturing here and there, by the way, isn't a bad way for a freelance writer to pick up a few coins now and then, and every time I do it I think of country singer Marty Robbins' description of working one-nighters: "Playing the road is like robbing Wells-Fargo; you ride in, take the money, and ride out."

At any rate, I found I was sharing the marquee with James Dickey, the poet-professor who was much in demand on the circuit due to the publication and filming of his Appalachia-oriented novel, *Deliverance*. Our pairing seemed justifiable enough, for a year earlier Dickey and I—along with such other Southern writers as Willie Morris and Marshall Frady and Bill Emerson and William Price Fox and Larry L. King, *et al.*—had been accused in an unsigned *Esquire* magazine essay of being charter members of a literary set known as the Pork Chop Conspiracy. In short, our happy little group of tape-wormed prophets was charged with capitalizing on the rest of America's fascination with the South. "It has been going on for some years," said *Esquire,* "and it pops out in funny ways, such as a New York cabbie or sort of intellectual listening to hillbilly music with wild, lustful eyes and slobbery, foamy lips." Flattered as I was to be mentioned in the company of such good writers as Dickey and the rest, I had been tempted to ask for equal time to counter with an essay about the Manhattanization of America.

But what the hell. Dickey spoke first that morning in the college auditorium, to a paying crowd of about 1,000, reciting and explaining his poetry and then closing his 90 minutes with a stirring reading of a piece of *Deliverance.* I took the podium that afternoon, to a nonpaying crowd of 500 drifters, repeating my Brother Dave Gardner jokes and tales of what a liberal Atlanta friend once called "those Southern creatures"—truck drivers, sheriffs, baseball bums, country singers, stock-car drivers, *et al.*—and then, in the late afternoon, Dickey and I sat in a spacious lobby, surrounded by college kids sprawled about the carpeted floor, and we answered their questions.

For all I know, the kid who pounced on me was the unnamed "contributor" who had written the *Esquire* piece. "You're nothing but a professional Southerner," he said, as the magazine had tried to say, "getting rich off writing about the crazies down here." Don't call my old man a crazy, I said. "Okay, weirdos," this kid said. And the debate cranked up. Finally, with it getting nowhere, I found myself suddenly having to fervently defend my decision to live in the South and write about it to some 19-year-old Queens College boy-friend as though I were standing before the Supreme Court. "I get a headache before I even get to the hotel every time I go to New York," I remember saying. "I live here because I love *and* hate to live here . . . I live here because it is the only place I understand. I'm too old [37, then] to start learning a new place all over again. I went to Philadelphia last month to interview about a newspaper columnist's job, and I wondered why I had even gone up there in the first place . . . All I know is truckers and hillbilly singers, if you insist on calling them hillbillies, and people who sell plastic Jesuses out on the highway. I don't understand Grace Kelly. I live in the South because I've got a sense of place here." The kid didn't ask any more questions. "That's pretty good," Dickey said, breaking the quiet. "A sense of place." I think some of them felt sorry for me.

The need for a book like this occurred to me at that precise moment, although I had started thinking about it a couple of years earlier when I returned as a columnist to *The Atlanta Journal* after a year as a Nieman Fellow at Harvard. The first thing I did upon returning to the paper was talk my way into a meandering two-month foray through the South. Driving the backroads and mailing back four columns a week, I wanted to capture the flavor of the region—to assemble a series of 1,000-word vignettes that would, as a body, characterize the South as it moved into the 1970s. "Hemphill Rediscovers the South," read the house ads as I made notes on the people and the places I was certain I would find: Dying Appalachian Town . . . Sat. Nite Road-house . . . Dirt Stock-Car Track . . . Moonshiner . . . Isolated Mountaineers . . .

It was frustrating. The dying towns were being revived, I found, by bland Chamber of Commerce types self-consciously concealing their drawls as they recited their mind-less Babbittry. The "fightin' and dancin' clubs" were being replaced by Holiday Inns. The stock-car tracks were now high-banked asphalt "superspeedways." The moonshiners had sold out to absentee syndicates. The isolated mountaineers sat in front of color television sets, laughing along with the East at the absurdity of "Hee-Haw." Over drinks one night in Greensboro, North Carolina, I told these things to a friend. "You're not 'rediscovering' the South," he said. "You're writing an epitaph to it."

God knows, we've been saying farewell to the South as a singular region long enough—paeans to a New South began with Reconstruction—but as a native son I have the distinct impression that this is it. No more tent revivalists blowing through town like rainmakers. No more fat-bellied sheriffs fleecing the Yankees out on U.S. 1. No more Crackers double-parking in front of the Grand Ole Opry House, coming out an hour later with a contract. No more governors with the audacity to tell the multitude they have "three friends in this world: God, Sears & Roebuck, and Eugene Talmadge." No more Junior Johnsons blowing out of the Carolina hills with a siren and flashing light to fool the Feds. It is all gone, or going, and about the only place where you can find that South these days is in the thigh-slapping novels of Carolinian William Price Fox (*Ruby Red* and *Moonshine Light, Moonshine Bright*).

This is not entirely bad, of course. There were aberrations in the soul of that Southern type first labeled as the "hell-of-a-fellow" by W. J. Cash in *The Mind of the South*. We began calling him the "good old boy" later—and to those questioning that label, I say if you don't know what a good old boy is, you never will—and he could be a mean son of a bitch: half-educated, vengeful, regressive, sadistic and, by all means, a racist. He could kill a dozen people with bad moonshine, then come out against fluoridation as a Commie plot to poison the water. He could teach his kids hymns on Sunday morning ("Red and yellow, black and white, they are precious in His sight . . .") and string up the church janitor that evening after prayer meeting. There is a theory, partly valid, that one reason racism in other parts of America was so late in being discovered was because our racists were more colorful than anybody else's racists. At any rate, there was a dark side to the good old boy, a side the South and the world could do without.

But what depresses me, as the South finally joins the Union, is that little of what was distinctive and good has been retained. The inevitable progress has put us into decent houses and fed our poor and educated us and even made us more tolerant of black people—however pragmatically—but it has also made us talk and act and dress and love and hate just like the people in, say, Denver. The good old boys are out in the suburbs now, living in identical houses and shopping at the K-Mart and listening to Glen Campbell (Roy Acuff and Ernest Tubb are too tacky now) and hiding their racism behind code words. They have forfeited their style and their spirit, traded it all in on a color TV and Styrofoam beams for the den, and I find them about as exciting as reformed alcoholics.

This book is a collection of some of the things I have written about the South, for newspapers and mostly for magazines, during the late 1960s and the early 1970s. The thread running through all of them is the theme I have expressed in this preface, and so the book is intended more or less as an epitaph to the good old boys. My favorite piece in here, and the most painful to write, is "Me and My Old Man." (When it was published, I am told, my mother ordered my old man to buy up every copy of the Sunday New York Times in which it appeared and to burn them in the backyard so she would not be embarrassed in front of her friends in Birmingham.) I am surprised to discover that I still like the collection of newspaper columns at the end, all of them written hastily in motel rooms all over the South while I was on that tour, and feel it is because that immediacy and freshness seems to endure. In few cases did I intend to update the writing, preferring to let it stand as it originally appeared.

PAUL HEMPHILL

St. Simons Island, Georgia
January 1974

"A good old boy . . . is a generic term in the rural South referring to a man . . . who fits in with the status system of the region. It usually means he has a good sense of humor and enjoys ironic jokes, is tolerant and easygoing enough to get along in long conversations at places like on the corner, and has a reasonable amount of physical courage . . ."

—Tom Wolfe, "The Last American Hero," in *Esquire*

But when the last moonshiner buys his radio,
And the last, lost wild-rabbit of a girl
    Is civilized with a mail order dress,
Something will pass that was American
And the movies will not bring it back . . .
—Stephen Vincent Benét, "John Brown's Body"

Bye, bye, Miss American Pie,
Drove my Chevy to the levee but the levee was
    dry;
Them good old boys were drinking whiskey and
    rye,
Singing, "This'll be the day that I die,
This'll be the day that I die" . . .

—Don McLean, "American Pie"

PART ONE

Growing Up

Redneck

1·ME AND MY OLD MAN

ICC is a-checkin' on down the line,
Well, I'm a little overweight
And my log book's way behind;
Nothin' bothers me tonight,
I can dodge all the scales all right;
Six days on the road
And I'm a-gonna make it home
tonight . . .

During the week, when he would be on the road somewhere, the days at home began with the muffled slapping of screen doors and the dull starting of cars and I could look through the living-room window and see the same thing happening up and down the block: the other men, wearing drab blue factory uniforms or plain gray suits, carrying lunch pails or briefcases, going off to shuffle somebody's papers or stand in somebody's production line, a stolid army of beaten men moving out under the orders of fate to absorb whatever the world had to dump on them today. And when I saw them return in the late afternoon, their lunch pails empty and their chalky faces more pinched than ever now, my throat would tighten and I would think, in the manner of a 12-year-old boy: *My old man is better.* Because I could not imagine then, nor can I imagine now, how a kid could get excited about a father like one of those; a father who wasn't visible, a father who merely functioned. And because I knew that during the same day, in that nine hours between the going out and the coming back of the other men of the neighborhood, my old man had been Out There—Ohio, Kansas, California? Outwitting the Interstate Commerce Commission? Saving a life on the highway? Overtaking a Greyhound?—a mechanized Don Quixote challenging the world, spitting into its face the juice of a Dutch Masters Belvedere cigar, giving it a choice of weapons and then beating it at its own game. And, too, because I was faintly aware that a snarling four-ton Dodge pulling a sleek aluminum trailer was, unlike the portfolio of the insurance agent or the samples of the salesman, something a kid could sink his teeth into.

Then, on a Friday afternoon, my mother would be standing at the kitchen sink and suddenly say, with a slight inward smile I did not yet know, "Your daddy ought to be home soon." And I would go out into the front yard, and shortly a mud-spattered red behemoth would top the long hill above the house, a clattering silver warehouse dragging behind, air brakes sneezing and air horns blasting at the wide-eyed kids gamboling on the sidewalks and the stunned old ladies swinging on their porches, the excitement swelling in my bony young chest until finally there was one final burp on the horns—*for me*—before the belching engine gasped and the whole rig shuddered to rest at the curb beside the house. "How-*dee*, I'm just so proud to be *hyar*," he would yelp, *Minnie Pearl at the Opry*, swinging down from the cab like a Tom Mix dismounting—sunburned face, grimy hands, squinty piercing pale blue eyes, greasy overalls and pirate boots, a half-chewed cigar jammed in the corner of the mouth—the leathery adventurer, King of the Road, home from the wars. Neighborhood kids crowding around, daring to touch the simmering tires, while my old man digs through dirty socks and Cleveland newspapers and kitchen matches to produce a novelty-shop key to the City of Akron for me.

A kiss for Mama and a hug for Sis, cowering, at the age of eight, in his presence. An hour in the vacant lot across the street, hitting mile-high pop flies until dusk over complaints from his wife ("Thirty-seven years old, acting like a *boy*"). Over supper, the stories of bad wrecks and truck stops and icy roads and outrunning the law and pulling the Appalachians at night, a born liar refining his art: "That fog was so bad I had to get out and *feel* that sign," and "They got watermelons in Texas grow so fast the bottoms wear off before they can pick 'em," and "She had a face so ugly it wore out two bodies." And afterward, a session at the old black upright piano in the living room, a self-taught Hoagy Carmichael: "I'd o' learned to play with the left hand, too, but before they could mail me my second lesson the Injuns shot the Pony Express." And finally to bed. Five days on the road, Birmingham to Akron and back, and he had made it home again tonight. He was my first hero and, the way things have been going lately, quite possibly the last.

So why, I am asking myself now, of all the good times we had together, why should I remember a bad one? The details are fuzzy. I must have been 18 or so. He came in off the road, but something was wrong. There was shouting. He talked about taking off again right after supper. My mother found a pint of booze in his overnight bag and, with hell-fire finality, flushed the contents down the toilet. He left. She and my sister were hysterical. *It's the son's place to go find him and talk to him.* Bewildered, I got into the car and raced into town, to the lot cluttered with tires and rusty engines and oil pans. I could see him sitting all alone in a dark corner of the cab, swigging from a pint, and when I pulled up and parked in the gravel beside the truck we tried not to look at each other. Blue lights laid a scary blanket over the lot. There was the desperate choking *putt-putt-putt* of a refrigerated trailer somewhere, broken by the occasional wail of a far-off train whistle, and after an interminable pause I heard myself say, "They're crying."

A gurgle, a cough. "Thought I'd get started early."

"How come you did it?"

"I don't know what you're talking about."

"Made 'em cry."

"What'd you come down here for?"

"Mama said. I don't know."

"She shouldn't o' done that."

"Well, she told me."

He tilted back his head and began draining the bottle, his Adam's apple quivering and some of the whiskey dribbling off to the side of his face, and his eyes looked like deep swollen ponds. I looked down and toed the gravel with my shoe while he finished. He sniffed and cleared his throat and then spoke in a frightened, vulnerable voice, a voice I had never heard come out of him before. "I'm not runnin' anywhere, son. There's a lot a boy don't know. I don't mean to make your mother cry, but sometimes a man's, a man's—" His voice had broken and when I dared look up at his face, bleached white by the pale lights on the lot, I saw that my old man, too, was crying.

Growing up is, of course, in line with the prevailing notion, a terrifying experience. But contrary to that notion, it is not accomplished in one giant symbolic leap, to the accompaniment of a dozen violins turning up full volume and the sudden brilliant dawning of a new and better day. Boys are not miraculously transformed into men through the first brutal sweaty defloration of a writhing rose in the back seat of a car, nor through the quaffing of eight beers without throwing up, nor by the stunning conquest of the neighborhood bully in defense of thy mother's good name—although all of those events play a part in the transformation, however exaggerated their importance later becomes. No, growing up isn't that simple. It may begin with a single pivotal moment, yes, but that moment is more likely to be one of defeat than of victory. In short, we must first discover that we do not know a goddamned thing and then take it from there. This has been known to take years.

Philosophically, theoretically, there is no good reason why it should take so long. Maybe one day we will become so sophisticated that we will modernize the whole system of maturing, organize it into an orderly program whereby young boys are weaned away from their childhood fantasies and patiently taught the mechanics of coping and therefore gently delivered into manhood as the grooming of young baseball players for the major leagues is done these days; you know, daily classes on Growing Up, regular weekly seminars with the old man where he speaks with candor about the times he screwed up and how it could have been avoided, and, finally, that ceremonial day of graduation into manhood just like the African tribes in television documentaries.

Maybe there are some fathers already doing that, but I doubt it. Because it is the nature of fathers to protect the old image, to set themselves up as infallible, and the nature of sons to swallow every bit of it. So growing up must begin with the shattering discovery that one's father is not perfect, a knowledge not easily extracted or believed; and then you have to learn why he is not perfect; and, finally, you are getting somewhere when you determine how he has managed to compensate for this pitiable shortcoming.

That night in the lot haunted me for a long time. It isn't easy to look on and see your father brought to his knees by mysterious devils. There was, indeed, "a lot a boy don't know." To this day—since it was a moment that embarrassed us both, we have never discussed it—I don't know who the devils were. That would have been around 1954, when he was 43: about the time the Teamsters were beginning to make it difficult for independent, free-wheeling "lease operators" of his breed to make it; about the time more money was needed for us than ever before, my having attained college age; about the time a woman's natural instincts for "respectability" were causing my mother to hack away at such issues as church and example-setting and a nicer house in a subdivision and a more secure job like driving a bus.

But the larger point is that I had seen him running scared, and it brought me to the first vague stirrings that life was not going to be easy or even fun; that life could be a bitch not above kicking you in the groin if you so much as winked at her; that there would be some terrible scars before it was done; that one day there would be a young boy looking up at me, wanting answers, and about all I might be able to give him in the way of solid advice would be to suggest he go into a clinch when they started working on the head. Here we had been working on the theory that he was un-beaten and untied, the last of the indomitable heroes, and now I knew differently and he knew I knew differently. From there, we began.

He has always seemed to treat everything that happened before he went into trucking as a prologue, which could explain why I have never been able to get much more than fragments about *his* growing up. I do know that he was born in 1911 at a tiny community in upper East Tennessee called Robbins, a then-prosperous but isolated mining and lumbering town that sat on a branch of the Southern Rail-road between the birthplace of Sgt. Alvin York and the in-augural dam on the Tennessee Valley Authority system. Left fatherless at the age of eight, he got on a train seven years later with his ailing mother and a sister and they went to live with relatives in Birmingham, never to return to the hills. He lacked a semester of English to graduate from high school, but instead of returning to finish—he has said he was a good student and could have gone to college if the money had been there, borne out every time I see him arrogantly complete the Sunday crossword of *The New York Times* with a ballpoint pen—he cut out for the Midwest to work at hard labor on the Rock Island Line. After a year or two he went back to Birmingham and married Velma Nelson, one of a husky coal miner's six children, whom he had met one night while hanging around the steps of a Baptist church.

The Depression had hit rock bottom by then, and it was a scramble to stay alive. For a while he and a Greek named Mike Manos set up a news-butch operation on the daily excursion train running between Birmingham and Chattanooga —splitting $50 a week from the proceeds of newspapers, soft drinks and snacks at a time when most men felt lucky to earn $15—and later on he established a back-breaking one-man coal-mining business. I have heard some of the stories: how he and my mother won a drawing that gave them a free wedding on the stage of the Ritz Theater and a night in the honeymoon suite of the Thomas Jefferson Hotel, how she would get up well before dawn to make sandwiches to be sold on the train, how he painted the doctor's house to pay for my birthing in 1936. I am sure that much of what he is today was shaped by those times, which is true with the great bulk of Americans who went through the Depression, but he is served well by a faulty memory of the whole thing.

Then, on a March morning in 1941, I awoke to the sounds of fierce sawing and hammering in the backyard. He was building wooden sideboards for a borrowed trailer and converting his dump truck to pull it, and with a war coming on he was announcing plans to go into trucking. "There's gonna be a lot of stuff needs haulin'," he said, "and I'm gonna help 'em."

It was the beginning, in a true sense, of his real life. He was born to drive a truck on the open road—a hard worker, a gambler, a fast talker, an adventurer with the eagle eyes and razor instincts and idiotic courage of a moonshine runner—and over the next 20 years he was to become something of a legend in that grim outback underworld of truck stops and loading docks and ICC checkpoints and cut-rate gas stations. Having a mountaineer's inbred distrust of big companies and organized labor, preferring to make or break on his own merits, he set himself up as a "lease operator." This meant he was a hired gun, a freelance trucker not on salary but on commission. The company, thus free of responsibility, couldn't care less if he was overloaded or otherwise illegal in the eyes of the ICC; if he got caught, that was his problem. Just deliver the stuff by Tuesday morning.

You can see, then, how quickly my old man learned the location of every weight station on the continent, not to mention the sleeping habits and personal financial conditions of the men who ran them. He would stand there at the dock and tell them to fill 'er up until she was bulging—with steel, tires, explosives, helmets, uniforms, whatever—and take off in the middle of the night, under the cover of darkness, like a bootlegger off on another run, twice as heavy as some states allowed but also twice as hungry. He knew every road in America by heart, and where to find the good coffee and the cheap gas, and how to make a gentleman's arrangement at a truck stop in regard to somewhat clandestine cargo; and it seemed to be about all a man had to know. By the time the war had blown over, he had paid cash for a three-bedroom house and a '46 Dodge automobile ("The 78th Dodge bought in Birmingham after the war"), started taking us on summer vacations to Florida and hired a driver to run a second rig. Those were the days of unblinking idolatry: that glorious time of puberty when I tried to wear my cap like his, and affected his hillbilly twang, and wondered what it took to be able to smoke and chew a cigar at the same time, and marveled at his ability to back a heaving trailer into the tightest hole. On summer evenings, at dusk, there was the great excitement of stuffing fresh socks and underwear into a bag and waiting impatiently for him to announce it was time to be going. "Now, Paul, I don't want him growing up to be a truck driver," my mother would say. "It's good enough for me," he would snap, "and I notice you ain't starving."

And a large part of growing up would begin to take place as we hit the open road, father and son, discovering the world and discovering each other together. Sleeping all day in the simmering Southern heat and riding all night to the songs of the whistling tires and the all-night country radio stations ("Ol' Ernest Tubb sings like a bullfrog, don't he?"). Seeing the big tankers parked at the Mobile docks, the traffic in Atlanta, the tarpaper shacks in Mississippi, the cattle in Texas and the mist along the Blue Ridge. The truck stops at 3 o'clock in the morning, with bug-eyed truckers so high on bennies they couldn't feed the pinball machines fast enough. "Your boy there looks just like you, Paul," and, in response, "Well, the kid can't help it." Donora, Pennsylvania, where Stan Musial was raised. Nashville, where the Opry was. Pittsburgh, where the Pirates played. Blowing past a Greyhound on a straightaway, walking around a curve to see if the scales were open, standing on the running board to relieve ourselves while crawling up the Smokies, the jouncing of the cab and the pinup overhead bringing a curious new sensation to the groin. The mysterious hand signals exchanged with passing truckers, the wrecks and near-wrecks, the Cardinals game from St. Louis broadcast by Harry Caray, the black laborers begging to help unload at the docks at New Orleans. "Naw, ain't got but a partial load o' tires on," to the ICC inspector and, a quarter-mile down the road, grabbing another gear, "Them boys just don't take their work serious enough." We had that to hold us together, and baseball—more than once we stood through Sunday doubleheaders to watch the Birmingham Barons play, then rushed home to work on my fielding until dark—and it seemed like a dream that would never end.

The breaking away began, of course, with that confusing night when I found him with his defenses down. We didn't have the trips together or the baseball any more—I had been jolted awake to the fact that I would never make it to the major leagues when I lasted only five days in spring training with a pathetic Class D club—and now I was cutting the umbilical, going off to college. In the college atmosphere, lost in a crowd of people whose fathers were doctors and architects and owners of legitimate businesses, I began to develop the notion that my old man was somebody to be ashamed of. It struck me for the first time that there had never been a book around our house, that my old man's English was atrocious and that his business associates tended to be unlettered itinerants spending their dim lives driving other people's trucks from one warehouse to another. I painfully learned that he, being a man of instinct rather than intellect, had been incapable of instructing me in any of the social graces now facing me, including sex. It occurred to me that while my friends were being staked to automobiles and off-campus apartments and fraternity initiation fees, I was having to serve up chow in a series of dining halls and work at summer jobs simply to stay in school. This was, remember, the 1950s, when we of the Silent Generation were in college for girls, football, parties and secure positions with big companies. Now my old man was no longer a character or a folk hero or even a champion to me; he was, as we say, tacky.

Which is not to say I had not been reminded of this before. He had always been the maverick in that great sprawling body on my mother's side referred to as The Family. One uncle sold insurance. Another was a career man with Internal Revenue. Another was a mechanic. The other uncle was, the best I could determine, a freelance inventor; but then, his wife hadn't let him out in years. It was a huge family, one that had in the early years knelt at the feet of my maternal grandfather—an imposing white-haired patriarch who reminded me of John L. Lewis and was respectfully called "Daddy Nelson"—and my old man had set the ground rules very soon after his marriage into The Family by refusing to cater to "the old man," as he doggedly called him. His irreverence on that score, and on dozens of others, had made him an outcast, a role he seemed to relish. He drank. He didn't believe in church. He talked loud and told blue jokes. He stated that the inventor had more brains than anybody in the bunch, he implied that being a deacon in the church was as good a way as any to sell insurance policies, and he was unable to fulfill his duties as a pallbearer at one relative's funeral when he warmed up to the task with a few snorts of bourbon on an empty stomach. He worked with his hands, often outside the law, and to a group bent on attaining respectability—garden clubs, Sunday school, college, newer cars and bigger houses—he was, more often than not, a pain in the ass.

Meantime, I had finished school, gotten married, begun to write sports and to understand that I hadn't seen much of the world at all. I had hitchhiked around a lot in pursuit of baseball clubs needing second basemen and I had covered a lot of miles in a truck with my old man, but it had been like running in place. After spending a year in France with an Air National Guard unit during John Kennedy's "Berlin Crisis," a year of enforced leisure in which I introduced myself to literature and found that a lot had happened in the world in 1946 besides the Cardinals' winning of the World Series, I returned knowing that I had to do two things: quit writing about games, and get the hell out of Birmingham. By 1965 I found myself a daily columnist on *The Atlanta Journal,* featured prominently on the second page and free to write about anything—politics, Vietnam, sports, strippers—a sort of Jimmy Breslin, Dixie branch. But the real issue then was, of course, civil rights, and I found I was poorly equipped to handle it. I didn't have the education or experience or, most important of all, the personal association with black people.

I had been raised by a Negro maid named Louvenia, never thinking to ask why she took her lunch on the back porch, and had grown up throwing rocks and jeering at a lanky fellow known as Nigger Charles as he ran from school to the shantytown that sat on a pile of scarred red dirt beyond our shaded neighborhood in Birmingham. My old man had always said they were shiftless and smelled bad and were not to be associated with, but the only opportunity I had to investigate that was when I played semipro baseball in Kansas with a dusky little local outfielder named Hank Scott; he turned out to be energetic, bright, deodorized and, to my astonishment, more of a soul brother to me than some of the white teammates from places like Chicago and St. Louis.

No, Louvenia and Nigger Charles and Hank Scott represented the only connections I had in what they were beginning to call the black community, unless you want to throw in the swarthy laborers who had always met my old man at the docks to help unload, and I had some homework to do. Not that I was alone in the South. Maybe the kids who grew up on a farm where there was nobody else to play ball with except the sharecropper's sons had prior relationships with the Negro, but most of my friends had never faced anything like that. We had blindly accepted the proposition that Negroes were inferior and should therefore be kept in their place—the back of the bus, the balcony of the theater, the "nigger bleachers" at the ballpark, and in their own churches and schools and restaurants—and now we had to make a decision: fight desegregation or work for it.

I must say that my old man made it easy for me. During the time I was living under his roof he had seldom felt it necessary to comment on the balance of the races, but the sight of those uppity folks actually demanding service in

white Southern restaurants during the early 1960s drove him
into a frenzy. This wasn't my old man. It was somebody else.
An autographed 8 x 10 of George Wallace showed up on
the family piano. He quit hiring blacks to help him unload—
at his age rolling into his trailer tires that sometimes weighed
500 pounds. He applauded the Birmingham Barons' decision
to drop out of the Southern Association rather than play
integrated baseball. He talked about reactivating his father's
old squirrel rifle, which hadn't been fired in at least 40 years.
He discussed moving out of the old neighborhood. Once, on
a visit with me when I was temporarily separated from my
wife, he raved on and on about Communists and niggers and
Catholics and Jews without addressing himself to my
anguish. A trip to visit the folks in Birmingham invariably
developed into an incredible one-way conversation: "This
old boy out in Texas was telling me all about Jackie and
those Secret Service agents . . . That's all right, I know old
Rastus McGill won't let y'all say anything when you get out
of Atlanta, but everybody knows he's getting paid by Moscow
. . . You talkin' 'bout Martin Luther Coon? . . . Now that
Strom Thurmond, that's a man for you . . ." Ralph McGill
paid from Moscow? Jackie Kennedy pleasuring the Secret
Service? I mean, there are times when it doesn't take an
expert to sort out the truth. I became a liberal, through the
back door.

During the last of the 1960s, then, our relationship, what
there was left of it, caved in from what should have been
peripheral pressures. He became just as convinced I was
a freaky Communist as I was certain he was the last of the
great racists, and one thing I did that I regret was to say it
in my column. Not because I consider it an especially cheap
shot to talk about your father like that in print or because it
might have disturbed him, but because it made him polarize
even further. Funny things were happening in The Family.
After being bombarded by Freedom Riders and Martin
Luther King and church bombers and police dogs, it seemed

as though everybody in Birmingham was preparing to give the world 24 hours to get out of town. There had been a time when my old man's audacious verbosity made him tacky, but now The Family was rallying around him as though he were some kind of proletarian prophet. "Well, now, Paul was telling me he heard over in Louisiana the other day how the nigras are being paid, yes, *paid*, to, ah, go looking for young white girls and, ah . . . ," said with some authority because my old man was, after all, as everybody knew, the one in The Family who traveled a lot and talked to different people.

Birmingham became a nice place for me to stay away from, what with one cousin being promoted to an executive position with the John Birch Society and my sister's husband building a house on an elevated cul-de-sac and actually saying, if I remember correctly, that he would be better able to "get a bead on 'em when they start coming." Jesus. How the hell do you talk with them, reason with them, when their nostrils are flaring and their mouths are clucking while we all sit around the color television watching Daley's cops riot in Chicago at the convention? *Communists, everyone of 'em.* Enraged: Hell, they're just kids. Calmly, smugly: *Prove they ain't Communists, then maybe I'll believe it.* Somebody, help.

> ". . . never even a book in our house when I was growing up, and Auburn was better known then for its football players and engineers than for its writers and thinkers. So I feel, in a sense, the Nieman program was made for somebody like me. I feel I can come to a better understanding of the South and people like my father by spending a year away from it all, in the academic atmosphere of Harvard . . ."

Each year a dozen newspapermen from all over the country are selected as Nieman Fellows, to spend a school year doing whatever they want to do at Harvard: reading, attending lectures, sleeping, drinking. The year is intended to put a spit-shine on promising young journalists, and it can be a good year if you handle it right. I mean, you don't have to lift a finger for a whole year. At the suggestion of Dan Wakefield, the writer, who had been a Nieman once, I started filling out applications in the spring of 1968. I had the vague notion that maybe a year away from the South and The Family would help me put some things into perspective—"Give 'em some of that poor-Southern-boy stuff and you're in," I was advised—but mainly I was running from the writing of six 1,000-word columns a week. I mentioned the possibility of a year at Harvard to my old man once, and all I got was a knowing smile. Then a wire came, saying I had been one of those picked, and I called Birmingham with the great news. "Mama, I won that fellowship," I yelled over the phone. "What school did you say that was?" she replied. "*Har*-vard, Mama." In the background I could hear my old man's response, and it didn't take much imagination to guess what he might be saying. *Went ahead and joined the damned Party, didn't he?* As far as he knew, the Nieman Fellows was an organization of Communist fags.

The joke was, as it turned out, on both of us. The atmosphere at Harvard was so academic it was overwhelming, eventually sending me into a shell I was unable to come out of. Among my fellow Niemans were two Moscow correspondents, a former Pulitzer reporter and a fellow who had once run errands for Scotty Reston at *The New York Times*. While many of the others had been fighting in the trenches of the civil rights push five years earlier, I had been picking up ten bucks a game as official scorer for the Augusta Yankees of the Class AA Sally League. Talk about your cultural shock. I was pretty good at drinking beer at Cronin's, but when they broke out the sherry at the Faculty Club and Galbraith started in on the industrial state I began getting a headache.

But there was more. It dawned on me, after too many

boring cocktail parties with too many terribly proper New Englanders, that what I was really missing at Harvard was the sweaty passion for life I had always taken for granted while growing up in the South. There was a superficiality, a sterility, in Cambridge—even among most of the Southern kids I met, who were, after all, from a different South than I—which was neatly packaged for me by a lady at one of those parties who told me, straining to be sympathetic, that she had been to the South and found it to be not nearly as bad as everybody thought: she and her husband had spent the night in Atlanta on the way to Miami Beach, and found the South to be altogether delightful. So I was able to develop a handy catch-all theory about life: that there are two kinds of people in the world, those who live life and those who ponder it. And I learned that a good way to break the routine at the parties was to get off in a corner and regale them with highly embellished stories about my old man and Junior Johnson and Roy Acuff—*How quaint. Tell us about Johnny Cash's years in prison*—and the time to go back home didn't come soon enough. The year at Harvard was the most profitable year I ever spent, for the wrong reasons.

Going back, then, I had a new frame of reference within which to view my old man. I had taken some 15 years to finally accept him for what he was—to discover why he wasn't perfect and then to determine how he made up for not being perfect. I knew, now, that I had to overlook his racial hangups—we would just have to ride that one out, it being too late for him to be changed—and search for the larger truths he had left me: an involvement with and a passion for life, a willingness to take on the world if necessary, the courage to endure. That's the word—*endure*—a word not so fashionable as it once was. Instead of bending or running when the blows came pouring down on his head —his wife harping on security and "respectability," his children acting ashamed of him, the unions killing his way of life—he stood and fought and, if forced to retreat, was still standing there, bloody, throwing rocks and cussing, when they found him. About all a man should be asked to do, when it comes to raising sons, is somehow to see that there is a slight improvement in the species. It's a hell of a burden.

He is 62 now, and those riotous days and nights of scrambling on the open road are faint memories. In the mid-1950s he chose to make it on his own rather than join a union or go with a big company, and by 1961 the unions were so strong that it was all over for the independent. Today he does some driving and bidding and odd jobs—"nigger work," he calls it—for a Syrian in Birmingham who owns a surplus tire company, lives in an $80,000 house and can't begin to understand what makes my old man tick. He and my mother live serenely in a comfortable brick house where there is an expensive organ for him to play, as well as a piano; they have plenty of friends their age, and they go to Florida several times a year to inspect the converted swampland they plan to retire to in two or three years. Not everything is right with him—his job is dull, and his wife makes more money working at the Social Security office than he ever made trucking—but he manages to keep up a façade.

Two weeks before the 30th anniversary of his entry into trucking, we took a trip together. A fellow in Louisville was selling out his tire business and my old man was going up to take the rest of the tires off his hands. On a Saturday afternoon we left in a pitiful faded red truck—no fuel gauge, leaky heater, bad brakes, no radio, dusty lopsided trailer behind—and for a while, chugging up the trough into Middle Tennessee, both of us were trying to pretend it was the same. "Call that Jew Overdrive," he cracked, cutting the engine to coast down a hill. We stopped off to watch the Opry from backstage—"Sure wish that pretty Jean Shepard ['A Dear John Letter'] was here"—before plugging on toward Louisville. From eight in the morning until two Sunday afternoon he loaded huge surplus aircraft tires into the trailer, in the rain, with the help of a couple of white boys and an aging Negro named Clem Miller ("Yessuh, yo' Daddy can go almost as hard as I can"), and after some sleep at a cheap motel across the river in Indiana we got up around two o'clock in the morning and headed back.

It wasn't really the same anymore. All I had to do was look at the truck he was driving, to observe the meaningless work he was doing, to see that. I noticed, when we stopped for breakfast at an obscure roadside diner, that he had trouble reading the menu. But we tried, passing a bottle of Scotch back and forth, laughing at the stories, creaking through Nashville as the streets jammed with Monday morning traffic: "Yeah, that time there was this fellow just handed me $150 cash up in Delaware and told me where to deliver these aircraft parts in Atlanta. Saved him some money, made me some . . . At least two and a half million miles without an accident chargeable to me . . . Hell, if you're driving a Greyhound they can fire you just because some little old lady didn't like your looks . . . I was representing all 82 of the drivers at Alabama Highway, see, and when I told this union organizer we didn't want to join up, he just looked at me real cold and said, 'Well, we can't be responsible,' and I said, 'For what?' and he said, 'If you get a brick through your windshield somewhere.'" And about the time the ICC almost nailed him in California, where he had some unpaid fines hanging: "Didn't want 'em to know my name, so I told 'em I didn't even have a license, was just helping out my buddy there who had passed out in the truck after drinking all night. 'Yeah, I'm from Tennessee, just came along to see California, can't get back home fast enough,' I told 'em. Never bothered to look in the truck. Think he just got tired of hearin' me talk." And disgust for the new breed of trucker: "Some of 'em been to college. Got credit cards now, company rigs, and if they break down they just call collect and have 'em send somebody out to fix it."

We got back into Birmingham in the afternoon, dropped

off the load of old tires and went by the house. While we waited for my mother to come home from work, we sat alone in the cool, darkened living room that I have never known and he sipped a beer and entertained me at the organ. "Mama's taking lessons," he said, "and I just watch and do what she does. Teacher says he's gonna start chargin' double." Then I said something about how it sure wasn't like it used to be, his work and his life, not knowing how he would take it, and he quit playing and slowly turned around on the bench. "If something was to happen to your mother, I'd be back out on the road in a minute," he said. "There's days I'll be sitting on the yard downtown, nothing to do but drink bourbon and chase it with a six-pack, and out on the expressway I'll hear some old boy in a rig whistle and get another gear, and it gets to me. Hell, yes, I miss it. It's the only thing I ever wanted to do. Tell your boy, David, he better hurry if he wants to ride with me."

2·"I GOTTA LET THE KID GO"

Cruising the barren streets one spring morning, 18 years after the fact, I found it ludicrous that as a boy my life could have been rearranged in such a place—that I would still be haunted, all these years later, by a dream shattered in a town like Graceville, Florida. "Nobody ever stops here on purpose," I was once told, and although the judgment seemed a bit flippant—people do, after all, come from miles around on Sundays to eat fried shrimp at the Circle Grille—it had the ring of truth. Graceville (pop. 2,500) squats just inside the Florida line, in the company of Noma and Chipley and Miller Crossroads, like a turtle broiling in the sun; the monotony of the oppressive Florida Panhandle broken only by occasional swirls of wind which lift the fine brown sand from the sidewalks and scatter it against the weathered frame buildings. Typical of most tiny Deep South farming communities, with their pickup trucks and feed stores and tattered storefront awnings under which leathery old white farmers share the shade with mute black laborers, Graceville is presided over by a bleak gray concrete hulk identified on picture postcards as the World's Largest Peanut

Sheller. Indeed, most of the changes that have taken place since the mid-1950s have been regressive. The movie house is closed now, leaving the Little Stag Pool Room as the center of entertainment, and to me there was a more poignant reminder of what had been lost: the sandwich-board sign that would have been propped up in the middle of the main intersection on another April morning—"BASEBALL TO-NITE, Oilers vs. Crestview, 7:30, Sportsman Park"—was there no more.

"Be right with you." Mike Tool was behind the counter at Cash Drugs, filling a vial with pills for a hunched old woman in a wilted cotton print dress and matching sunbonnet. When the Graceville Oilers were members of the Class D Alabama-Florida League during the 1950s, making Graceville the smallest town in professional baseball, Mike Tool was in charge of selling tickets and buying balls and paying the players and handling anything else that came up. "Medicare day, busiest day of the month," he said when the woman had left. "Say you played for the Oilers?"

"In 1954. Spring of '54."

"Hemphill." He tried to remember. "There were so many."

"I didn't last but a week."

"Guess that explains it. Writer now, you say?"

"In Atlanta."

"Writer in *Atlanta*," he said, arching his eyebrows. "Lot of boys had to go to work. *Hard* work. Know what I mean? Bob Odenheimer, he works in a plant or something up in Illinois or Indiana. I forget which. Comes through just about every summer on vacation." Another customer was at the counter now, wanting a prescription filled. Tool flattened out the wrinkled scrap of paper, squinted to read the scrawl, then reached for a jug of capsules. "Sometimes," he said, "it's like the Oilers never happened."

Later, having driven across the railroad tracks to the ballpark, I waded through the weeds to where second base used to be and it started to come back—Joaquin Toyo chattering in broken English from shortstop, Al Rivenbark doing the splits at first base, manager Cat Milner drawling that all you had to do in baseball was "hit the ball and run like hell." Now the park lay like an abandoned farm. The light poles had been moved around for football, the rickety frame bus-shelter dugouts were gone, the tin left-field fence was buckling under foliage, and the hand-painted letters saying SUPPORT GRACEVILLE OILERS BOOSTER CLUB were flaking off the concrete-block wall that had been our centerfield fence. Even in its time it was one of the worst parks in organized baseball, and now it was a washed-up whore. What a place it had been, I thought, to join the company of men.

The game of baseball doesn't magnetize kids today as it did 25 years ago. Basically a measured and innocent diversion, baseball simply doesn't offer the pizzazz to grab a generation raised on color television and automobiles and weekends at the lake. The game hasn't changed, the kids have. Early on, they become sophisticated to a degree of cynicism which leaves no time for the unblinking worship of heroes that baseball always thrived upon. They play Little League ball, sure, but by the time they reach puberty they have had it all—the best equipment, manicured parks, publicity, night games, crowds of 1,000—and there is no need to go on.

For those of us born in the 1930s, however, it was an entirely different matter. Our pleasures were simple—double-dating on the trolley, roller skating, bowling, spending marathon Saturday mornings at the neighborhood picture show rooting for Hopalong Cassidy and the Green Hornet—and one of those pleasures was baseball. The game may never have it so good as it did in 1948, when five cities had at least two major league teams (New York had three) and out across the land there were 59 minor leagues; most of them in the South because of its warmer climate. Surrounded by baseball, we played it in the morning, watched it in the afternoon and listened to it at night.

I was fairly typical of my generation of Southerners, I suppose. I got hooked on the game when I heard Harry Caray's tense description of Enos ("Country") Slaughter of the Cardinals winning the '46 World Series over the Red Sox by scoring all the way from first base on a single. Baseball became my life one day the following spring when a young YMCA worker named Bill Legg came by the Minnie Holman Elementary School in Birmingham to give birth— amid cracked Arkansas Traveler bats and scarred baseballs and smelly sneakers—to the Woodlawn Blues.

Those were marvelously innocent times. Spring training began on Christmas Day, when my cousin and I gingered onto the lot behind the fire station to try out our new spikes. By mid-January I was taking the trolley downtown to the Thomas Jefferson Hotel for the weekly Hot Stove League meeting in hopes of a glance at such local heroes as Red Mathis and Tommy O'Brien in their two-tone shoes and silk buttoned-at-the-neck sport shirts. And, finally, the summer: hitching rides on the hood of Legg's Terraplane Hudson, playing games on rutted city playgrounds, replaying them over Coke Floats at Hudson's Drug Store; catching the old man's pop flies until dark in the vacant lot across from the house, stumping him with trivia from the *Sporting News* and *Baseball Register* at suppertime, retiring to hear Gabby Bell's imaginative ticker-tape recreation of Birmingham Baron road games; papering my entire bedroom with full-page color "Sportraits" from *Sport* magazine; quickly delivering my 78 copies of the *Birmingham News* so I could reach Rickwood Field early enough to see racoon-eyed Eddie Lyons of the Barons get out of a cab for another night's work. At some point in there I developed a fixation on Jacob Nelson (Nellie) Fox, the runty, tobacco-chewing second baseman for the Chicago White Sox—I gamely tried to ape Nellie's huge chaw until the day I caught a bad hop in the throat and threw up on the spot—and when my parents casually mentioned they had almost named me James *Nelson* Hemphill I sulked for three days.

By the time I was 15, I had determined that my fate was to play professional baseball. Nothing else mattered. One year I saw 50 of the Barons' 77 home games, usually sitting alone in the bleachers so I could dissect every move on the field, and coaxed my parents into making trips to Atlanta and Memphis and Chattanooga for Baron road games. "A man can do anything he makes up his mind to do," my old man once told me, avoiding the facts about my frail body. I merely got by in school, sketching uniforms and ballparks on sleepy spring afternoons when I should have been listening to the science lecture. I had no hobbies and no interest in girls (except for one, for a while, whom I ventured to kiss on the sixteenth date). Once I had delivered my newspapers after school on days when the Barons were on the road, I would bicycle home and continue preparing for my life's work: perfecting the hook slide in the rocky "sliding pit" I had scraped out beside the house, building up my forearms with a pair of mail-order Charles Atlas hand grips, greasing the pocket of my Bob Dillinger glove with neat's-foot oil, swinging my Jackie Robinson model Louisville Slugger in front of a full-length mirror, topping off the ritual by downing a pint of creamy half-and-half milk and a dozen fudge brownies and a raw-egg milk shake.

What was happening did not occur to me at the time, of course, and would not occur to me until several years later. I had closed myself up in a fantasy world—a world where anything happens if you simply *think* it—just as easily as I nightly closed my bedroom door to go to sleep listening to Gabby Bell broadcasting the Baron game from Mobile. I put off asking swishy little sophomores for a date until it was too late, because I was afraid they would say no. I did not go out for the high school baseball team—choosing, instead, to work and save my money so I could attend summer baseball camps—because I was afraid I wouldn't make it. By avoiding all the commitments, I avoided the possibilities of failure. Perhaps no one realized this and suffered from it like my mother, who dreamed of my going to college and marrying a nice girl and getting a respectable job someday. "Don't you think you're missing out?" she said to me once. "On what?" I said. "On *life*," she said. I had no earthly idea of what she was talking about.

The time to expose myself, to put it on the line, came early in 1954 as midterm graduation neared. During the fall I had clipped an ad from the *Sporting News* that told of the Jack Rossiter Baseball School in Cocoa, Florida. For 16 years Rossiter, a part-time Washington Senators scout, had been running the school during January and February for hopeful young unsigned players who worked out under the supervision of former major leaguers and scouts. "Players showing promise," the ad concluded, "will be signed to professional contracts."

The last month of high school was spent in a fog—doubling up on the exercises, honing the bat with a soup bone, buying a new pair of spikes and breaking them in—and on the final day of classes a teacher invited all the graduating seniors to stand up and tell their plans for the future. "Spread the word of the Lord," said one girl, drawing giggles. "Sleep about three months," drawled an acne-faced basketball player. When it came my turn I nervously bolted to my feet, solemnly said, "Play professional baseball," and upon falling back into my seat had the impression my classmates were noticing me for the first time. I had committed myself.

A week after the graduation ceremony, I threw my gear into my old man's truck—he had a load going to Miami and would drop me off in Cocoa—and we left home. The occasion was every bit as momentous for him as it was for me. He had never been allowed to play baseball as a kid in Tennessee, his mother being afraid he would get hurt, so he had lavished his love for the game on me. He had absolutely no doubt that I would someday play in the major leagues. Not an articulate man, now he could understand the need to say something lasting and important to send me into manhood with. As the tires whined toward the Atlantic coast, we talked about Cocoa and baseball and the minor leagues. And we must have been skirting Jacksonville in the middle of the night when he went quiet for a while and finally—with a great clearing of his throat and much shifting around in his seat—blurted out the best piece of advice he could think of at the moment. "Always use a rubber, boy," he said.

I was deposited before 8 A.M. in front of the shabby tin-roofed Seminole Hotel, where all players had been told to report. Lugging a new cardboard suitcase in one hand and my bat and glove in the other, I checked into a room with wooden floors and a creaking overhead fan. Then I nervously walked the streets for an hour before I returned to the Seminole, went to the end of the hall on the first floor and knocked lightly on the door. "It's open," a voice rasped, and I stepped inside. Jack Rossiter—a fat, garrulous man with bronze skin and blond wavy hair—was sitting at a desk in his shorts and undershirt, looking every bit like Sidney Greenstreet in one of those Oriental espionage thrillers, sipping something from a hotel-room tumbler.
    "Checked in yet?" he said after introductions.
    "Yeah." *Be cool.* "I got something upstairs."
    "That's strange."
    "What? Sir?"
    "You don't look like the type."
    "Hunh?"
    "Blonde, brunette or redhead?"
    "A room," I said. "I've got a *room* upstairs." Jack Rossiter, the major league scout, was laughing uncontrollably now,

his raucous strip-joint howl pounding away at me while I wondered what to do with my hands.

If Roger Kahn's postwar Brooklyn Dodgers were the Boys of Summer, then we were the Boys of Spring: the culls, the ones who now had to pay somebody to look us over. One was already 25, just out of the service, figuring he might as well give it a shot before going to work the rest of his life. Another was a deaf left-handed pitcher from North Carolina whose hometown had paid his tuition and given him a magnificent banquet before putting him on the train. A half-dozen had real ability and were quickly signed by Rossiter for the Senators, but the rest of us had little more than desire. As the weeks passed at the local ballpark, working out and playing games under an ex-shortstop named Eddie Miller and an old pitcher named Pete Appleton, a frantic dread set in with those of us who remained unsigned. Where do you go from the Jack Rossiter Baseball School? We might make the rounds of the Class D leagues, or we might stay another month in Cocoa, or we might say to hell with it. With less than a week remaining, we got our chance. A scout representing the Panama City Fliers of the Class D Alabama-Florida League came through with a stack of standard player contracts calling for $150 a month if you made the club, lined up about a dozen of us who appeared ambulatory and broke out a pen. It must have looked like a straw boss signing up grape pickers off the back of a flatbed truck. That night, unable to sleep, I wrote cards and letters to a half-dozen friends and relatives to advise them that I could probably arrange tickets for the Fliers' opening game of the season.

Nothing went right at Panama City. Anxious to get away on the big adventure, I bummed a ride from Cocoa with a rangy lead-footed outfielder named Ron Horsefield and we left late one night, having convinced ourselves the long ride across Florida would be cooler then. We ran out of gas in one town, got stopped for speeding in another, and when we arrived at the Dixie-Sherman Hotel we discovered we were a day late for spring training. It turned out the scout had signed at least 40 boys like us, put them up barracks-style on the rooftop terrace of the hotel and when Horsefield and I walked in they were walking out for the morning workout. In a panic, we eschewed sleep and rushed out to the ballpark. My legs wouldn't take me to ground balls and my arms couldn't swing the bat. "Jesus, kid," said a hairy veteran named Bob Karasek when I nubbed a looper to rightfield, "you'll hit .300 in this league if your thumbs hold out." On the morning of the third day, with an exhibition game scheduled that night for Tallahassee against a Class B club, we gathered around the pitcher's mound. "Those whose names I call," said the manager, a career minor leaguer named Roy Sinquefield, "can stay." My name was not called.

It had not gone at all like I had hoped it would, of course, but I easily rationalized what had happened. Panama City had not been a fair test. I still felt I could play. Reluctant to go back home after all the boasting to my friends and relatives, I spent the next week at the home of my favorite aunt and uncle in Dothan, a shaded town in the southeast corner of Alabama, which had a club in the same Alabama-Florida League. It was a listless week of sleeping late, playing catch with my eight-year-old cousin, watching soap operas and counting the stars. No one said anything about what had transpired, knowing I must be working things out in my mind. After about a week there, my uncle made a call to a friend of his—the director of the Dothan Recreation Department—who arranged a tryout for me with the Graceville Oilers, just over the Florida line, about 20 miles below Dothan. I hitched a ride into Graceville on a sultry morning in early April and started asking around for the manager of the Oilers, B. Holt (Cat) Milner.

Class D baseball is a faintly remembered piece of Americana that will never come our way again. It was at once the beginning and the end in organized baseball's classification system, a grubby underworld where young players began to climb to the top and where old players completed their slide to the bottom. Class D meant dim yellow lights and skinned infields and rooming houses and wild young pitchers whose fast balls could kill. You rode from town to town on condemned bulb-nosed church buses, watched out for beer bottles flying from the rickety wooden bleachers, showered ankle-deep in cold water, wolfed down hamburgers in desolate all-night truck stops and—if you'd hit a home run the night before—got out on the streets early the next morning in hopes of a free meal from an appreciative fan. Class D was a survival of the fittest, a mean place to grow up, and if it was anything it was democratic. There were more than 100 Class D towns in the country in those days, and on any given day in any of those towns a bus would stop long enough to let out a young man carrying a battered suitcase and a baseball bat, a young man looking for the manager, looking for a chance. "We got three teams," goes a saying which probably originated in the low minors, "one going, one coming, one playing." The nucleus of most clubs was formed by the playing manager and the two or three others officially listed as "veterans"—their bodies having all but quit them, they led their league in hitting or pitching on savvy—but the real tone of Class D was established by the kids, the "rookies." It was their enthusiasm and their hopelessly wild dreams and their pubescent recklessness that gave Class D baseball a reason for being.

There were strong Class D leagues and there were weak ones, and the Alabama-Florida League belonged to the latter group. In the history of the league, only two players had ever graduated to the majors for any appreciable time—pitchers Virgil Trucks and Steve Barber. In 1954 only two of the league's six teams had working agreements with major league organizations, and the others were forced to scramble on their own for uniforms and players and expenses. Dothan and Panama City each had a population of around 35,000, but the others were obscure little towns lost in the barren stretches where Alabama and Florida run together. There was Andalusia in Alabama, and Fort Walton Beach and Crestview in Florida and—the baby of them all, the town that would lead the league in attendance in 1954—Graceville.

When I tracked down Cat Milner, a droll old man who was the only nonplaying manager in the league that year, I discovered why I had been welcomed to try out. Only nine days away from the Oilers' opening game of the season, there was not a second baseman among the 14 players in camp. "How come you got that hole cut in the pocket of your glove?" he asked me. When I explained that Eddie Miller had recommended it "so you can *feel* that goddamned ball," Milner shrugged like a man who had heard it all. Depositing my suitcase at a rooming house where the players were being put up, I walked on down to the ballpark and was told to pick out—from the clothesline strung to the low-slung concrete clubhouse down the rightfield line—a uniform that would fit me. They were old gray road uniforms with patched knees and frayed sleeves and, across the shirtfronts, the dim outline of stitches left years earlier when the felt letters spelling CINCINNATI had been ripped off. I wondered, as I slipped into the shirt with the number 10 on the back, what Cincinnati Red had buttoned up the same uniform. I shook hands with two or three of the other players as they drifted in; finished dressing, poked a chew of Beechnut into my jaw, whapped my fist into the pocket of my glove, felt the smooth hickory of my Jackie Robinson bat, stomped my spikes on the rough concrete clubhouse floor, tugged at the bill of my Chicago White Sox cap and burst out into the sun of the Florida Panhandle to begin my real life.

In retrospect, those were the most gloriously giddy days I have ever known. Most of the others were first-year players like me, and when we were not going through the two-a-day workouts at the park we were hanging around the Circle Grille or riding in somebody's convertible or merely sitting on beds talking baseball. "Hey, roomie," my roommate, a catcher named Tommy Doherty, would whisper through the mask while I lunged away during batting practice, "drop that stick and get your glove on. You don't want to overexpose yourself." With Joaquin Toyo, the tiny brown shortstop who knew virtually no English, I worked out a sort of pidgin English-Spanish so we could let each other know what was going on. "This game's simple boys," Cat would say during a break. "All you gotta do is hit the ball and run like hell." I couldn't hit a basketball with a paddle, as we say, but I could field. On my second day Cat came around asking everybody what model and weight bat they used so he could put in the order for Louisville Sluggers. That night there was a supper for the ball club at a local church, during which I was introduced as the Oilers' second baseman. In one week, on the night of April 15 at Wiregrass Stadium in Dothan, the season would officially open and I would become a professional. Again the cards and letters went out to Birmingham.

The third night, we had an exhibition game in Graceville against a Fort Benning, Georgia, team, stacked with players who had been pulled out of the minors to do their service time. "Jesus H. Christ," one of them barked when they arrived at our little park. "I forgot how bad Class D was. They fed you guys this week?" I didn't know where I was most of the night. By the time infield practice was starting the little ballpark was crammed with more than 1,000 fans, and one of them was my uncle from Dothan. The moment of truth had come for me, that ultimate commitment when I would finally become *experienced,* and when the crowd roared as

49

we bounded onto the field to start the game I felt an elation I had never known.

We got the hell beat out of us, and I struck out all four times I came to bat against Fort Benning's lefthanded pitcher. Cat was morose after the game: "How do y'all think you're gonna hit old Onion Davis up at Dothan if you can't hit this *private?*" I had done well in the field, turning the corner on two double plays and nearly throwing out a runner at third on a relay from the outfield, and I was not especially long-jawed when Tommy Doherty and I gobbled our hamburgers afterward at the Circle. "Hey," he said, "if *you* don't play second base, who is?"

On the morning of my fifth day at Graceville, Tommy and I were the last to finish running in the outfield and break for lunch. The heat was like an oven, stilling the air and turning our uniforms into wet blankets. Cat Milner stood down the rightfield line, handing each man trudging toward the clubhouse his $2.50 meal money for the day. Exhausted but happy, we strolled up to get our money.

"One of y'all got change for a five?" Cat said.

"Not me," said Doherty. I shook my head, too.

"Gotta bust this thing somewhere."

"Hey, Skip, me and roomie'll split it," Doherty said.

"Won't work."

"Naw, see, we'll just take the five and—"

"I gotta let the kid go."

The blood went out of my body. I didn't know what to say. I wanted to lash out at Cat Milner, but when I looked back at him I saw that after all those years it was still a messy business for him, having to swing the ax. I would never be able to hit Onion Davis, he said, and on top of that there was a second baseman coming in from Class C that afternoon.

The rest of the day was a mirage: jumping in the shower so nobody would see the tears, trying to tie my shoelaces with quivering hands, pats on the back and observations that I'd been screwed. Within an hour I had gone by the rooming house, had collected my things and was standing beside the road leading north to Dothan. It was only then that I let it fly, the huge tears streaking my bony cheeks and splaying my see-through nylon shirt. A farmer in a pickup stopped for me, surely noticed the tears and didn't speak for several minutes. "You a ballplayer?" he finally said, seeing my bat and glove. "Sort of," I told him. They were the only words spoken until he let me out on the edge of Dothan and wished me luck.

Unlike Panama City, Graceville's dismissal was absolute. When you can't make it with the Graceville Oilers—the smallest town in baseball, in one of the worst leagues, at the bottom of the line—the message is clear. I drifted on back home to Birmingham, and while my old man was trying to lift my spirits I was numbly stripping my bedroom walls of the "Sportraits." For the next three summers I would dabble at baseball, playing two seasons in a semipro league in Kansas and a final year in an amateur industrial league in Birmingham, but I never again gave a serious thought to making my living at the game.

In a sense, my first life ended and my second life began that moment in Graceville when Cat Milner broke the news to me. There is a saying in sports that I had always had drummed into me, from Bill Legg to Cat Milner: "You don't learn when you win, you learn when you lose." In missing the brass ring, in having my dream fall in around me, I had learned. For the first time in my life, I had to consider something besides baseball. I reluctantly agreed to try college, became sports editor of the Auburn University newspaper, started reading books for the first time, graduated, went into sports writing for a living, switched to writing general "human interest" columns, won a Nieman Fellowship to Harvard, wrote two books and then became a freelance writer. It hasn't been bad.

But a first dream doesn't die easily. I left too much of myself on rocky playgrounds and in splintery bleachers to forget. At least one night a week I go to a batting range near our house to flail away for an hour or so at baseballs being fired by a mechanical arm, pretending this is Graceville and that is Onion Davis of the Dothan Rebels out there on the mound. When I am covering baseball and see a great play at second base, I feel it is I—not Glenn Beckert or Felix Millan —making the spectacular stop and whirling to fire toward first base. Driving through the somnolent Southern towns which had minor league teams, I am compelled to pull up at the decaying little ballparks that are left to see how they are doing. It is a bittersweet memory, my love affair with the game of baseball, and I am still haunted by Cat Milner's words: *I gotta let the kid go.*

The other day my son and I—David is only seven, the smallest player on his Little League team, but a pretty good little hitter already—went out to the vacant lot at the end of our cul-de-sac to play catch. I had my old Bob Dillinger glove with me, now wrinkled and stiff, and for 30 minutes we laughed and threw in a world of our own. As we sat under an oak tree afterward, catching our breath, David slipped his tiny hand in my glove and awkwardly pounded the pocket. "Daddy, why did you cut a hole in it?" he said. I started explaining about the Jack Rossiter Baseball School and Eddie Miller and Panama City and Graceville. He was interested for a while, but then he got bored. "I betcha *I'll* be good enough to play," he said. Knowing better, I told him I hope to hell he is.

PART TWO

Rasslin' and
Other Diversions

3·WHAT EVER HAPPENED TO WHATSISNAME?

It promised to be another one of those days on that softly undulating farmland where Oklahoma, Kansas and Missouri run together. By three o'clock in the afternoon the temperature was moving on 100, and there was a peculiar suffocating stillness in the air. Grasshoppers hustled inside every time a screen door opened. Newspapers in the scattered towns and villages warned against the watering of lawns, lest there be no water by August. Trying to ward off the heat, Bruce Swango loosened his tight orange Banlon at the neck and stuck his head out the window so the wind created by the speed of his pale-green camper would whistle through his crewcut. When you are born in a land like this, you learn to cope. "Thought I'd stop by at the folks' place for a minute," Swango said, jamming a Roi-Tan Blunt deeper into one corner of his mouth. He is 35 now and has seen a lot of America since he got $36,000 from the Baltimore Orioles and went off to find fame and fortune 17 years ago. But he remains pure Okie, with a massive upper torso and a red face and barn-door ears and a way of making the words "hired" and "tired" come out *hard* and *tard*.

"They used to write how a scout seen me warm up in the barn, but I think it was some of them New York writers that never seen a barn," he said, bouncing onto a dusty gravel road leading ·to the white frame farmhouse where he was born and raised, on a 240-acre spread outside the community of Welch, Oklahoma (pop. 500). "Right here's where me and my brother used to play ball. It was a home run if you hit the ball from the barn to the water pump."

"It's a long way from here to Baltimore," I said.

"Yeah, well, that was part of my problem."

"I talked to Richards the other day."

The mention of Paul Richards, the former Baltimore general manager, stunned him. "What'd Paul say?"

"Didn't want to talk about it."

"That figures."

Finding both of his parents gone, Swango stood in the center of the darkened living room staring at the clutter of old family portraits and photographs. "Reckon why Paul done what he did?" he said, as though talking to himself. "I wasn't no big-league pitcher. Heck, no, they wouldn't a-let me go if I was a big league pitcher. It's just the way they done it. See, when Baltimore signed me that made it five bonus boys they had to keep on their bench. There was this rule. You get more than $4,000, right away you got to stay on the big-league roster two years. Well, you can't win no pennant like that. So what Richards wanted to do, he wanted to release me and then sign me back again a year later. When he released me he said, 'Don't pay any attention to anything you read in the paper.' Well, the next day when I got home I read that Swango was too wild and couldn't pitch in front of crowds. I don't know whether Paul told 'em that or not, but somebody sure did. That's what disgusts me. There wasn't none of it true. They was just trying to scare off the other scouts. But two months ago, right here in my home town, they had an Associated Press story in the paper saying how crowds frustrated me and Baltimore released me and nobody ever heard of me again. Seventeen years later, I'm still trying to live it down."

"At least you got some money," I said.

"Did that, all right."

"What'd you do with it?"

"Built a house. Bought some cattle."

"You seem to regret the whole thing."

"Naw," he said, closing the door to the house and walking back to the camper. "Not really. You can't turn down that kind of money. I think I had big-league ability, but I needed experience. If you were a bonus ballplayer you didn't have the chance to go out to the minors and learn how to pitch. I do wish I'd a-kept on playing instead of quitting like I did. I think I could have made it back up to the big leagues. Oh, well," he said, cranking the engine, "working the graveyard shift in a *tahr* plant may not sound like much, but it pays good and I get to hunt and fish a lot." With a Babe Ruth League game to coach in a couple of hours, Swango slithered down the gravel road. "Had a big traffic jam on this old road when I was a boy," he said. "One day we counted nine cars parked out here, a big-league scout in every one, all of 'em waiting his turn to go in the house and talk me into signing."

Now, almost two decades later, Bruce Swango and scores of others seem like antiques: names and faces, vaguely recalled, from another era. Teenagers transformed into legends before they were old enough to shave, they live today with the memories of shattered expectations and broken dreams. They were the original "bonus babies" of baseball, as they came to be called, precocious young athletes who were given anywhere from $35,000 to $100,000 as bonuses to sign contracts with major league clubs suddenly gone bananas over the improbable idea of buying themselves instant pennants or, at the very least, instant superstars.

It was a time unlike any other in American sport. Football and basketball bonus babies of later years were college men, older and comparatively more sophisticated, already tested by top competition. The baseball phenoms were uneducated high school kids, their experience often limited to American Legion games in ballparks where cows grazed behind the outfield fence. They were pursued not by one team from each of two competing pro leagues but by every team in major league baseball. Although there were some bonus players before and after, the period ran roughly from 1947 to 1955. During that span some 100 players received over $6 million in bonuses. In general, the players' overnight affluence was the only positive result. Nobody ever won a pennant with bonus players. Baseball almost went broke. Fans lost respect for owners. Veteran stars protested the reckless spending, bringing some clubs to the brink of mutiny. Most of the young players, pressured to produce, had their careers stunted from the start.

Exactly how it all began, no one seems to know, but once bonus fever set in there was no stopping it. The first pure bonus baby was Dick Wakefield, who had a couple of good wartime seasons with the Detroit Tigers after signing in 1941 but folded when the men came back home. The true beginning of the era came in the late 1940s when the Braves gave $65,000 to an 18-year-old lefthander named Johnny Antonelli and the Phillies shelled out some $145,000 for pitchers Robin Roberts, Curt Simmons and a Georgia country boy named Hugh Frank Radcliffe. When all except Radcliffe showed immediate promise in the major leagues, everybody went crazy.

It was a zany, hysterical, frantic time. The day after high school graduation, strapping young prospects embarked on a summer tour of major league ballparks, where they would pitch or take batting practice for the brass before finally—around World Series time, when there had been enough time for the bidding to get completely out of hand—signing for something like $75,000. The scouts out in the boondocks, well aware that they could be stamped as lifelong geniuses by finding just one kid who made it, lost their perspective: laying intricate smokescreens for their peers, beating the bushes, finding "another Bob Feller" on every farm, turning in embellished reports on kids who didn't even own a pair of baseball shoes. The owners, too, became addicted: they signed one bonus baby, then had to have another and then another. To the initial delight of the baseball hierarchy—which enjoyed being portrayed as spending enormous sums to bring its fans a winner—the press regularly exaggerated the size of bonus payments and created dozens of premature folk heroes out of kids who had never batted against a curve ball. Despite the exaggerations, the spending was prolific. By the early 1950s the owners were moved to legislate against their own greed and recklessness. Any player signing for more than $4,000 had to take a place on the big league roster for two years before he could be shipped to the minors. Typically, the "bonus rule" had only negative results. The huge payments continued unabated—though sometimes under the table—but the young prospects' chances for success were drastically reduced. Forced to sit in big league dugouts—gaining no experience, ostracized by jealous teammates, eventually a source of humor for fans and press—they waited while their potential (assuming they ever had any) stagnated and often disappeared. Many youngsters became convenient scapegoats for scouts and executives who publicly ridiculed them (even inventing fictitious explanations for the players' failure) to cover up for their own poor judgment.

Of the hundred or so bonus babies of that era, no more than a dozen made it in style: Al Kaline, Sandy Koufax, Harvey Kuenn, Roberts, Simmons, *et al*. They are far outweighed by the ones like pitcher Billy Joe Davidson, who got $60,000 from the Indians in 1951 when he was 17 years old, hurt his arm, never pitched a major league inning and at 25 was back home in North Carolina pitching to his father in the backyard. In 1955 the Orioles had more than $200,000 tied up in five bonus players they had to keep in Baltimore, and the results were catastrophic: Swango never pitched a big-league game and the other four had a composite Baltimore production of 5 home runs, 49 runs batted in and a .190 batting average. "I swore then," says Paul Richards, "that I'd never sign a kid without seeing him with my own eyes." For most of the bonus babies it was a matter of taking the money and running, usually back to the minor leagues for a while, where they labored as curios until they had proven to themselves that they would never go back up, finally dropping out and going back home to dull jobs and yellowed press clippings and childhood sweethearts. And memories.

"Nothing like a danged old tight T-shirt to let everybody know how fat you're getting." Bruce Swango had poured himself an iced-tea-glass full of Canadian whiskey and water before going back to the bedroom to change, and now he was padding into the living room in the uniform of the "Rebels," the local Babe Ruth League team. The Swangos and their two young children live in a Permastone-front house, close to town and the B. F. Goodrich tire plant, where Bruce is "just an ordinary laborer" from midnight to 8 A.M. He owns two lots at the end of the block so he can keep his four bird dogs penned up. "I must be twenty pounds overweight," he said.

Swango's wife, Joanne, is a petite blonde from nearby Commerce, Mickey Mantle's hometown. She met Bruce the summer he came home from Baltimore and married him a year later. Possessed with that fierce, frontier resiliency of Oklahoma women, she was calmly laying out a huge, rushed-up country dinner of roast beef and vegetables so Bruce and 14-year-old Scott, who plays second base for the Rebels, could make it to the ballpark on time. Cara Jo, their nine-year-old daughter, was at the moment playing a softball game. "Yeah," said Bruce as everybody sat around the table, "if old Scott had his desire and Cara Jo's talent, he'd be something else."

Swango swallowed a roll. "I've tried not to push Scott," he said. "I've seen too many boys who wanted to play real bad and just didn't have the talent. Heck, I was like that. You can fool around too long at something you aren't good at, and it'll mess you up. Scott, now, he's real good with that saxophone. Been talking about giving it up because it's 'sissy,' but I tell him he better keep on playing that saxophone." After a second helping he shoved away from the table. "Be ready soon as I get my spikes," he said. "Hey, you know what? They're the same spikes I *retahrd* in."

Of all the stories about the bonus babies, the most bizarre —and yet, because it contains so many universities, the most nearly typical—is that of Bruce Swango. He grew up working in his father's fields and walking back and forth a mile each way to a country school that had 13 kids in its eight grades, and never played any organized sports until he enrolled in the tiny high school at Welch. One spring his coach told him if he would try pitching he might be able to get a college baseball scholarship. "That taught me a notion," says Swango.

In his first game as a pitcher he beat arch-rival Miami, 1–0, with 13 strikeouts. He was a bit wild, but what farm boy with a blazing fastball isn't? He continued to pitch, for the strong Tri-State Miners and other semipro teams in the area. This is baseball country, where such major leaguers as Mantle, the Boyer brothers and Ralph Terry were spawned —and by the time Swango was finishing high school there were a dozen scouts in the stands every time he pitched.

"They all wanted to fly me up to the big leagues for tryouts, but I didn't want to mess with that," he says. Eventually he signed with a fellow named Dutch Dietrich of the Baltimore Orioles.

What really happened at Baltimore? It could be there is a little truth from both sides. "Hell, he got so wild after a point," says one ex-Oriole who was there, "that we just refused to take batting practice against him." Swango says pitching coach Harry Brecheen tried to make him change everything he was doing, from his windup to his grip, and had him utterly confused after two weeks. "You can't believe how scared I was up there and how much I had to learn," he says. "One day I started pitching batting practice without a catcher. They had to tell me you don't never do that. Heck, I didn't know."

At any rate, two months after receiving his $36,000 and joining the Orioles he was given his unconditional release. The newspapers were having fun with him, but when he got home to Oklahoma the next day he had calls from five scouts. "I kinda felt obligated to go back and sign with Richards if he wanted me, because of the money they'd give me, but my parents and my coach didn't think I should." He played occasional games with semipro teams here and there, and late in the summer signed with the New York Yankees organization.

He spent the next eight years in a frustrating odyssey through the minor leagues. In 1956 they tried him as an outfielder at McAlester, Oklahoma, in the Class D Sooner State League, where he hit only .240. From then on he was a pitcher. Greenville, Texas; Fargo, North Dakota; Greensboro, North Carolina. Amarillo. Charlotte. Binghamton. Drafted from the Yankee organization after a good year at Nashville in 1961, he went to spring training with the Twins but he was sent out to Vancouver in Class AAA.

Swango's last year was 1963. He had a strong spring training and started out 2–2 with Dallas–Fort Worth. He thought he had found it, but then he was abruptly shipped out to Charlotte in the Sally League. "That kinda destroyed my confidence. I was 26 and I'd done a lot of traveling. I thought maybe it'd be better, you know, if I did something else." Minnesota asked him if he would be interested in going down to the winter instructional league during the off-season. "What do you want me to do," Swango asked them, "go down there and take care of them young boys for you?" It was over.

Not all of them went off to the big city as confused country boys, of course, although the majority of America's professional baseball players *have* come from small towns in the South and Midwest, and, recently, from California. One who was just as savvy as the next guy, and who kept up a running battle with organized baseball throughout his fiery 10-year career, is Frank Leja. Already six-foot-three and 210 pounds when he graduated from high school in Holyoke, Massachusetts, Leja was wanted so badly that three clubs were fined heavily by commissioner Ford Frick for holding secret tryouts before his American Legion season had ended. "That," says Leja, now an articulate man doing a booming insurance business in Nahant, Massachusetts, "is how my career began." Soon after blasting a 485-foot home run into the center-field bleachers at the old Polo Grounds during an intrasquad game, he signed with the Yankees for $50,000 during the World Series of 1953. Leja was 17 years old.

Two decades later, his recollections have a vividness that comes only with pain. From the start, Leja felt put upon. When he checked into his first spring training, he found dollar signs, rather than his name, painted on every piece of equipment in his locker. The Yankee veterans—cold, proud, defending World Champions—treated him with icy contempt. During batting practice, when Leja inevitably popped the ball over the infield, manager Casey Stengel would dip into his reservoir of sarcasm and wheeze: "Look at that kid *hit that ball!"* Coach Bill Dickey changed his entire batting stance, Leja says, and he never felt comfortable at the plate again.

Finally, when the season opened and he saw his first paycheck, Leja took on the baseball commissioner. "They were paying me based on *last* year's minimum for rookies," he recalls. "It's no big deal. I just thought I ought to get what was due me. It was the principle of the thing." The buck passed all the way up to Commissioner Frick's office. "I was told to report there and right away I knew I was in trouble." Leja remembers. "'Now what the hell is this about your salary?' Frick said to me, and when I tried to explain he cut me off. 'They gave you enough money,' he says. 'Now go on out there to the stadium and play ball!' "

During his enforced two years with the Yankees, Leja went to bat just seven times. He got one hit, was sent out to the minors and—except for a brief shot with the Angels in 1962 when he went hitless in 16 trips—never came back. "You can't tell me baseball's not a family business," says Leja, still puzzled and angry at not being advanced during a sometimes dazzling eight-year career in the minors. "My composite totals for those eight years were 290 home runs, over 800 runs batted in and a .263 average, but every time I turned around I was being sent out to Amarillo. In '56 I'm at Binghamton for two months. I'm third in the league in home runs and second in runs batted in, hitting .240. So they tell me to go to Winston-Salem. O.K.? You follow me?" The way Leja sees it, the Yankees' East Coast scout, Paul Krichell —the one who had originally signed him—died and the next day it was Winston-Salem for the rich kid who makes trouble.

The era of bonus babies is ancient history. The track record on young phenoms is so bad owners are no longer willing to gamble wildly. More important, all eligible amateurs are now placed in a free-agent draft—somewhat similar to football and basketball—and can bargain with only one team at a time. And teams can no longer keep young players on ice in the minor leagues. Each winter, clubs are allowed to protect only 40 men in their entire organization—majors and minors—leaving all others open to a draft by other teams.

"Scouting's different now from what it was back then," says Mercer Harris, a Cardinals and Tigers scout in the Southeast for 27 years. "The whole game's changing fast. Used to be, you'd find yourself a real *phee*-nom out in the country and keep him for yourself. It was a lot of fun. We didn't talk to each other any more than ballplayers stood around talking to the opposition at the batting cage. But you can't hide 'em anymore, and when you get 'em you can't hold onto 'em because of the draft and all." College baseball, in fact, could become the new minor leagues: a place where kids get educated, finish growing and play close to 100 games a season under former major leaguers before moving straight into the big leagues. "Scouting was a lot more work then," says Harris, "but it was a lot more fun."

Astronomical bonuses didn't disappear completely after the mid-1950s, when the owners abandoned the "bonus rule" and the official bonus baby era ended. Players like Rich Reichardt and Bob Bailey still signed six-figure contracts. But the $100,000 bonuses have now become a distinct rarity. Blue-chip prospects can still get bonuses—but the vast majority are now in the $30,000 range.

Mark Pettit got $30,000 from the Baltimore Orioles last year. He had to choose between going to college first or immediately turning pro. His father called it "the biggest decision we as a family ever had to make." His father should know. In 1950, Paul Pettit was the first six-figure bonus baby, signing amid great fanfare with the Pittsburgh Pirates. Pettit was a monumental bust. Today, like so many of the original bonus babies, he is still trying to get over what happened to the dream, wondering where the money went, wishing he could have given it one more shot. Yet he was pleased that his son signed and chose to attend college only in the off-season. "If you play four years at Arizona State," Paul Pettit says, "you've still got to prove you can do it. They want to see if you can play pro ball."

When Paul Pettit signed with the Pirates for $100,000 in 1950 he was immediately sent to New Orleans in the tough Southern Association. "I think I could've become a good pitcher in the big leagues if I'd had a chance to come along slowly," he says. Instead, he hurt his arm that first year and pitched only 30-⅔ innings in the majors. Then came a decade all over the minors, later even a switch to first base in Class C.

Now he coaches baseball in the Los Angeles area, making a good living off that and the rental property bought with his bonus, and says somewhat resignedly that he is "still plugging away." Sometimes, says his wife, "Lefty sort of drifts away into his own world, like nobody else is around." It seems to be a pattern. Do people still remember him? "Just the other day I went into a drugstore with a prescription and when the woman waiting on me saw the name she said, 'Aren't you a basketball player?' I said no, that I used to play baseball. They still get me confused with Bob Pettit, the basketball player."

The Rebels had beaten the Chiefs by one run, with the help of some late-inning maneuvering on the coach's part, and now the cool night air cloaked northeast Oklahoma. Bruce Swango had rushed home, spent a few minutes taking a needling from the kids about his crewcut, grabbed a bath and suited up to work at the tire plant all night. His wife had offered to run me up to Joplin so I could make my early-morning flight, and after a detour to pick up her sister for company on the road back, we were out on the highway.

"I guess it's been pretty rough for you," I said.

66

"What?"

"The traveling and moving around."

"Oh," Joanne said, "you don't know the half of it. Remember the cattle he bought with some of his bonus money? Well, every time we ran out of money we'd just go out and sell another cow. They're all gone."

"I don't guess you miss that."

"No. I sure don't miss that part."

"How about Bruce?"

Joanne blinked her lights for a diesel to pass. "He doesn't sleep well sometimes," she said. "I don't know if it's what happened or what, but a lot of times he just sits and stares off somewhere. Oh, I'm sure he misses it. He wishes he'd kept on trying so he could prove himself. I feel bad about that. Maybe I should've talked him into playing longer. He only quit because of us."

"Us?"

"Me and the kids. He's a good man, a family man. He wants to move to a farm, and I think maybe that's what we should do. Move back to the farm. Then maybe he'll get it off his mind."

4·PUNT, 'BAMA, PUNT

A bit haggard and stooped now from 14 years of whiskey and cigarettes and past-due bills and late nights at type-writers, The Old Grad sprawled out over the skeletal bleachers at the trim little Auburn University baseball park and let the memories whirl through his head. In the late 1950s it was called Alabama Polytechnic Institute, and it was then a "cow college" heavy on the sciences of farming and engineering and veterinary medicine. The rich kids and the city kids and even some Jewish kids from Up East had traditionally gone to the University of Alabama, across the state at Tuscaloosa, but Auburn, over on the high farm-pond plains between Montgomery and Columbus, Georgia, had always been the domain of rough-handed Georgia and Alabama country boys who trod dirt paths in scruffy boots while slide rules slapped the legs of their khaki trousers. Those, of course, were the days of skinny Wembley ties and white bucks and flattop crewcuts and see-through chartreuse nylon shirts with a pack of Luckies tucked away in the rolled-up short sleeve, getting drunk for the first time at a grimy roadhouse beer joint called the Casino, peeping into the upstairs windows of the women's dorms, shooting pool up on College Avenue, necking in a '54 Ford convertible down on condom-littered Biggio Flats, while Kitty Kallin crooned "Little Things Mean a Lot." Chubby Checker, the Platters, Fats Domino and Elvis. Every now and then, when the situation demanded it, some studying, or, at the very least, frantic cramming for an exam.

Through it all, however, the ritual of big-time football in the Deep South had dominated The Old Grad's life during those years. Nothing better than a batting-practice pitcher for the baseball team, he had quit to become sports editor of the school paper and, to pay his way, gotten free room and board in the jumble of cottages called Graves Center, where the scholarshipped athletes lived, by serving meals in the dining hall there for a flighty lady dietician known as Hoot Gibson ("Hey," the frat boys would sneer, "you still slopping hops over there?"). He had once shared a cottage with a strapping tackle from Eufaula named Ben Preston, who would, after dinner on lazy spring evenings, roll up a mattress and go off in a car with a bronze coquette from Dadeville or Heflin or Lineville to spend the night under the stars at Lake Chewacla. He had lived next door to a sadistic toothless halfback named Bobby Hoppe, who occupied his mind at dusk by sitting on the porch and aimlessly popping pine cones out of the trees with a .45. He had known an All-American end named Jerry Wilson, who gleefully took into battle at the Casino his heavy diamond-studded ring signifying Auburn's 1957 national championship ("Boy," he said on one such occasion, sitting out in the gravel, happily rubbing the ring and gazing moonward, "I bet that sumbitch really hurts"). And he had seen the hasty home-made poster nailed to the downtown telephone pole on the Sunday morning in 1956 when the news broke that Auburn had once again been slapped on NCAA probation, this time for allegedly offering a trifle more than tuition and laundry money to an exceptional high school quarterback: "Auburn," read the sign, the only hint of student protest The Old Grad could recall from those days, "Gives the World 24 Hours to Get Out of Town."

Outwardly, he could now see, much had happened since 1959. All of the old buildings like Samford and Tichenor and Brown still stood, but were obscured by the newer ones: the glassy library holding nearly a million books, the contemporary Haley Center, where a liberal arts major could spend his entire four years, the huge circular coliseum replacing the old 2,400-seat converted World War II Quonset hut, the stadium addition that ran football seating from the 34,000 of the late 1950s to the current 62,000. Enrollment was up from 8,500 to 14,000 now, including about 150 black students. The study of engineering and agriculture no longer dominated, there being a lot who came now to study medicine or law or journalism, and such big-name liberal personalities as Julian Bond and George McGovern were likely to show up for speaking engagements. There was not a sign of Graves Center, it having been replaced by a Holiday Inn-ish dormitory, and Hoot Gibson was last seen helping ex-halfback Fob James sell barbells over in Opelika. The Casino was still crowded, out on the edge of town, but in the place of a family-style eatery named The Green House squatted a franchised Jack's hamburger joint.

Still, The Old Grad could see, not everything had changed. Auburn's baseball team was playing a doubleheader on that lush spring afternoon against the University of Alabama, which had just locked up the championship in the Southeastern Conference's Western Division, and as he sat with a capacity crowd of some 500 students he felt the same old tingling that always accompanied an Alabama-Auburn match in any event. Auburn still attracted its fair share of red-faced yahoos, even if they *were* majoring in English these days, and he could see the blood in their eyes when they spotted a red-and-white Alabama uniform through the wire backstop. A full five months earlier, in the most memorable football victory in Auburn history, Auburn had blocked two Alabama punt attempts in the last six minutes and returned both for touchdowns in an incredible 17–16 win. The score, and bumper stickers saying PUNT, 'BAMA, PUNT, still adorned everything in the quiet town of Auburn (the city name comes from a Goldsmith poem that notes "Auburn, loveliest village of the plain"), and now, as Auburn jumped on Alabama for three quick runs in the first game, a swell of raw leathery voices began to chant. "Punt, 'Bama, Punt." Baseball, on a lovely April afternoon five months later, and they wouldn't let it alone. "PUNT, 'BAMA, PUNT . . . PUNT, 'BAMA, PUNT." Forget, hell. 'PUNT, 'BAMA, PUNT. PUNT, 'BAMA, PUNT. PUNT, 'BAMA, PUNT, 'BAMA . . ." No, The Old Grad smiled, some things never changed at all.

Up East and throughout much of the rest of the nation, they like to point out with disdain that colleges like Auburn are little more than "football factories." It is true that 23 Auburn players have made All-American, that 12 of them were in pro football last season, that the last five Auburn teams have been in postseason bowl games, that Auburn is accustomed to being on network television at least once a year (not counting the bowl game), and that it expects to finish somewhere in the nationwide Top Ten poll. It is true that football is the only sport that really counts at places like Auburn and Alabama and Georgia and LSU and Ole Miss, and that, team for team and year to year, the Southeastern Conference has virtually dominated college football since the days of Gen. Robert Neyland at the University of Tennessee and Bobby Dodd at Georgia Tech. But a football factory? The term denotes that they go out and buy or otherwise snare the best football talent available in the land, whipping them into a well-oiled semiprofessional machine, but on Auburn's 1972 roster (including freshmen) only one of the 86 players was from other than a Deep South state. Of the total, 58 were from Alabama alone, where football is less a way out than a way of life. No other sport has a chance in Alabama. In a lot of towns, a kid's father hangs his head in shame if the boy doesn't make the high school team.

With that in mind, it is easier to understand the frenzy that undermines the entire state of Alabama as the annual season-ending Alabama-Auburn game approaches. Interrupted back in the dark ages when a blood-letting erupted, the series picked up again in 1948 and has become one of the premiere cross-state rivalries across the land. Both squads take off for a week before the game—to lick wounds, watch films, put in special strategy and hate the other side—and then they come together on the first Saturday of December in front of more than 70,000 people at Legion Field in Birmingham (FOOTBALL CAPITAL OF THE WORLD, says a massive poster on the double-deck facing), usually with bowl bids and national rankings and the conference championship on the line. Undecided prep stars usually cast their futures with the winner, giving the pendulum of power a crazy tilt each recruiting season, adding even more significance to the game.

Not surprisingly, the game didn't reach such prominence until Paul (Bear) Bryant went back to coach at his alma mater, Alabama, in 1958. Auburn had put together some of its strongest teams in the mid-1950s—the Tigers, or Plainsmen, had outscored Alabama by 128 to 7 points in winning the last four prior to Bryant's arrival—and Bryant was hired to head them off. His first team—the remnants of the one which had lost to Auburn 40–0 the year before—lost The Game by only 14–8, and his next four threw shutouts in Birmingham. Bryant was king in Alabama during those years, getting all of the players and winning the national championships and going to the big bowl games, while Auburn—coming off two successive NCAA probations totaling five years for recruiting violations—slithered to a 4–6 record in 1966, its first losing season since 1952. There were the inevitable jokes about Bryant and Auburn coach Ralph (Shug) Jordan, under fire from alumni for the first time, the best one about the two of them turning over in a boat while fishing together and Jordan pulling Bryant to safety. "Shug, do me one favor and don't tell any of my folks I can't *really* walk on water," Bryant says in the story. "I'll promise you that, Bear," says Jordan, "if you won't tell *my* folks I pulled you out." Bitterness reigned, especially at Auburn, where they still grumbled that it was Alabama which had blown the whistle in both recruiting scandals.

Jordan managed to survive it all, of course—the NCAA probations, the seven losses in eight years to Alabama, the poor record of 1966, not to mention a serious bout with cancer a couple of years ago—and today, at age 62, is ranked fifth nationally in winning percentage (155–69–5) among active coaches with 20 or more years. More important, at least to him, is the rejuvenation he has undergone. "You think about a lot of things when you don't know whether you're going to make it or not," he says of the endless cancer surgery, "and if you come out of it alive there's no way you won't be a changed man. I used to spend all day Friday and that night before a game with alumni, hanging around and being nice. Since the illness, I've gone out to the movies with the boys. Let somebody else hang around the alumni." Indeed, Jordan refused to give up coaching and move into the athletic director's office two years ago when everybody in Alabama figured he would upon long-time AD Jeff Beard's retirement. "I wanted 'em both, the AD job and coaching, but when they wouldn't let me have 'em both I took coaching."

The differences between Bryant and Jordan are striking, and it seems certain that a more widely publicized and/or charismatic figure would not have finished second in the national Coach of the Year voting, as Jordan did to Southern Cal's John McKay, on the basis of the coaching job he did last season: stripped of the scintillating Sullivan-to-Beasley passing attack, picked to win no more than three games, Auburn went to defense and safety-first offense to go 9–1, upset Alabama at its own game, blew beefy Colorado out of the Gater Bowl and finished fifth nationally. Bryant is blunt and quotable, Jordan gentlemanly and a bit ponderous (his favorite phrases are "down through the years" and "my cup of tea"). Bryant is dynamic, Jordan rather bland. Bryant is Patton, Jordan is Eisenhower. While Bryant is likely to be on his office phone to his New York stockbroker at noon, Jordan goes home for a glass of tea and a 20-minute nap. Bryant is an innovator, Jordan still gripes about artificial turf ("I did learn last year," he grins, talking about the two blocked punts picked up for touchdowns against Alabama, "that the ball bounces beautifully"). Bryant, Jordan, Bryant, Jordan. The comparisons are endless. But in Alabama they are unavoidable.

What we have in Auburn's Shug Jordan, then, is the very opposite of the Woody Hayeses and the Bear Bryants of the world: a gentle man who has spent some 40 years of his life as a player and a coach in the same little sleepy east Alabama college town, one who has met the devils of defeat and death and beaten them both, an old-fashioned coach who loves his "boys" and the tingle of being out there on the sidelines with them on Saturday while a crowd of 60,000 roars *at* them or *for* them, a man who discovered a sense of place two decades ago and has spent the rest of the time reveling in it. Late one April afternoon, on a break during spring football practice, he sat in a modest paneled office and reflected on it, sounding less the operator of a "football factory" than a paunchy intramural director:

• *On Auburn*—"I wanted to come here in '48 when there was an opening and I was at Georgia, but they seemed to have their minds set on a Notre Dame man or somebody else from outside. I told 'em, 'If you don't believe in Auburn people, you ought to close the place down.' Then, in '51, Jeff [Beard] had to beg me to apply. I just wrote out a note saying, 'I hereby apply for the position of head football coach at Auburn.' They took me on—I insisted on a five-year contract, figuring at the age of 40 this would be my one chance —but I didn't become established for two or three years."

• *On Bryant*—"It's tough, being in the same state with him, but there's no doubt in my mind that it has made better football teams out of both of us. I feel close to him. There's no animosity. He called me just this afternoon, just to chat, and we always call each other before the season starts to wish each other luck, except in the last game. The Auburn-Alabama game wasn't the classic it is today until he came. It's a healthy competitive situation. The cruel stuff only takes place maybe at drugstores and quarterback clubs."

• *On Pat Sullivan*—"There was never any doubt about him, from the moment he came here. He has wonderful poise, pride and confidence. There was a strange thing his senior year, with a lot of people who didn't know him actually pulling *against* him in the Heisman Trophy thing. They couldn't believe that his sincerity was for real, that he really was just a nice young gentleman. They thought he would be maudlin with this 'Yessir, nosir' business. I think he finally captivated the Easterners at the Heisman banquet, when they met him. They couldn't believe it."

• *The 1972 Team*—"I don't like to compare my teams, but that raggedy-ass bunch had to be my favorites. For three years nobody had talked about anything but Sullivan-to-Beasley, and they decided they wanted to prove something on their own. We knew we had some fine defensive players —after all, they had been practicing for three years against the most explosive offense in America—plus fierce pride and spirit, and if we could stick our noses in the ground and avoid mistakes we could win. About all we had for offense was five running plays and two or three play-action passes, but we knew those plays forward and backward. I'm worried about this year because we don't have that psychology of being the underdog."

• *The Five Years' Worth of Probation in the 1950s*—"I think if it happened today, with all of the interest in civil rights, the courts would look out for us. We gave the Beaube twins in Gadsden $500 apiece to offset the offer of apartments for both made by Alabama, and Alabama didn't get punished because the boys hadn't actually moved into the apartments. In the case of Don Fuell, they [the NCAA] never once showed us any concrete evidence of all those things we supposedly gave him. There was a used air-conditioner sold to Don at cost-plus-ten by an alumnus, and that was it. They were looking for us, and we got caught. I tell you one thing, they said they would let us off if we would fire [assistant coach] Hal Herring in the Beaube case, but Jeff [Beard] refused to do it on the basis of loyalty."

• *The Player of the 1970s*—"You can't do some of the things now that you used to do. I mean, when practice is over they don't necessarily want to spend the rest of the night on football. They're more independent and free-thinking—smarter, maybe, overall—and you have to give a little. We don't worry about the hair or the dress. I just get 'em together before fall practice and ask 'em to act like gentlemen. Last year's group was so dedicated to playing football that we never had a single disciplinary problem. That's the first time that's ever happened since I've been here."

• *On the Auburn Program*—"The year before I got here we had lost to Wofford and Southeastern Louisiana, with only 10,000 bothering to come to the games. We were $75,000 in debt, had 18,000 seats and practically no advance ticket sales. Pretty soon we were out of debt, were winning and had to enlarge the stadium. The way I see it, the object here is to have an interesting football team that wins and brings credit to Auburn. Look at how the university itself has grown, along with the football program. They can go hand-in-hand. They *should* go hand-in-hand. That thing called the 'Auburn Spirit' has always come out of adversity—the losing years, the NCAA probation, the coming of Bryant—and it's been a beautiful thing to watch. Only I don't need any more adversity for a while."

During football practice the next afternoon, the day of the Auburn-Alabama baseball doubleheader, The Old Grad wandered over to the lush new 14-acre football complex. Auburn people tend to go back home, sooner or later, and all over the field were coaches who were Tiger heroes in the 1940s and 1950s and even the 1960s ("When you're too tired to eat, you're tired," said ex-quarterback Bobby Freeman, recalling the first Jordan team's shakedown period), men looking as at home as organdy curtains in a country kitchen. The 150 candidates for the 1973 Auburn Tigers pranced about the bright green field, now and then the hysterical voice of an incensed line coach rising above the measured grunts. A cloudless blue sky smiled on it all as Shug Jordan, in khaki trousers and a powder blue T-shirt, climbed into his canopied golf cart and invited The Old Grad to hop in.

"Sixty-five of these boys are walk-ons, just trying out," he said with a grin. "I look at that as a tribute to our program, that they want to play and we want to give them a chance to make it. Some do, most don't. But at least they've tried." Bumping around the edge of the field to the far side, where the interior linemen were pounding each other, he stopped and pointed to an impressive stand of pines planted in a steep bank. "We could go into the pulpwood business if things got bad," he said.

"A lot of us were surprised," said The Old Grad, "when you didn't quit coaching a couple of years ago. With Sullivan gone, it would've been a good one to quit on. That, and the cancer."

"Well," Jordan said, "I told you about how the illness affected me. I did a lot of thinking, lying in the hospital, and I had to determine what was important to me and what wasn't. I wouldn't want to stand over a cash register or have to keep my thumbs on the money. The older I've got, in a way, the younger I've become. Or at least the more I've wanted to taste youth again. I want these boys to come by my house. I want to go to the movies with 'em. I want to laugh and to cry with 'em. They're *my* boys. Every one of 'em."

5·THE MAD, MAD, MAD, MAD WHIRL

It is five degrees below zero on a mid-January Saturday night, but nobody inside the cavernous Cincinnati Gardens is thinking about that right now because the Roller Derby has come to town. Down on the portable banked track the ladies of the Pioneers and the ladies of the Bombers have already bent themselves to the business of trying to kill each other off in the first game of a doubleheader. Elbows are flying, skates are clacking, fans are screaming for blood, and all of it is being orchestrated by an hysterical trackside announcer who sounds a lot like Howard Cosell: *Weston coming up on the outside, Forbes with a blow to the head of Tucker . . . Twenty seconds to go, Bombers lead by two . . . Forbes forms a whip, starting the play . . . Eight seconds, eight seconds left . . . Here's Garello, Garello SCOOORES!* Pandemonium. Everybody up. *Official decision, two Pioneer points. Tie game! Tie game!* Unable to contain herself any longer, a lady in pink doubleknit toreador pants and blue hair charges the lip of the track and pastes little Jackie Garello in the left breast with a rolled-up Dixie Cup.

Charlie Knuckles is watching the games this night with considerable interest. Five days from now he will take a plane to the West Coast and enroll in the official Roller Derby training school. With a name like this they can make him a star. A slight 18-year-old with shaggy unkempt hair and a pimply face, he made the big decision as soon as he got out of the Job Corps in October. He has been cleaning out condemned houses for a construction company, hoarding his money, and he has it all worked out. "It's just a buck a day for the school. You can live at the YMCA for four a day and a buddy told me you can pick up twenty-five or thirty bucks unloading a truck." The product of a broken home and never much interested in the basic sports, he has been "messing around at little dinky rinks" since he was ten. In many ways he is typical of the Derby stars he has followed for nearly half his life.

"Yeah, I been planning for this a long time," he says as the period ends and the male Bombers and Pioneers take over the track. "I'm on their mailing list, watch 'em on TV, even hitchhiked to Cleveland to see 'em once. Ain't never smoked. Got my knee busted up speed-skating one time and took walks in the hospital at three o'clock in the morning to strengthen it. You know, build it back up."

"Never skated a banked track, then?"

"Naw. That's what the training school's for."

"How long does that take?"

"Depends. They gotta teach ya how to fall, how to block, how to jam. Some guys get signed up in a week. Others, they'll maybe get put on an amateur team for a while." Out on the track a Bomber is chasing a Pioneer through the infield with a metal folding chair. "Jesus, I hope he kills him."

"C'mon. You don't believe that."

Blinking incredulously, Charlie Knuckles doesn't bother to dignify that with a reply.

Essentially it is—as the title of a Derby-sponsored paperback book reads—"a very simple game." Two teams of five players each skate counterclockwise around a banked track,

310 feet in circumference, that can fit into a 50-by-90-foot rectangular space. Each team has two skaters at the rear of the pack called "jammers." When a jammer breaks through the pack, the countdown begins and the jammers have 60 seconds to lap the pack. Every time a jammer laps an opposing skater he scores a point for his team. There are certain finer points in the rules, of course, but that's about the size of it. The Roller Derby isn't so much a sport as it is a caricature of sport—pure show business, a higher form of "Friday Nite Rasslin'," pregnant with scowling villains and glamorous heroines pulling hair and cracking skulls almost every night inside some auditorium somewhere in a melodramatic morality play that sends thousands of proletarian fans into delirious frenzy. "I never heard them say, 'Tonight we win, tomorrow night you win,'" says author Frank Deford, who spent considerable time traveling with the Derby caravan for a book called *Five Strides on the Banked Track*. "But I never saw a lopsided game. There's almost an unwritten rule that you let up when you get 'way ahead. There are always bits of business to be done, like throwing a chair or sending [Ann] Calvello through somebody's legs or knocking over the water cooler. The hitting is seldom for real."

But never mind. There is a sizable underground in America that *wants* to believe in the Derby, just as it wants to believe in professional wrestling. This belief has made it one of the hottest entertainments going. Six teams play one-nighters on the road for seven straight months and are seen by more than 3 million paid customers. (Last year, when the Derby went into New York's Madison Square Garden for the first time, there were three consecutive sellouts.) A total of 132 television stations carry weekly syndicated taped Derby games. Upward of 1,000 fan letters reach Derby headquarters in Oakland, California, each week. Every Monday an average of 100 hopefuls like Charlie Knuckles check into the Derby training school, straining to find the brass ring.

At least two movies—one of them starring Raquel Welch as queen—were being done by two major studios. Charlie O'Connell, the Derby's top drawing card, earns around $60,000 a year. The Bay Bombers franchise was recently sold to a Texas group for a reported $1 million. And Bay Promotions, Inc., the parent company for the entire operation (funded in the late 1950s with $500), last year grossed nearly $6 million. "Well, gee, let 'em go watch lacrosse," says Bay Promotions president Gerald E. Seltzer of purists who scorn his game.

I am reminded of Cowboy Luttrell, whose company I shared when I was a young newspaper sports editor in Tampa and he was the local wrestling promoter. A rollicking old codger who had lost one eye in an exhibition boxing match with Jack Dempsey, Cowboy was a fixture in steamy downtown Tampa, where he lived in a fading hotel and lunched in dark bars and terrified shoppers by lurching down Florida Avenue at high noon in his magnificent white sharkfinned Cadillac.

Cowboy was your basic wrestling entrepreneur. He had a stable of athletes with outrageous pseudonyms like Klondike Bill and Kublah Khan, and on any night of the week they could be found practicing their vaudevillian routines in small-town auditoriums all over the upper part of Florida. Seldom was there anything short of a capacity crowd for their shows, no matter where or when they performed, bringing great wealth and a sort of underground celebrity to Cowboy and his men. Stuck deep in Cowboy's craw, however, was the fact that we gave the fuzzy Class A Tampa Tarpons baseball club top play almost daily while burying our scant mention of pro wrestling among the tire-recapping ads.

"Hey," he said one day while we fished the Gulf in his 24-foot boat, "great story on us yesterday. Two paragraphs."

"Okay, Cowboy," I said.

"The Tarpons. What'd they draw?"

"You read. 112."

"My boys," he smiled, "4,000. *Power of the press.*"

Jerry Seltzer is a suave, 40-year-old Northwestern graduate who took over the business from his father, Leo, 14 years ago when the Derby, badly overexposed nationally during the early days of television, was drawing crowds of 200 at the Cow Palace in San Francisco. The Derby had sprung out of the walkathon and marathon bike-race crazes of the Depression years (indeed, such present-day Derby terms as "jamming" are holdovers). Leo Seltzer patiently nursed it into a popular, offbeat and fairly legitimate sport until the honeymoon ended and he disgustedly turned the whole thing over to his only son. Jerry had been slogging along as a salesman, announcing Derby games for pocket money, and there wasn't much to recommend him as a savior except that he came armed with the instincts of a newer generation that had been teethed on television. He was wise enough to know that baseball, for one, was being killed by too much television and too much devotion to tradition. In 1960 people wanted action and the trick was to keep them hungering for it. Going on his instincts most of the way, Jerry Seltzer hit upon a formula that is a classic study in successful promotion.

On the surface it is difficult to comprehend that a venture could be so successful with virtually no help from the usual publicity sources, principally newspapers. "We asked the wire services if they would carry our standings this year. UPI said they ought to wait and see how it worked out. AP never answered," says Derby publicist Herb Michelson. On the day of most games in most towns there will be at best a three-paragraph mention of the Derby on the local sports page. Seltzer couldn't care less; he has gone straight to his audience, amassing a mailing list of 250,000 fans who regularly receive press releases about the league and when *their* team will next play in *their* area. The six Derby teams represent definite geographical areas; the Midwest Jolters, for example, are the "home" team wherever they play from Michigan to Kentucky.

Bay Promotions is an awesome machine—it covers the Derby itself, the TV syndicate, an ad agency, the training school, a skate factory, a publishing house and a movie production company (whose *Derby* was rated by some critics in the top 10 films for 1971). "The San Francisco *Chronicle* runs a long boxing column once a week," says Michelson, "but what do we care? Boxing crowds in the Bay area average around 1,800 people, and everybody *knows* what we draw. We've got our own thing going." Indeed they do. On the night before the Cincinnati doubleheader, which drew more than 8,000 in subzero weather with only an obscure two-column newspaper ad, the National Basketball Association game between the Cincinnati Royals and the Atlanta Hawks enticed only 3,908, even with the help of a lead story on Friday's sports pages.

Like most of the Chiefs and Jolters, Ann Calvello and Margie Laszlo get away from Cincinnati by 10 o'clock in the morning. That night the two teams will play at the Convention Center in Louisville and Ann and Margie want to reach the downtown Holiday Inn in time to watch the Super Bowl (and the Roller Derby tape) on color television. Calvello, who signs her autograph just that way, is 43 and tired of traveling. Laszlo, already a veteran of 13 years with the Derby, is 29 and would like to get married. Bushed from five straight nights of skating in five separate towns—not to mention a hard Saturday night of carousing in Cincinnati— Calvello has turned over her car to somebody else (its special California license plate reads L-O-V-E-R) so she can catch up on her sleep. Before the season ends in April, they will have driven nearly 50,000 miles. Laszlo tanks up at a gas station, meticulously records her mileage in a black diary, then heads out to the southbound interstate highway.

There are roughly 100 skaters employed by the Roller Derby—half of them women, a third of them black (although, curiously, black fans tend to huddle together in small knots during road dates). Even though a lot of ink is given to O'Connell's $60,000 salary and statuesque Joan Weston's $50,000 (Calvello is the third highest-paid at around $35,000), rookies begin at $8,000 and the great bulk of them earn in the teens. The Roller Derby Program Yearbook has fascinating things to say about them all—"Won't back down from a battle" and "Has a variety of often-painful crunching moves"—but the truth is that the average skater comes from a tumultuous lower-class background, wasn't much at other sports, has little education and is painfully shy when off the track. "Most of us are pretty quiet and I guess it is a release to get out on the track," says one demure female skater. There is some homosexuality, male and female, but not much. There is usually at least one flaming love affair taking place on each tour, especially when some young stud has just joined the troupe. About a third of the men have nonskating wives back home and there are but four married skating couples on the road. For most the Derby is an endless cycle—skate, drive 400 miles, catch a nap in a motel, skate, move out again—that leaves little time for hobbies or marriage or thinking beyond next week. Few skaters stay at it for more than four or five years. "The road, that's what gets to you," says Calvello. "I had a week off at Christmas, but it wasn't worth it to go all the way to the Coast. Me, I spent Christmas at a Holiday Inn in Chicago."

There has been but one death on the track in Derby history, but only two survived a massive bus accident in the 1930s and several others have died or been ruined on the open road. Traveling is especially hazardous now that the season runs from October through April. "One time it took me five hours to make the 129 miles from Saginaw to Battle Creek," recalls Laszlo. And what happened once in a 35-

below night in Canada isn't entirely out of the ordinary: the rental truck carrying the portable track (the Derby keeps eight of them in circulation) got snowbound, there was a sellout crowd waiting and the skaters turned down the frantic promoter's suggestion to "just draw a track on the floor" of the gymnasium and skate. "When I started out I was making $40 a month, plus room and board," says Calvello. "Now I've got a phone bill of $150 a month, just calling my daughter."

Ann Calvello is a story in herself. The oldest of a sailor's six kids, she joined the Derby in 1948 and is one of only 18 members of the Derby Hall of Fame. Unlike most of the female skaters, she is an extrovert—an astrology buff, a friend of Bay area professional athletes, a born villainess ("I don't want to be a cigarette," meaning one content to "sit back in the pack"), a walking commercial for Roller Derby (featured in a Public Television *Great American Dream Machine* spot on the Derby) and an expert on everything ("What's wrong with this generation is they got no discipline. I saw a guy yesterday eating a salad with his hands"). She has had raging affairs with more than one Derby star but now goes with a San Francisco fireman. She and her teenage daughter share an apartment featuring a psychedelic toilet. The constant traveling and skating have cost her her looks—she has gone through broken noses, stitched eyes and torn lips, and wears braces on both knees— but she is still the most singular figure in the game: blonde polka-dot hair (sprayed on by Margie Laszlo before each game), deep-freckled, animated face.

"Ahh, sometimes I think it's no life for a girl," Calvello is saying as we reach the outskirts of Louisville. She is sprawled over the front seat in flowery bell-bottoms and a Notre Dame letter jacket and scruffy brown Hush Puppies. "You come back off the road and find yourself opening car doors for men. I have to remember to act helpless."

"I may have to get a divorce before I get married," says

Laszlo. "I've been going with this one guy since I was six-teen."

"Hey," says Calvello. "You know that movie Raquel is doing?"

"The Derby movie?"

"Right. Well, I want to tell you that she's actually playing me. Calvello. How 'bout that? She may have bigger tickets [Derby slang for breasts] than me, but I can outskate her."

Another day, another town. If it's Sunday, this must be Louisville. They played here two weeks earlier, celebrating New Year's Eve by running up and down the streets at midnight outside a crummy little beer joint on a lonely street, and here they are again. The crew of younger skaters goes out in midafternoon to assemble the track (for three hours' work, putting it up and taking it down, a man earns around $30) while the others crawl in bed and watch the Super Bowl game from New Orleans. There is that familiar two-column ad on the sports page of the Louisville *Courier-Journal*, plus a slightly longer story because one of the Derby rookies hails from Louisville, and then there is the Derby on television later in the day. As in Detroit and Fort Wayne and Cincinnati, a poster outside the Louisville Convention Center reminds fans to come and see "Your Jolters" do battle.

Joan Weston and Ann Calvello are big, but nobody in the game is as big as Charlie O'Connell. At the heart of Roller Derby is the ability to play a part, to lull the crowd into a never-never land of good guys and bad guys—in short, to make them either love you or hate you—and nobody can anger a crowd like "Bomber Great Charlie O'Connell," as the Derby press releases always call him. He is the classic heavy: big for a skater (six-foot-two, 200 pounds), moody and sullen, sort of a malevolent John Wayne on wheels. He has the crowd on his back the moment he rolls out for warm-ups with a white towel tucked tightly around his neck and stuffed into his jacket collar like a prizefighter. He is No. 40, an All-Star every year since 1958 and the only other active skater besides Calvello who is in the Hall of Fame.

O'Connell represents one case where no flackery is needed. He is truly a villain, not only with the fans but with many of the skaters and the people back in the front office at Oakland. They refer to him there as "GSB," which stands for "Greedy Son-of-a-Bitch." He stays to himself on most of the tour, the majority of the time bringing along his wife. While almost all of the skaters live on the West Coast, and O'Connell himself has a spacious home overlooking the Bay area, he now prefers living in a suburban community an hour north of New York City. He got burned on a couple of investments in bars and restaurants and now simply puts his $60,000-a-year in the bank and lives the good life when not on the road. He has come a long way. He grew up poor on Manhattan's Lower East Side and says most of his boyhood pals are today "on one side of the law or the other."

Tonight, in Louisville, O'Connell is not in a good mood. He was late getting into town and as soon as this game is over he and his wife will have to drive 500 miles straight to Springfield, Missouri. At 36, he is suffering injuries more regularly. He has just returned from a five-month layoff with a broken forearm and is surlier and 15 pounds heavier than usual. He thinks he just might quit all this stuff.

"Hell, I'm skating against 20-year-old kids now," he says. He is sitting in a narrow hallway outside the dressing room. The game has already started, ladies first, and you can hear the bellowing of the crowd through the heavily guarded door.

"What would you do if you quit?"

"Coach, I guess. Hell, I'd like to be one of them rich landlords, to tell the truth. Anything but working."

"You wouldn't miss skating, then."

"Yeah, I'd miss it." He wraps the towel around his neck and crosses his legs. "Stuff gets in your blood. I tried to quit once and about went nuts. I can honestly say I'd be in a hell of a fix if it hadn't been for skating."

"What do you say to people who call the Derby phony?"

He spins a wheel on one of his skates. "They're crazy."

"It's all on the up-and-up, then."

"Naw. Look. What about Ted Williams? There was a great athlete, but do you think he'd have made all that money if he hadn't been a little something extra? I mean like giving people the finger and spitting toward the press box? Hell, there's a little bit of show business in everything. Okay, we have a little fun now and then. I'll tell you one thing, though. This damn broken arm ain't no put-on."

Having spoken thus, "Bomber Great Charlie O'Connell" pushes the door aside and skates across the broad expanse of concrete to the banked track. Although the girls are still whirring around, all eyes turn to him and the auditorium reverberates with boos and cheers. He gives them their money's worth. In the first minute of play he belts a black Jolter with a forearm chop, showing princely disdain as the skater flies all the way over the cushioned rail and sprawls out cold on the slick concrete floor. As the first half ends, O'Connell is sitting out his second one-minute penalty and an out-and-out brawl breaks out in the infield. *Both coaches are fined $100! Both coaches are fined $100!* the announcer keeps shouting above the roar of the crowd. Nobody hears him because the same black Jolter is taking a folding chair over the head this time, cops are trying to head off the hundred or so fans swarming down on the track, and both teams are bursting through for the dressing room. When Charlie is 20 feet from the door a pretty girl in yellow stretch pants comes running up to him and—thinking the vilest of thoughts—rears back and unloads a full cup of chipped ice right in his face. "Bomber Great Charlie O'Connell" smiles benevolently at her before going on inside to see how badly he hurt the guy.

6·MOTIVATIN' WITH JABE

There were three of them, and they had left the mountains beyond Roanoke at four o'clock in the morning, the glistening new Dodge and the extra tires and all their tools sitting atop the bed of their truck, sustaining themselves on Dr. Pepper and candy bars on the twisting five-hour drive down to the flatlands, and when they got into Richmond they drove straight to the state fairgrounds, where the race would be run on Sunday, the next day. All of the big-name drivers like Petty and Allison and Yarborough had already qualified and wrapped the tight vinyl covers over their cars, and while those lolled around the infield sucking on Nehis and acting humble for the good old girls the racing team of Jabe Thomas hunched earnestly amid oil pans and lug nuts and carburetor parts trying to get the car set up for business. Some racing team. Petty had 13 mechanics there, in matching uniforms, but Jabe had only his partner—a body-shop operator from Roanoke named Don Robertson—and a brooding mountain mechanic known only as Stinky. All day long they crawled over the car's innards, Jabe flitting around the pit area playing grab-ass with the other drivers ("Hey, this woman had a baby born with a mustache and she was tickled to death"), and they got it ready in time for him to

89

be one of the last of the 30 drivers to qualify for the Richmond 500.

Now, bone tired, they were checking into a Holiday Inn on the fringe of town, three of them in one room to cut down on expenses, and they were just in time to catch the previous week's Daytona 500 on *Wide World of Sports*. Jabe had finished 15th in that one, one of his best ever at Daytona and worth nearly $2,000 to him when you count it all up, but he also nearly had been creamed when a car in front of him spun out at 170 miles per hour. "I want to watch and see how I didn't get killed," Jabe was saying. Robertson slumped next door to filch a drink of whiskey from another mechanic. Stinky, already homesick for the hills after only 14 hours away from them, was sprawled out in a fitful sleep on top of the covers and would later refuse to leave the room for so much as a hamburger.

"Tenth," Jabe said as Robertson came back into the room with a tumbler full of warm Scotch.

"What say?"

"We're shootin' for tenth place."

"Uh-hunh."

"Naw, lookie here, I got it figured out. Expenses ought to go nearly $700. Tenth pays $625, plus that $250 we got for qualifying. Finish tenth and we make a little money. Hey, here it comes," he said, pointing at the television set as Scottish racing star Jackie Stewart, wearing a black tam on his shaggy head, described the Daytona wreck. The car ahead of Jabe blew the engine and began spinning out of control. Jabe guessed the car was going to spin up high on the track so he went down on the apron, but so did the crippled car. "*Wheew-weeee*," Jabe chortled as his yellow-and-red No. 25 came through it unscathed, "I don't know how I done it. Fella told me the announcer on the radio said, 'There's a veteran driver for you.' Why, heck, all I did was close my eyes and stomp on it and pray he'd be gone when I got there."

In the beginning there were the good old boys, primal sons of Appalachia who came howling down out of the Southern hills on weekends to bang around quarter-mile dirt tracks under pale yellow lights in a celebration of life which perfectly mirrored their relative position in American society. They were poor and hungry and violent, and more than one of them used the car for bootlegging moonshine whiskey during the week ("When not racing, Mr. Seay divided his time between Dawsonville and Atlanta," deadpanned the obituary for one of the early idols, murdered in a shootout with a cousin over a sack of sugar), and they represented a raw slice of this country's history. "What they ought to do," said one when tighter regulations were added to the sport, "is give everybody a drink of liquor and drop the green flag." Back then, which was some 30 years ago, Southern stock car racing meant fender-banging vendettas on the curves and tire-iron fights in the infield and whiskey in the skittery skeletal bleachers. The roar of the engines, the smell of the crowd.

The changes, barely perceptible at first, began in 1948 when the National Association for Stock Car Auto Racing was formed. NASCAR was intended to upgrade the sport, to preen its image and to make it profitable for the drivers and the promoters. They started paving the tracks. They started building "superspeedways," pushing speeds past 100 miles per hour. They started paying prize money in the thousands rather than the hundreds. Detroit came in, throwing financial backing behind the better drivers. Television deals were made for the bigger races, such as the Daytona 500. Some of the more prominent drivers bought planes and flew from race to race. The whiskey and the primeval feuding disappeared, as did most of the other rough-edged Southern reflexes, and all of a sudden it had become a dead-serious business.

Today, of course, Southern stock car racing is quite another animal from what it was in the old days. Expenses being what they are, the hell-raising poor country boy has been forced aside by the drivers with sponsors like Coca-Cola and STP. Bobby Allison, of Hueytown, Alabama, won $273,000 in prize money last year. Richard Petty, who started driving in the halcyon days of the dirt tracks, employs dozens of mechanics at Petty Engineering in Randleman, North Carolina, which maintains a fleet of identical cars making him virtually unbeatable on the NASCAR circuit. The circuit itself is sponsored by the Winston cigarette people, who put up a "point fund" totaling $120,000. An average of 43,000 fans paid to see each of 31 races last year, and this year's Daytona 500 drew a record 103,000. At the new track in Talledega, Alabama, drivers pull two and three gravity forces on one high-banked turn, developing vertigo and sometimes blacking out as they hurtle down the backstretch at more than 200 miles per hour. "It's got so you can't have no fun anymore," you will hear a driver say these days, but then he excuses himself to go off and cash a first-place check for some $5,000. The good old boys, like the South that nourished them, are all but gone.

The last of them, in fact, may be one Cerry Ezra (Jabe) Thomas, who is 42 and runs Jabe's Gulf service station in the small western Virginia town of Christiansburg. A poor boy who "ain't never had nothin' to speak of," Jabe has been driving race cars since 1950, and in eight seasons on NAS-CAR's "Grand National" circuit for big late-model cars he has never finished better than fourth in 261 races. He has never had any sort of help from Detroit or anywhere else substantial ("The only thing close to a sponsor I've had is this fellow who pays me $100 to paint the name of his used-car place on the side of my car") but is partners with Don Robertson. They have about $35,000 invested in a truck, two '73 Dodges and tools and tires. What Jabe Thomas does is finish a race, which he did often enough two years ago to win $31,500 and place sixth in NASCAR's overall point standings. Making every race on the circuit, not pushing his car hard enough to blow it, cutting down on expenses, Jabe and Don are able to break even nearly every year. "We do it," says Robertson, "to get away on weekends and have some fun. It's a hobby."

In the process, Jabe Thomas has carved out a place for himself as "the clown prince of stock car racing." Loose-jointed and angular, with mischievous eyes behind a pair of thick black horn-rimmed glasses, he is probably the best-liked driver on the circuit among his peers and the fans. He is liable to sign off over the phone with, "Okay, buddy, ten-four." He describes his racing strategy thus: "It's kinda like squirrel hunting, where you sneak around and get what you can." He is saddened by Detroit's recent pullout, and the other sponsors with it, because "you can't even turn the *tahr* carcasses in no more." Once in Texas he bought a Geiger counter for $100 and bet two fellows at a rest stop on the highway that he could find money with it, but wound up losing the bet and a dollar when he couldn't find the four quarters he had hidden on the ground under a layer of dust. Another time, in North Wilkesboro, North Carolina, he had a bucket of water dropped on his head from the third floor of a ragged hotel when he went outside to use the pay phone on the sidewalk. He once slipped a rock into another driver's tight racing uniform pocket, and the driver carried it for 500 miles with his seat belt digging it into his thigh. Remembering his heavy-drinking father, he has never touched a drop of liquor or smoked a cigarette; but he makes up for that and qualifies as a good old boy with his irrepressible wit and soul. He drives a modest little Datsun and works his service station while his wife holds down a job at the overall plant in Christiansburg, and he is thoroughly at peace with the world. "Every time we start up the engines, I just thank the good Lord I'm behind the wheel," he says. He is an inherently good man without a bad word about anybody, and he has a simple explanation for what makes him tick:

"Anybody who knows how I grew up knows why I'm like I am."

Growing up is never easy in that rugged hill country west of Roanoke, and it was twice as tough for the Thomases. "We was probably the poorest folks in the county," says Jabe, "and that's really saying something around there." He was the oldest of three boys and one girl born to a part-time farmer and odds-and-ends man, and except for an occasional piece of pork the family subsisted on home-grown vegetables. He remembers going for three days without anything at all to eat, and except for a hamburger now and then he still can't develop a taste for meat. He also recalls only two Christmas gifts during his childhood: a 15-cent toy truck and a cap pistol. He dropped out of high school after the second day of his sophomore year, to go to work at $3.20 a day in the local chair factory, spent eight months in the Army before being discharged with a bad back, delivered milk door-to-door, worked for five months as a welder in Cleveland, Ohio, and finally settled down back home in 1958 when he took over the service station.

All along, he had been into racing. "I used to sit in school, drawing pictures of cars," he says. His first race had been in 1950 at Victory Stadium in Roanoke, the same place the legendary Curtis Turner had started, in the days when stock car racing was still a frontier shootout. The machines were "ordinary street cars hopped up as much as you could get 'em," and Jabe's first one had no roll bar. He won a lot of races over the next 15 years, but they were all on small local tracks in the "modified" and "sportsman" divisions that didn't pay much money. Hankering to go onto NASCAR's Grand National circuit, he worked and saved and then went in with Don Robertson. They are as compatible as two grown men can be with each other, each in racing for the same reason and each enjoying a loose good time, and there has seldom been a strained moment between them. Jabe joined the Grand Nationals in 1965 and has at least broken even financially every year but 1972, when he blew two engines within nine days.

Sitting in the cab of the truck with nothing to do but wait for the race an hour and a half away, Jabe was jotting down figures on the back of a promotional picture postcard of him put out by a company in Indianapolis. "See here," he was saying, "our expenses at Daytona came to $2,350 and we didn't win but $1,970 all told. A man's not racing for the dollar he makes. If he did, it'd come out to 50 or 75 cents an hour." Is it possible for an independent to win in NASCAR these days? "If I ran the race like I run to qualify I'd take the lead on the first caution flag, but I can't afford to run like that. If I blow an engine or tear up the car, I'm out of racing. If a fellow with big backing does that, he just gets another car given to him." Ever since the factories pulled back on their support four years ago and more independents got into the act racing hasn't been as much fun. "Everybody's tense. It's become a business now. Why, shoot, I can't even kid 'em like I used to do. They're panicky and tight, worrying about winning and worrying about paying their bills."

Wandering toward the pit area for the ritualistic prerace drivers meeting, he rambled on as though he preferred to joke and tell stories more than drive in a race that day. One of his brothers, he said, had gone on to become a college professor. One year, Jabe's Gulf was the No. 1 Gulf station in the district. To pick up a little spending money he goes into the hills in search of a medicinal root called ginseng, washes and cleans and dries it, and ships it to Greensboro. North Carolina, for $50 a pound. "Back home," he was saying, "they read in the papers how much I won in a race and they figure I'm rich." He once spent $700 of his own money going to Nashville for a recording session and a shot on the *Hee-Haw* television show, neither of which ever materialized. Right now, he said, checking, he had a grand total of $2.63 in cash to his name.

"Well, Jabe Thomas, ain't you speaking?" It was a gaggle of middle-aged women in bouffant hairdos and tight toreador pants, holding clipboards and sitting on the back of a truck.

"Well, hey there, ladies. How y'all?"

"We're gonna be scoring for you, Jabe Thomas."

"Better look close, 'cause I'm gonna be motivatin'."

"When you be on *Hee-Haw*, Jabe? I been takin' off work to see it."

"Well, now, we're still trying to get all that worked out with my agent up in *Noo Yawk City*."

"Get out of here, Jabe Thomas."

At the drivers meeting a somber NASCAR official went over the rules they had heard a thousand times as Jabe tried to enliven it: "Hey, that ain't fair, no passing the pace car. That's the only thing out there I can pass." Each driver was introduced to the crowd of nearly 20,000, Jabe being roundly cheered and Petty—the closest thing in racing to the New York Yankees of the 1950s—being hooted by at least half of them. The crowd was given a breakdown of the makes of cars entered ("We've got 13 *Chevys* . . .") and they cheered the cars, too. Finally, with the crowd on its feet under a crisp blue Virginia sky, the engines were cranked and off they flew on their 250-mile journey. The last car in the lineup of 30 was No. 25, Jabe Thomas' Dodge, passed on to him by Richard Petty.

It was a classic Jabe Thomas race. On the second lap he moved up to 28th when two cars tangled and went out for the day. The "hot dogs" inevitably burned out, and inexorably came Jabe as if he were on a Sunday drive: nursing the machinery. Down in Petty's pit there were 13 crew members and a crew chief with a headset in radio communication with Petty, but down at Jabe's there were Don and Stinky. On the 251st lap Jabe came in and found there was clutch trouble ("He'll just drive as long as he can, I guess," said Robertson), and after 267 laps the field was down to 21 cars. When it was all over, more than three and a half hours from the start, Petty had won and Jabe had finished 13th to take $495 to go along with the $250 he had gotten for qualifying. It meant a net profit of $71 for Jabe.

Even so, nobody signed as many autographs after the race as Jabe Thomas. A black couple, a rarity at a Southern stock car race, shoved their shy little girl up to shake hands with him. A wild-eyed young fellow who claimed he once raced against Jabe kept hanging around, jabbering. A little girl had pasted up a poster in school with the names of her two favorites on it: PETTY and JABE. "I couldn't make it turn over 5,000 and had to baby it all day," Jabe told one fan, "but I finished." His fans, who seem to perfectly understand Jabe Thomas' motivations in racing, nodded knowingly. "Hey, Jabe," some old boy cracked from the pits, "how much did Petty pay you to throw this race?" Jabe grinned and said, "You wouldn't believe it if I told you."

Streaked with grease and sweat, then, the three men strained to lift a spare engine onto their truck to take back home and put in the car for the next Sunday's race. The crowd was gone now, as were many of the drivers and mechanics, and only an echo rang through the deserted track as a reminder of the hours of roaring and cheering and gnashing of metal on metal. Scraps of paper were picked up and whirled about by the scattered wisps of wind. Bobby Allison's crew was headed out to the airport to get on a jet and order up some cocktails and ogle the stewardesses on the whistling flight back through Atlanta to Birmingham, but Jabe Thomas and Don Robertson and Stinky had the long haul back into the mountains ahead of them. "Y'all come see us, now, if you get up our way," Jabe called as they loaded up the truck to go. They would shower when they got home.

7·YESTERDAY'S HERO

> "A week never passes that the Alumni Office fails to receive news highlighting the good works of former football players. So many of them reflect credit on our University."
>
> —University of Tennessee Football Guide

> "What is fame?
>   An empty bubble;
> Gold? a transient,
>   shining trouble."
>
> —James Grainger, 1721–1766

The evening began with an expedition to the friendly neighborhood liquor store four blocks away, where a purchase of four quarts of sticky-sweet Wild Irish Rose red wine was negotiated with a reedy gray-haired man behind the cash register. When the man saw who was shuffling through the front door his jaw tightened and he glanced nervously around, as if checking to be sure everything was nailed down. "When you start drinking that stuff, Bob?" he asked. "Since the last time I woke up and didn't know what month it was," said Robert Lee Suffridge, inspiring a doleful exchange about his drinking exploits. It was concluded that cheap wine at least puts you to sleep before you have a chance to do something crazy. Paying for the $1.39-a-quart bottles he trudged back out the door into the dry late-afternoon July heat and nursed the bleached 12-year-old Mercury back to his apartment.

It is an old folks' home, actually, a pair of matching six-story towers on the outskirts of Knoxville, Tennessee. At 55 he isn't ready for an old folks' home yet, but a brother who works for the state arranged for him to move in. Most of the other residents there are well past the age of 65, and to the older ladies like Bertha Colquitt, who lives in the apartment next to his and lets him use her telephone, he is their mischievous son. More than once they have had to call an ambulance for him when he was either drunk or having heart pains, but they don't seem to mind. "Honey, if I was about 10 years younger you'd have to watch your step around me," he will say to one of them, setting off embarrassed giggles. God knows where he found four portable charcoal grills, but he keeps them in the dayroom downstairs and throws wiener roasts from time to time. He grows his own tomatoes beside his building, in a fiberglass crate filled with loam and human excrement taken from a buddy's septic tank.

Getting off the elevator at the fourth floor, he thumped across the antiseptic hallway. The cooking odors of cabbage and meat loaf and carrots drifted through doorways. Joking with an old woman walking down the hall with a cane, he shifted the sack of wine bottles to his left arm and opened the door to his efficiency apartment. A copy of *AA Today,* an Alcoholics Anonymous publication, rested atop the bureau. A powder-blue blazer with a patch reading "All-Time All-American" hung in a clear plastic bag from the closet doorknob. The bed, "my grandmother's old bed," had not been made in some time. Littering the living room were old sports pages and letters and newspaper clippings.

"Not a bad place," he said, filling a yellow plastic tumbler with wine and plopping down in the green Naugahyde sofa next to the wall. "Especially for $42.50 a month."

"What's your income now?"

"About $200 a month. Social Security, Navy pension."

"You don't need much, anyway, I guess."

He stood up and stepped to the picture window that looks out over the grassy courtyard separating the two buildings. In the harsh light he looked like the old actor Wallace Beery, with puffy broken face and watery eyes and rubbery lips, his shirttail hanging out over a bulging belly. "I'm an alcoholic," he said in a hoarse whisper. "I've done everything. Liquor, pills, everything. I don't even like the stuff. Never did like it, not even when I was playing ball. Hell, only reason I used to carry cigarettes was because my date might want a smoke." He drained the wine from the tumbler and turned away from the window, and there was no self-pity in his gravelly voice. "I came into the world a poor boy," he said, "and I guess I'm still a poor boy."

The 1970 Tennessee Football Guide was generally correct, of course, when it boasted about the steady flood of "news highlighting the good works of former football players." The good life awaits the young man who becomes a college football star. He gets an education, or at least a degree, whether he works at it or not. He becomes known and admired. He discovers the relationship between discipline and success. He makes connections with alumni in high places: men who, in their enthusiasm for football, cross his palm with money and create jobs for him. About all he has to do is mind his manners, do what he is told, and he will be presented with a magical key to an easy life after he is finished playing games. The rule applies to most sports. "If it hadn't been for baseball," a pint-sized minor-league outfielder named Ernie Oravetz once told me, "I'd be just like my old man today: blind and crippled from working in the mines up in Pennsylvania." For thousands of poor kids, particularly poor kids in the South, where football is a way of life, athletics has been a road out. Look at Jim Thorpe, the Indian. Look at

Babe Ruth, the orphan. Look at Willie Mays, the Negro. Look at Joe Namath.

But look, also, at the ones who couldn't make it beyond the last hurrah. Look at Carl Furillo and Joe Louis and the others—the ones who died young, the ones who blew their money, the ones who ruined their bodies, the ones who somehow missed the brass ring. Fame is an empty bubble, easily burst if not handled with care. What happens when the legs go, the arm tires, the eyes fade, the lungs sag? Some cope, some don't. The reasons some don't are so varied and sometimes so subtle that they require the attention of sociologists. But the failures are there, and they will always be with us.

Few bubbles have burst quite so dramatically as that of Bob Suffridge. A runaway who had been scratching out his own living in the streets of Knoxville since the age of 15, Suffridge went on to become one of the 11 best college football players of all time. He weighed only 185 pounds, but he had killer instincts and rabbit quickness and the stamina of a mule. "He was so quick, he could get around you before you got off your haunches," says one former teammate. "Suff was the archetype," says Knoxville sports columnist Tom Anderson, "of the Tennessee single-wing pulling guard." Playing both ways for coach Bob Neyland, averaging more than 50 minutes a game, Suffridge was in on the beginning of a dynasty that became one of the strongest traditions in American college football: the Tennessee Volunteers, the awesome single-wing offense, "The Big Orange," those lean and fast and hungry shock troops of "the General." During three seasons at UT, 1938–39–40, Suffridge never played in a losing regular-season game (though the Vols did lose two of three bowl games, the first of many postseason appearances for the school). He was everybody's All-American in 1938 and 1940 and made some teams in 1939. In 1961 he was named to the national football Hall of Fame, and during

101

college football's centennial celebration two years ago joined the company of such men as Red Grange and Jim Thorpe and Bronko Nagurski on the eleven-man All-Time All-American team. "Bob," says George Cafego, a Vol tailback then and a UT assistant coach now, "had every opportunity to be a millionaire."

There may be no millionaires among the Vols of that era, but there are few slackers. The late Bowden Wyatt was head coach of the Vols for eight seasons. Ed Molinski is a doctor in Memphis. Ed Cifers is president of a textile company. Abe Shires is a sales coordinator for McKesson-Robbins. Bob Woodruff is the UT athletic director.

All of which makes Suffridge an even sadder apparition as he drifts in and out of Knoxville society today, an aimless shadow of the hyped-up kid who used to blitz openings for George Cafego and who once blocked three consecutive Sammy Baugh punt attempts in a brief fling with the pros. Over the past 25 years he has tried working—college coaching, selling insurance, hawking used cars, promoting Coca-Cola, running for public office, and running a liquor store (in that order)—but something would always happen. He hasn't worked now in about five years. He has had two heart attacks, one of them laying him up for eight months. He has engaged in numerous battles with booze, winning some and losing others. He has gone through and survived a period with pills. Now a bloated 250 pounds, he lives alone at the Cagle Terrace Apartments (he lost his wife and four kids to divorce 12 years ago, although now and then one of the children will come to see him), where he seems to have made a separate peace with the world. He made the local papers recently by protesting when two armed guards showed up to supervise a July 4 party there. ("Bob Suffridge, a former All-American football player at Tennessee, complained that elderly residents were frightened at the sudden appearance of the men with guns. . . . Suffridge serves on a committee to help set up socials for elderly residents and also lives at Cagle Terrace.") He spends his time hanging around the sports department of the Knoxville *Journal,* going fishing with buddy Tom Anderson, writing spontaneous letters to people like Paul (Bear) Bryant, talking old times with Cafego and publicist Haywood Harris at UT's shimmering new athletic plant, and sitting for hours in such haunts as Dick Comer's Sports Center (pool hall) and Polly's Tavern and Tommy Ford's South Knoxville American Legion Club No. 138.

Except for a handful of sympathetic acquaintances, some of whom have battled booze themselves, Knoxville doesn't seem to really care much about him anymore. When a woman in the upper-class suburbs heard a magazine was planning a story on Suffridge, she said only, in a low gasp, *"Oh, my God."* There is a great deal of embarrassment on the part of the university, although officials there recognize an obligation to him and have, over the years, with fingers crossed, invited him to appear at banquets and halftime ceremonies. "It's really pretty pitiful," says another Knoxvillian. The newspapers generally treat him gently—"He is now a Knoxville businessman," the *Journal* said after his Hall of Fame selection in 1961—and mercifully let it go at that.

Even when you talk to those who know him best you get little insight into what went wrong. Says Tom Anderson: "He's smarter than you'd think he is, and I thought for a while he was going to straighten up. But I guess you have to regard him as a great athlete who never grew up. It gets worse when he starts talking about the old days. He can get to crying in a minute. Some of those big guys are like that." George Cafego is clearly puzzled by it all: "I don't believe the guy's alergic to work. I've *seen* him work." Ben Byrd of the *Journal* paints a picture of a man who has always marched to a different drummer: "He used to drive into town, park his car anywhere he felt like it, pull up the hood like he had engine trouble, and be gone all day. That time Coke hired him to do PR he got fired when they had a big board meeting and he put a tack on the chair of the chairman of the board. He doesn't mean to cause trouble. Maybe he just never understands the situation. I mean, like when he was sergeant-at-arms for the state legislature one time and didn't like the way a debate was going he demanded the floor."

Perhaps the best friend Suffridge has is a lanky Knoxville attorney named Charlie Burks, a friend from college days who is a reformed alcoholic himself and deserves some credit for the occasions when Suffridge is in control of things. "Oh, Bob's a great practical joker all right," says Burks. "But what do you say about him and his troubles? He's looking for something, but he doesn't know what it is."

There was a time many years ago when Bob Suffridge knew exactly what he was looking for: three square meals a day and a place to sleep at night. He was born in 1916 on a farm in Raccoon Valley, then a notorious hideout for bootleggers, situated some 20 miles from Knoxville. As one of seven children he often had to help his father carry sacks of sugar and stoke the fire for a moonshine still, but that didn't last long. Bob wanted to go to school and play football, against his father's wishes, and one day when he was 15 there was a big fight between the two and Bob left home. He wandered into Fountain City, a suburb of Knoxville, where he fended for himself.

"I was living on a park bench at first," he recalls. "One day I went into this doctor's office and got a job going in early in the morning to sweep out the building and start the fire, for $2.50 a week. I noticed they had some bedsprings next to the heater in the basement—no mattress, just springs—and since I had a key to the place I started sleeping there." The doctor, a Dr. Carl Martin, came in unusually early one morning on an emergency call and found Suffridge asleep in his clothes and saw that he got a mattress and some blankets. Soon another doctor hired him to clean up his office, too, meaning an additional $2.50 a week. "For two years I lived like that. I carried newspapers, worked in a factory, cleaned out those offices and even joined the National Guard so I could pick up another $12 every three months. I didn't go hungry. I was a monitor at school, and took to stealing my lunch out of lockers."

In the meantime, he was asserting himself as the football star with the Central High School Bobcats. "Maybe I was hungrier than the rest of them," he says. He was almost fully developed physically at the age of 18, an eager kid with tremendous speed and reflexes, and in 1936 he captained the Bobcats to the Southern high school championship. Central won 33 consecutive games, and Suffridge became a plum for the college recruiters.

Tennessee was the school he wanted. "They already had a lot of tradition. Everybody wanted to play for General Neyland." Something of a loner, a poor country boy accustomed to fighting solitary battles, he spent every ounce of his energy on the football field. "I couldn't get along with anybody. I couldn't understand them." Although he and Neyland were always at odds, there was a curious, if unspoken, mutual respect between the nail-hard disciplinarian and his moody, antagonistic little guard.

Once the last cheers of the 1940 season had died, Bob Suffridge appeared to have the world in his hands. He earned a degree in physical education ("I guess I thought maybe I'd be a coach one day"), married a UT coed and signed to play with the Philadelphia Eagles. He was named All-Pro for the 1941 season, but more important than that was what happened in the last regular game of the year. It was played on Sunday, December 7. "That was the day I blocked three of Sammy Baugh's punts," he says, "but nobody paid any attention the next day. At halftime somebody had come into the dressing room and told us Pearl Harbor had been bombed by the Japs. I'd have been the hero of the day except for that." Suffridge immediately joined the Navy.

In retrospect, that announcement of the attack on Pearl Harbor was the pivotal moment in Suffridge's life. As executive officer on a troop attack transport, he suffered only a slight shrapnel wound to his right leg and went through no especially traumatic experiences. What hurt was the timing of it all. He was 25 and in peak physical condition when he went in, but a flabby 30 when he came out. He tried to make a comeback with the Eagles during the 1946 season, but he weighed 225 and was soon riding the bench. The bubble had burst, and he was confused. There would be occasional periods of promise, but once the 1950s came it was a steady, painful downhill slide.

Giving up pro football, he tried college coaching: at North Carolina State under ex-Vol great Beattie Feathers, and at the Citadel under his old high school coach, Quinn Decker. Next he went to work as an insurance agent for a company in Knoxville, and after three good years he decided to open his own agency. The business did all right for a while, thanks to his name and contacts in town, but he started in on the pills and the booze and soon had to unload it. ("I sold out for a good profit," Suffridge says, but others say the business fell flat.) And the wandering began. He went to Nashville to sell used cars. He blew the public relations job with Coca-Cola. He was divorced by his wife in March 1960, a year before his election into the football Hall of Fame. The chronology of his life became a blur after that. He ran for clerk of the Knox County court and nearly defeated a man who was considered one of the strongest politicians around and who later became mayor of Knoxville. He had to be literally propped up, to the horror of UT officials, at numerous occasions when he was being paraded around as the Vols' greatest player. He drifted to Atlanta, where, for a year, he drank more than he sold at a friend's liquor store. He worked briefly for the state highway department. Finally, around 1965, shortly after the private publication of a boozy paperback biography entitled *Football Beyond Coaching*—composed in various taverns by Suffridge and a local sports-writer known as Streetcar Edmunds—he suffered two heart attacks.

"Yeah, me and Streetcar had a lot of fun with that book," Suffridge was saying. It was almost dark now, and we had driven out to Tommy Ford's American Legion club. This is the place where Suffridge's Hall of Fame plaque had hung majestically behind the bar for several months before out-raged UT officials finally got it for display in a glass show-case on campus, and the place where Suffridge has spent many a night locked up without anybody knowing he was there. He was saying farewell to his friends, for in the morn-ing he would leave for a month's vacation at Daytona Beach as the guest, or mascot, of his attorney friend Charlie Burks and a doctor from Jamestown, Tennessee. He had dropped a couple of dollars at the nickel slot machine and now he was sitting at the bar, playing some sort of game of chance for a bottle of bourbon.

"How'd the book do?" somebody asked.

"Damn best seller," he said. "Hell, I made about $17,000 off that thing. Sold it for $2. We'd have done better than that if we hadn't given away so many. I'd load a batch in the trunk of my car and head out for Nashville, Memphis and Chattanooga. Sell 'em to people I knew at stores and in bars. Then I'd come back home and find Street sitting in Polly's Tavern and I'd ask him how many he'd sold while I was gone and he'd say he'd gotten rid of 200. 'Well, where's the money?' I'd ask him, and he'd say he gave 'em away. Street' was almost as good a businessman as I was."

"Go on, Bob, take another chance," said a blonde named Faye.

"Another? Honey, that's getting to be expensive liquor."

"Price of liquor never seemed to bother you much."

"Guess you're right about that." A phone rang. "Get that, will you?" he said. "Might be somebody."

And so it goes, an evening with Bob Suffridge. They are all like that, they say: aimless hours of puns and harmless practical jokes and, if the hour is late enough and the pile of beer cans high enough, those infinitely sad moments when his eyes water up as he talks on about the missed opportunities and the wasted years. How can anyone pass judgment, though, without having gone through the pressures he has? *I came into the world a poor boy and I'm still a poor boy.* What a man has to do is be grateful for the good times and try to learn to live with the bad.

We were finishing steaks at a motel dining room, washing them down with beer, when the waitress could stand it no longer. A well-preserved woman near Suffridge's age, she had been stealing glances at him throughout the meal. She finally worked up her nerve as she was clearing the table, turning to me and saying with an embarrassed grin: "Excuse me, but didn't I hear you call him Bob?"

"That's right."

"Well, I thought so." For the first time she looked directly at Suffridge. "You're Bob Suffridge, aren't you?"

He wiped his mouth and said, "I guess I am."

"I was Penny Owens. I went to Central with you."

"Penny . . .?"

"Oh, you wouldn't remember me. You never would even look at me twice when we were in school."

They talked for a few minutes about old times and former classmates. There was an awkward silence. "So," she said, "ah, what are you *doing* now, Bob?"

"Nothing."

She flushed. "Oh."

He suppressed a belch and then looked up at her with a mischievous grin. "You want to help me?"

"Aw, you."

"Awww, you."

8·PRAISE THE LORD AND PASS THE BALL TO FUQUA

It isn't easy, being head basketball coach at Oral Roberts University. Ken Trickey has accepted an invitation to meet a writer in the bar at the Camelot Inn in Tulsa, Oklahoma, and the minute he walks into the place he starts wishing he hadn't come along. "This is one problem other coaches don't have," he is saying as we weave past perfumed ladies standing at the bar and take a conspicuous table right under the nose of the guy playing the piano and leering and telling raunchy jokes to a horny crowd of fat cats in town for the Tulsa-Houston football game. Trickey's Coke hasn't even arrived when a middle-aged businessman points out the coach to his leggy blonde friend and they begin to giggle.

"Hey, coach," the man howls, "lemme buy you a drink."

"Thanks. I just ordered one."

"Bourbon and Seven?"

"Just a Coke."

The guy and his date are breaking up now, and all Trickey can do is smile and sweat. "I'll tell you one thing," he says, "my life has sure changed since I took this job. You don't

THE GOOD OLD BOYS

work for President Roberts and drink, and you don't throw
any temper tantrums on the court. When I was at Middle
Tennessee I'd go into the dressing room at halftime and the
first thing I'd do was pick up a bottle and throw it through a
window." The comedian's jokes are getting rougher, and
Trickey is tightening his jaw to keep from laughing. "Yeah,
everybody laughed at me when I took this job, but nobody's
laughing anymore. How many coaches would want to be at
a place where it's a *school rule* not to smoke or drink or fool
around? Look, we've probably got over a million alumni.
You've gotta figure everybody who ever came into contact
with Oral Roberts is an alumnus. And, hey, can you imagine
what it's like to have him recruiting for you? I mean, you're
trying to get a great basketball player and Mr. Roberts goes
into the living room with the boy and the parents, and he
bows his head and starts praying? Preachers always used to
turn me off, but this man is something else."

The idea that a university run by the world's most famous
faith healer and evangelist would have a big-time basketball
team leads to the usual jokes, of course ("With Oral Roberts,
who needs a trainer?"), but the time has come to consider
the ORU Titans as something more than a curiosity. For
five seasons, they had piddled along in relative obscurity,
stuck out there in the eastern Oklahoma outback and playing Ouachita Baptist and Sacred Heart and Oklahoma
Christian. Oral Roberts himself had made noises about wanting to win a national championship by 1975—"Expect a
miracle," he would say, parodying his favorite slogans, "because something *good* is going to *happen* to *you*"—but such
a possibility must have appeared as ludicrous to people like
Johnny Wooden and Al McGuire as the curing of a broken
arm through prayer.

But then came the 1971–72 basketball season. Going with
a modest bunch of kids from places like Chattanooga, Tennessee, and Inola, Oklahoma—they were predominantly

black, too, which seemed another curiosity—ORU started off by winning its first four games against minor opponents by a total of only 14 points. When the Titans lost their first substantial test—by seven points, at Murray State in Kentucky—everybody figured they had reverted to form. But from that point on, ORU never looked back. They won the next 21 games they played, finishing the regular season with a 25-1 record and obliterating tough Memphis State in the first round of the National Invitation Tournament at Madison Square Garden before losing to St. John's. Led by a slippery black six-foot-four guard named Richard Fuqua, whose 35.9 scoring average was second in the nation to the 36.6 of Southwest Louisiana's Dwight Lamar, the Titans set an all-time NCAA scoring record of 105.1 points per game. Fuqua made some All-American teams, and ORU was ranked 16th in the final Associated Press major-college rankings. "Something good," headlined a postseason press release, "happened to us."

And from the looks of it, better things are in store this year. Graduation losses from last year's team are minimal— 84 percent of the point production is back—and two new men should give Trickey the beef under the backboards that he needed last year, even though ORU did lead the country in rebounding ("Because we shoot more"): a seven-foot former prep All-America named David Vaughn, and a six-foot-eight, 225-pound junior college All-America named Greg McDougald. The schedule is tougher, sprinkled this time with names like Jacksonville and Long Beach State and Eastern Kentucky, which will help in the ratings if ORU can win or play them close. The late-February match with Southwest Louisiana will be nationally televised, giving the rest of us a chance to see the country's top two gunners shoot it out. And this year the fanatical ORU fans in Tulsa will be able to watch it all from the plush bucket seats of the new 11,000-seat Special Events Center, rather than in the dinky little 3,000-seat gym the Titans have been enduring on their way to prominence. In anticipation, some 9,000 fans had paid for season tickets in advance of the opener.

Oral Roberts University itself is remarkable enough. Early in the 1960s, Oral Roberts began laying the groundwork for building a nonsectarian private liberal arts school on the dusty undulating flatland south of Tulsa. "I think people thought I was crazy," he says. It wasn't that much of a gamble, once you grasp the breadth of the Oral Roberts Association, which stands behind the university. One Tulsa banker has estimated that the foundation takes in $40,000 a day, or some $15 million a year, in donations from all over the world. The foundation handles more mail than anybody else in town, including Shell Oil's national credit-card operation. Such a response is generated, of course, by the dynamic personality of Roberts himself and his modern brand of sleek evangelism: the endless books he publishes, the magazines and other regular publications, and above all the nationally televised programs such as Oral Roberts Presents. With all of that behind him, in 1965 he opened the $30 million university on 500 acres.

What you have today is a futuristic campus that looks more like the site of a World's Fair than a place for study and worship. The student body has risen to some 2,500 now. ("We had 1,800 kids apply this fall," says the registrar, "and we could only accept 900 of them.") They come from all over: Only 26 percent are from Oklahoma, 30 denominations are represented, and 5 percent are black. The campus is dominated by the glassy 200-foot Prayer Tower, where a switchboard is manned every minute of the year by workers who counsel and pray for callers all over the world, and if the students who walk beneath that tower share anything it is a well-scrubbed joy right out of the 1950s. In the student handbook the rules are quite specific: church on Sunday, chapel meetings twice a week, coats and ties for boys, skirts for girls ("They tried to enforce a skirt length code," says a faculty member, "but wisely gave up the idea"), no smoking, no drinking, no "fornication out of marriage," even a curfew for the girls. "We had to let only ten kids go last year for breaking the rules," says the dean of men, Jack Wallace, a former college football coach at Northeast Oklahoma, pointing out a theory shared by all administrators at the college: that kids today want discipline and rules to work under. ORU students comport themselves as a master race, wearing their hair trim but modishly long (as Roberts himself is doing these days), opening doors for each other and disarming visitors with Huckleberry Finn grins. "Any kid on this campus could cash a personal check anywhere in Tulsa," says one school official, "because everybody knows who stands behind them."

Standing behind it all, of course, is The Man: Granville Oral Roberts, a son of the Oklahoma soil. Born into a Pentecostal preacher's family 54 years ago, he was given the middle name because his mother hoped he would grow up to be a preacher like his father. But he developed a speech impediment and didn't particularly care for church as a boy, and it took a serious illness to change all that. Driving in for a layup during a high school basketball game when he was 16, he suddenly collapsed. Tuberculosis, they said, with not much hope for survival. Desperately, one night his parents wrapped him up and took him to see a faith healer at a tent revival in Ada, Oklahoma, and he says today that he recovered because of the faith put into his body by the preacher. He began preaching in the Pentecostal Holiness Church in the 1940s, but soon dropped out and hit the road on the tent-revival circuit. By the 1950s he was the biggest name in the business. Like most evangelists, he has begun to soften his approach and modernize his methods—no more tents, no more hell-fire preaching, no more hysterical boasts of instant miracles—to become a sort of poor man's Billy Graham. Roberts is what he is today because he recognized earlier than most that Americans had a new set of interests, not to mention television and air conditioning, and evangelism had to fold its tents and go to the people.

With that in mind, Roberts included big-time basketball in his earliest plans for the new university. "Sports is probably the biggest thing going in this country today," he says. "A game like basketball is healthy, and it can also be a strong witness for God." The first ORU Titans began playing during the 1966–67 season, going 17–9 the first year and 18–6 the next. They were winners, sure, but the competition was small stuff and something was lacking. Roberts discovered what he was wanting when his team hosted Middle Tennessee State in the second game of the third season. Running a wild fast-break and a pesty full-court pressure defense, Middle Tennessee embarrassed ORU by a score of 115–98. Roberts was so turned on by the free-wheeling Ohio Valley Conference team that he went down on the court as soon as the game ended and button-holed the Tennessee coach, a young fellow named Ken Trickey. "I decided," Roberts says, "that that was the kind of team I wanted." By the early spring he had hired Trickey as basketball coach and athletic director, upped the athletic budget to around $300,000, and started talking about a national championship.

Although he deliberated over the job before accepting ("All my coaching friends were saying, 'What's an Oral Roberts?' ") Trickey has never looked back. "I've got everything going for me here," he was saying on his last day in the old gymnasium, prior to the move into the gaudy new coliseum. "I've got the city of Tulsa, which is beautiful and clean and accessible to both coasts. It's a place a kid from a small town or a ghetto would like, and that's where the players come from nowadays. I've got this kind of school, which has got to appeal to parents. I've got all of those built-in alumni like Notre Dame and West Point have. And I've got Oral Roberts on my side. I could call him right now and say, 'President, I've got this five-foot-ten guard from

Ohio over here and I want him,' and he'd be over here talking to the boy in five minutes."

Ken Trickey is a delightful, candid man of 38 years who
is popular anywhere he goes. He was the New York press
corps' boy last year during the NIT meeting at Madison
Square Garden, drawling one-liners right and left ("Defense
is something you do when you don't have the ball") like a,
well, like a colorful evangelist would. A two-time All-Ohio
Valley guard at Middle Tennessee, he played in the 1954
NAIA tournament before coaching high school teams in the
Midwest and then going back to Middle Tennessee as an
assistant in 1962. When he took over the head job there three
years later, he quickly gave the school a colorful winning
team. "You're not too smart if your livelihood depends on
five kids running around in their underwear," he has cracked,
but he is another of those hyped-up coaches basketball seems
to breed. "I'm not nervous," he says, "just quick."

Every time one of these obscure little schools suddenly
bursts forth with a winning basketball team (as Jacksonville
did three years ago), the coaching establishment across the
country begins talking about methods of recruitment and
suggesting investigations and questioning the level of opposition. "I know," says Trickey. "When I took over it was
April 1, and I had one game on my schedule and eight ballplayers. We were a little Christian school, and we weren't
accredited in the NCAA. If we keep on winning, nobody's
going to want to play us and everybody's going to be saying
we're buying players and all of that stuff." Actually, Trickey
says, he virtually fell into the team which ranked 16th in
ORU's first year as a "major college." Richard Fuqua, for
example, was headed for Middle Tennessee to play for
Trickey when Ken took the ORU job. "I thought I'd lost
him, that he wouldn't want to come out to Tulsa." Fuqua is
a poor black kid from Chattanooga, one of eight kids from
Tennessee on the 23-man roster for this year. The coach at

115

Riverside High in Chattanooga, which had won 60 straight games, told Fuqua that ORU would be a good place to play, "so that's how I got the best basketball player that ever came out of Tennessee," says Trickey. Most of the others found their way to ORU the same way, through Trickey's acquaintances and his ability to turn the kids on to ORU's future.

"I don't really have that much trouble recruiting here," he said as he sat in an office filled with pictures and busts of the Kennedy brothers, John and Robert, behind the inevitable placard saying EXPECT A MIRACLE. "Most of those kids want to play pro ball, so I tell 'em to come here because we're already playing the pro game. I want my boys to shoot and score. We try to shoot at least 100 times a game, on the theory that if you make half of them [ORU shot 45.2 percent from the field last year] you've got 100 points right there. On top of that, the game is just more fun that way. Who wants to go watch somebody win 60–50? We put it up, and play a full-court press and work a lot on positioning for the rebound, and we'll pass the ball all the way from one end to the other for a layup if we can. If I'm going to win by ten points, I want it to be 130–120." Indeed, ORU and Union, Tennessee, in a game last year won by ORU 155–113, set an NCAA record with their 268 points. It interests Trickey little that his Titans led the nation in scoring and rebounding, yet were next-to-last in defense: "If I'd known we were that close, we'd have gone for the record." He delights in pointing out that three ORU games had to be halted last year so trainers could get cramps out of the officials' legs.

The star of the show, and the man most likely to benefit from ORU's style of play ("We Run and Gun," or WRAG, reads the publicity), is Richard Fuqua. "Look," says Trickey, "I'd play five Indians if they could win. The only time people start talking about color is when you lose." Richard

Fuqua is a shy, 21-year-old black who had taken his share of licks before arriving at Oral Roberts University, never really finding himself until he came under Trickey's wing. He is one of five children, father unaccounted for, whose mother tried to support them on $6 a day as a maid. He had to hold down jobs while going to school and playing for Riverside, an all-black high school in Chattanooga. He wasn't much of a scorer at Riverside, primarily because the starters were usually pulled midway through the second quarter to keep scores down. "He would only shoot eight or nine times a game," Trickey recalls.

Playing as a freshman, back when ORU was rated small-college, Fuqua showed flashes of what was to come. "He's such a good, modest kid. I had to beg him to shoot," Trickey remembers. That first season, Fuqua took 483 shots in 31 games, hitting 47.2 percent, for an 18.1 scoring average. Between seasons, Trickey went to work on him. *You want to play pro ball, don't you? You want to make All-America, don't you?* "I told him if he shot the ball every time he got it, we would win and all these things would happen for him." The next year he put it up 701 times making 50.4 percent, and last season he averaged 34 shots a game from the floor, making 44.4 percent. Rather frail at six-foot-four and 175 pounds, Fuqua makes it on silky moves and an incredible long-range touch; most of his shots are from 20 to 30 feet out, where he springs high in the air and falls back as though he were unloading from the dollar seats. "Richard," says Trickey, "is the greatest shooter I have ever seen."

Fuqua very definitely wants to play in the pros, and during the past off-season turned down a couple of feelers from ABA teams on the advice that a sensational senior year at ORU would drive his price out of sight. Married since he was 16, he has had trouble piled on trouble with his four-year-old daughter: first she had spinal meningitis, which was nearly fatal, and then there was eye surgery. He makes passing grades in Health-and-PE, while his wife works to bring in some money. Although he understands Trickey's strategy, it still bothers him a bit to be getting all the glory.

"Naw, there hasn't been any race problem for any of us," Fuqua was saying one rainy day, two weeks before practice would officially begin. "People out here are real nice. They're interested in you—Mr. Roberts, coach Trickey, everybody."

"Did you want a big school?" he was asked.

"I thought about it some, but not much."

"You had offers?"

"Yeah, I had some. But, see, me and Baker and Taylor, we decided to stick together. We all came here."

"You want to play pro ball, I guess?"

"Man," he said, shoving a funky rain cap over his forehead and whistling. "Poor boy like me? Do I want to play pro ball?"

Whether Oral Roberts University can make it all the way to the top any day soon remains to be seen. They have already come to the stage where nobody—not the big-time powers like UCLA, at any rate—is aching to take them on. Trickey and Roberts are currently thinking of expanding the athletic program enough to enter the tough Missouri Valley Conference so they won't have to sit around and hope for at-large bids to NCAA tournaments. Certainly Trickey's recruiting will come easier now, after what happened last year. "I felt we were going to make it about halfway through my first year," says Trickey. "I felt like we could play anybody except the Top 15 that year, and the next year I thought we could play all except the Top Ten. Now I think we can play anybody." UCLA, he says, turned down an invitation to play the opener this fall in the new colliseum. "The day's going to come when they'll *have* to play us."

Whatever happens, ORU has already made its own unique contribution to college basketball in an era when violence has become a way of life. There has been only one fight in Trickey's tenure, and in that one a Titan simply couldn't bring himself to turn the other cheek. Acting the good Christians they proclaim themselves to be, ORU fans never boo. When both teams are announced before a game, they are accorded equal applause as they prance to the center of the court on a red carpet. "They beat us," said one visiting coach last year, "but that crowd had our kids thinking they'd *won*." ORU uses Missouri Valley Conference officials for its home games and, says publicist Mal Elliott, "It's the one time all year that a lot of 'em bring their wives to watch 'em work." If that isn't enough, ORU players are instructed to raise their hands and *smile* when a foul is called.

Which is just the way The Man meant it to be. The influence of Granville Oral Roberts on the basketball program is every bit as pervasive as it is on the workings of the rest of the university. He makes every game he can, even on the road, and sits prominently on the second row behind the scorer's table. "He doesn't go off chasing basketball players all over the country," says Trickey, but he is always there to do what he can: talk to a prospect, lead the halftime prayer in the dressing room, fly away with Trickey on a scouting trip. With an extra office in the coliseum, where he can be found one-fourth of the time during the season, he acts about this team like a boy with a litter of puppies.

"Chapel was real good this morning, President."

"Aren't those World Action Singers wonderful?" Roberts said to Trickey. The coaches and athletic-office people had been standing around at the end of the day, sipping coffee and talking, when he stuck his head through the doorway. The twice-weekly chapel, all students and faculty required to attend, had been held that morning. There had been the jazzy World Action Singers, from the Oral Roberts television show, and some preaching and an announcement that George Wallace was feeling no pain—that announcement followed by thunderous applause—and a further notice that next week's chapel guest would be black mayor Charles Evers of Fayette, Mississippi.

The basketball program, Roberts was saying, is simply another part of ORU's ministry. "You know, we almost lost America there for a while," he said. "Discipline was shot, and people were talking about tearing America down. Now, I don't think they really meant that, do you? We have to be clean and pure and disciplined. That helps you to live life, and"—he looked at Trickey and winked—"and it helps you win basketball games, doesn't it, Coach?" From there he drifted out onto the gymnasium floor, and he was last seen shooting two-handed set shots from 25 feet out with Richard Fuqua. Not badly, either.

PART THREE

The Poets

9·OKIE FROM MUSKOGEE

If it's Friday, this must be Dayton. Laid out like a sheet of rolled steel on the Great Miami River, a major industrial center plopped down on the placid, undulating farmland of southwestern Ohio, Dayton is about as Middle America as you can get. "Middle Voter," says the book *The Real Majority,* "is a 47-year-old housewife from the outskirts of Dayton, Ohio, whose husband is a machinist." There has been some rumbling in the black ghettos and some posturing by isolated hippies, but Dayton is still dominated by two singular classes: substantial law-abiding Midwestern businessmen and alienated white Appalachian migrants dismissed as "Briarhoppers." The businessmen bank the money and ridicule the workers ("The first thing Neil Armstrong saw when he stepped on the moon was two Briars in a '57 Ford, looking for the Frigidaire plant"), while the latter mind the factories by day and smash the Rebel-flagged honky-tonks of disheveled East Dayton by night. But no matter how much the two groups may differ in life styles, they stand together on what are, to them, the larger issues. Hippies, draft dodgers and pot. The flag, police and apple pie.

Little wonder, then, that Memorial Hall, a bleak granite hulk dedicated to the area's war dead, is bulging on a blustery Friday night when the new king of country music comes on. It is Merle Haggard, a wiry ex-convict whose Okie parents endured the same degradation in Depression California that the Briars suffer in Dayton, and when he strolls out in a flared black Western suit and $350 rattlesnake-skin boots from Nudie's in Hollywood, they wildly applaud. His "Workin' Man's Blues" touches nerves ("I ain't never been on welfare, that's one place I won't be"), but as he moves on to his autobiographical ballads about liquor, ladies and the law, you can sense the crowd's restlessness. They have come for one thing this night. " 'Okie,' 'Okie,' " they are pleading. Personal-sized American flags begin coming out of purses. Haggard grins nervously. "Hey, Merle, how 'bout 'Okie'?" Finally, having teased them long enough, Haggard lays it on them—"We don't smoke marijuana in Muskogee, and we don't take our trips on LSD"—and suddenly they are on their feet, berserk, waving flags and stomping and whistling and cheering, joining in on the chorus: ". . . we still wave Ol' Glory down at the Courthouse, white lightning's still the biggest thrill of all," and for those brief bombastic moments the majority isn't silent anymore. "It will," a liberal friend had promised, "scare the living hell out of you."

Country music was always the folk music of the white Southern working class—"white soul," if you will—an earthly commentary that rang out over rural radio stations and roadhouse jukeboxes for truckers, farmers, mill workers and their bored housewives. Even in recent years, when the music began to modernize into "pop-country" and spread out from the South to become the nation's most popular form of music, its basic appeal was in its simple answers to every-day problems. Country artists continued to sing about divorce and drinking and a fiery hell, leaving the more complex contemporary problems to the politicized young folk-rock crowd. But they had to react, sooner or later, when America went through the traumatic social upheaval of the late 1960s.

Suddenly there were more pressing social problems than booze and broken homes to deal with: campus riots, drugs and war protests. There was an America out there, weary of complexities, looking for a simple answer to it all. It was inevitable that country music would get around to offering up an answer.

The response was "Okie from Muskogee," and when Merle Haggard first sang it in public—to a beery crowd of Green Berets at the Fort Bragg, North Carolina, NCO Club—the reaction to the song scared him, too: "They started comin' up after me on the stage, and I didn't know what was gonna happen next until they said we'd have to do it again before they'd let us go." But when "Okie" was released in 1969, followed by the more explicit "The Fightin' Side of Me" ("If you don't love it, leave it, let this song that I'm singin' be a warning; when you're runnin' down our country, hoss, you're walkin' on the fightin' side of me"), it stamped the handsome 33-year-old Bakersfield, California, native as a proletarian poet and fired his career into another orbit. His average price for a one-nighter on the tire-busting country music circuit quadrupled to nearly $9,000, and his gross annual income tripled to $1 million. The "Okie" album qualified as a gold record, his first and a rarity in the country music marketplace, and when the annual Country Music Association awards show was televised from Nashville's Grand Ole Opry House the next fall, Haggard swept the boards, as Johnny Cash had the year before. He got a letter from President Nixon applauding "Okie," and there were indications that he would be invited to perform at the White House. There was talk of a network television show, and National Educational Television rushed out with a Haggard profile. "He is sort of the Spiro Agnew of music, the poet laureate of the hard hats," wrote a Dayton columnist after Haggard's performance there.

Predictably, most liberals were livid. "Okie" and "Fightin' Side" came along precisely when students and rock musicians were beginning to picture Haggard as a potential Woody Guthrie of the 1970s—a raw populist tale-spinner more concerned with singing honest songs than with cutting gold records—but the two new songs blew it for them. "Somewhere, some night, some guys are going to sit around in a tavern, prime themselves with beer, 'Okie' and 'Fightin' Side,' and go out and get some hippies," said the *Great Speckled Bird,* an underground paper in Atlanta. "I hate Merle Haggard," a Hollywood writer-friend closed out a letter to me. "One ground rule," the wife of my publisher said over drinks at their Manhattan apartment, "don't mention the Okie's name." Liberals were accusing Haggard of capitalizing on Middle America's frustrations and adding to the nation's polarization. In retaliation, several rock groups unsuccessfully solicited Haggard's permission to record parodies to the tune of "Okie," and Arlo Guthrie, son of the folk singer Haggard, was supposed to succeed, began opening his concerts with the song, to the delight of his long-haired audiences.

Haggard, then, had become caught in this crossfire between the hard hats and the hippies, both of whom seemed intent on remaking him into their image, and he didn't like it one bit. Claiming no special knowledge about Vietnam, campus disorders or hippie culture—"except what I read in the papers or see on TV"—he swears "Okie" occurred to him on the bus one day while he and his band rumbled over the drab Oklahoma flatlands en route to a date: "There was this sign that said 'Muskogee, thataway,' or whatever, and somebody said something like, 'I bet they don't smoke marijuana in Muskogee.' I thought it was a pretty funny line, and we [Haggard and Roy Burris, his drummer at the time] just started making up some more. It probably took 20 minutes to write the thing, if you add it all up." When the furor arose after its release Haggard got scared—"Boy, I tell you, I didn't realize how strong some people felt about those things"—and backed off, wondering what manner of monster he had wrought. He turned down George Wallace's invitation to work the Alabama gubernatorial campaign, eluded reporters and shied from network television talk shows. But at almost every stop he was collared by liberals and began to hear the other side, like the night in Buffalo when a pair of college students waited in the wings for him between shows: "The girl was kinda hippieish, but the boy looked like a pretty sensible kid. Anyway, we got onto the war thing, and I said to the boy, 'You mean you wouldn't fight for your country?' He said, 'Oh, yeah, I'd fight for my country. But I don't believe I'm fighting *for* my country, I'm fighting *against* it.' So I said, 'Well, if you'd said anything else I'd o' walked off, but I'd like to hear what you got to say.' I spent the next two hours listening to 'em, squatting right there in the hallway. I have to be truthful; after I talked to 'em I wasn't too sure they wasn't right. They made me understand some things that possibly I never understood before."

It is a shame, in a way, that Merle Haggard had to be the one to give us "Okie" and "Fightin' Side," because those two songs have obscured the fact that he is one of the few genuine folk heroes in American popular music today. " 'Okie' notwithstanding," said *Rolling Stone*, the folk-rock journal, "Haggard is no racist cracker spewing out Johnny Reb songs for the segs . . . As a writer he is gifted with an ability to capture the life of the common man with a certain dignity." He has no racial hangups ("I got that out of me in prison"), no politics (he hasn't told anybody whom he supported in the presidential election, if he supported anyone at all), and few concerns about his image. Restless, moody, chain-smoking, intense—as real as the tattoo of a spider web on his back ("He did it when he was young and felt trapped," says his wife)—he is a good old boy who put himself through a lot of trouble as a kid and lived to write and sing about it. Technically, his voice is second only to Marty Robbins' in country music, and when he meanders onstage he is a supercool, almost reticent troubadour—no sequins, no ten-gallon hat, no hokey ad libs—with wavy black hair and slightly bowed legs and a high shiny forehead and a story to sing. Maybe he *did* turn out "Okie" and "Fightin' Side," but sandwiched around them were two splendid albums with little chance of commercial success: loving tributes to Jimmie Rodgers and Bob Wills (he taught himself the fiddle in only six months for the latter), which he did because he thought they were historically and musically important. "To brand him for those songs is wrong, man, because he's written some of the best folk songs that's ever been written," says Kris Kristofferson, leader of the new breed of folk-country songwriters in Nashville. "What he oughta do now is an album based on *The Grapes of Wrath.* That'd bring 'em back to roost."

Indeed, the early history of the Haggard family reads like John Steinbeck's novel about the farmed-out Okies' desperate migration to California during the 1930s, and much of this is reflected in Haggard's songs. The Haggards and their two children were living on a farm near Checotah, in eastern Oklahoma, when they awoke one morning in the spring of 1934 to see their barn and almost everything else they had burning to the ground. Although they managed to plant their spring crop with the aid of neighbors, the worsening drought killed it, and a year later they made the decision to leave. They were, as it said in Jimmie Rodgers' "California Blues," "going to California, where they sleep out every night."

Relatives who had gone ahead two years earlier to work on a cotton farm sent them $40. Mr. Haggard swapped all but the essentials for a 1926 Chevrolet and a rickety trailer, and while his wife packed home-cured bacon and other nonperishables, he bandaged the crippled automobile and loaded the trailer. On a blistering Monday morning in mid-July, the four of them set forth on the treacherous journey across the country, joining the antlike train of refugees creeping westward along Route 66. "I remember we broke down in the middle of the desert," says Flossie Haggard, the mother, who is in her 70s now and lives with Merle and his family in Bakersfield. "We were out of water, and just when I thought we weren't going to make it, I saw this boy coming down the highway on a bicycle. He was going all the way from Kentucky to Fresno. He shared a quart of water with us and helped fix the car. Everybody'd been treating us like trash, and I told this boy, 'I'm glad to see there's still some decent folks in this world.' He rode the rest of the way with us, and I still write to him."

On Friday they limped into Bakersfield. "A lot of our friends were already there," Mrs. Haggard recalls, "and some of them were living in 'Hoover Camps,' all bunched up and starving in old cardboard boxes." The Haggards moved into a makeshift farm cabin with her sister's family and found work—their children, 14 and 12, not excluded—milking cows for rent, $50 a month, and "all the milk we could drink." After two months of that, Mr. Haggard caught on with the Santa Fe Railroad as a carpenter and found more permanent lodgings. "One day Jim saw this railroad car sitting on concrete blocks out in the sagebrush, and he talked the lady that owned it into letting us live in it free while we made it into a house. He was always a good worker, good with his hands. The only thing we ever took on welfare was a sack of flour a friend gave us that time the barn burned. Nine months later, he'd turned that old boxcar into a right nice little house, and we bought it for $500. When Merle sings 'Hungry Eyes' ['a canvas-covered cabin, in a crowded labor camp, stands out in this memory I revive: ' 'cause my Daddy raised a fam'ly there with two hard-workin' hands, and tried to feed my mama's hungry eyes'], almost every word of it really happened like that."

The same can be said of "Mama Tried," another Haggard composition: "One and only rebel child, from a fam'ly meek and mild, my mama seemed to know what lay in store; 'spite of all my Sunday learnin', towards the bad I kept on turnin', 'till mama couldn't hold me anymore." Merle was born in the spring of 1937 and grew up, in that converted boxcar, closer to his father than to his mother. His father taught him how to fish and hunt, while his mother, a fierce member of the Church of Christ who had made Mr. Haggard cease fiddling in honky-tonks when they got married, felt duty-bound to see that her baby grew up a Christian. Mr. Haggard died when Merle was nine, and trouble was imminent. "A psychiatrist has said that's what started it," says Mrs. Haggard. Past 40, she had to take a job and leave a rambunctious boy at home alone.

When he was 14, he started skipping school, to go fishing and taste grown-up vices with some of his buddies, and it was felt that a juvenile home would scare him into his senses. "It was the wrong thing to do," Mrs. Haggard says now. Merle simply walked out of the place the next day ("Well god-*damn,* they practically *invite* you to escape"), giving him a police record and touching off a nomadic spree that didn't end until some nine years later. "Wild hair, that's all it was," Haggard says. "I was curious, and I wanted to feel like a man. Like, while I was in jail I could smoke if I wanted to and didn't have to eat if I wasn't hungry. It's really hard to say what makes a kid do that, but it's certainly not as unappealing as it may seem." The dossier on Merle Ronald Haggard grew quickly: stolen car in Kingman, armed robbery in Bakersfield, bogus checks in Phoenix, escape here, petty theft there. And when he wasn't in jail, he was exploring the great Southwest: driving a truck, pitching hay, hopping freights, picking grapes, working oil fields, lying about his age so he could pick guitar in what Glen Campbell calls "fightin' and dancin' clubs." The authorities finally nailed him late in 1957 when he and some pals tried to burglarize a Bakersfield bar ("We got drunk waitin' for it to close, thought it was three in the morning when it was eleven at night"). He was charged with second-degree burglary and escape and told to say good-by to his mother and his wife—an impromptu marriage had produced non-stop fights and four children—since he was off to San Quentin for six months to 15 years.

He stayed in trouble until he spent a week in solitary confinement, in a dark bunkless cell across a narrow hall from Death Row, for involvement in a moonshine whiskey scheme. "A week of hearing those guys talk about how one thing led to another scared the hell out of me. The first thing I did when I got out was ask for the roughest job in the house." He worked overtime in the sweaty prison textile mill, minded his manners, got a high-school-equivalent diploma, and even joined the warden's country band. And he got to see his idol when Johnny Cash came through to entertain the troops. (Actually, Cash has spent only one afternoon and one night in jail, both times for pep pills, and Haggard says he is "always asking me about prison." Haggard doesn't play prison dates because "it'd look like I was copyin' John.") He was paroled after two years and nine months at Quentin and drifted back home to Bakersfield in November 1960, 23 years old and much wiser. "I'm not so sure it works like that very often, but I'm one guy the prison system straightened out. I know damned well I'm a better man because of it."

Music was about the only serious interest Haggard had as a kid. His grandfather had been one of the top fiddlers in Oklahoma, and his father continued to pick and sing around the house after he quit the clubs. Merle grew up listening to the Grand Ole Opry broadcast on Saturday nights, and became a fan of such early stars as Wills, Rodgers and Lefty Frizzell. "By the time I was 11," says Haggard, "I felt like I might go into music. I remember, one day my brother came by the house with this old guitar some guy had left at the service station as mortgage for some gas or something. Mama showed me a couple of chords, and I taught myself the rest. About the time I started to screw up I'd learned to play pretty good guitar."

When Haggard returned to Bakersfield from prison, the town was beginning to blossom as a minor center of country music. A musician could make a decent living playing on local radio shows, at weekend dances and in the rowdy taverns catering to ranch hands and oil workers. Country stars like Glen Campbell had served apprenticeships there, and singer Buck Owens had come in from Arizona and established such an empire that the city was being called "Buckersfield" by some. Haggard first took a job with his brother, an electrical contractor, driving a truck for $80 a week—playing at different clubs on weekends for an extra $20—but it wasn't long before he went into the clubs full-time and ran into Fuzzy Owen.

Fuzzy was an angular Arkansan with pearly teeth and jet black hair and flashing eyes—the small-town dandy you see in a shiny suit and a string tie, slapping used-car hoods on local television—who had been in Bakersfield for 10 years, playing the clubs and Cousin Herb Henson's television show, enjoying moderate success. He had bought the Tally record label from a cousin and was making plans to cut some records in a converted garage when he and Merle met. They became fast friends, and Fuzzy helped Merle with his singing and his bookings. Haggard went off to Las Vegas for a while in 1962 to play in a band, and when he returned he began to record. The first release sold about 200 copies, but the second slipped into the charts, and when Haggard recorded "All My Friends Are Gonna Be Strangers," the doors blew open for him. The song made the country Top Ten, and Capitol Records came calling. "I was over there doing a live album on Cousin Herb," recalls Capitol producer Ken Nelson, "and one of the warm-up acts was Haggard. I knew he had it, and I offered him a recording contract. You know what he said? 'I appreciate it, but I've got a contract with Tally Records, and if it wasn't for Fuzzy I wouldn't be anywhere today.' I never heard of such loyalty." But Haggard named Fuzzy his personal manager and arranged the sale of Tally Records to Capitol. Divorced since his return from prison, he married Bonnie Owens, a pleasant Oklahoma farm girl who was once the wife of Buck Owens. He rounded up a band, moved up from a station wagon to a used bus, and they hit the road. He started writing his own stuff, running into Hollywood to record, hitting the top of the charts with every release, turning them into albums, and became by 1968 one of the top stars in country music with a fanatical following in America's factories and bars and prisons owing to songs like "I Take a Lot of Pride in What I Am" ("Things I learned in a hobo jungle, were things they never taught me in a classroom; like where to find a handout, while thumbin' through Chicago in the afternoon"). He was, to that forgotten mass out there between New York and Los Angeles, relevant.

Since "Okie" and "Fightin' Side," Haggard has been able to immerse himself in the trappings of the superstar. He has built a rustic $250,000 lakeside estate on the 280-acre spread he owns at the mouth of Kern Canyon outside Bakersfield. There is a recording studio on the land, and a 42 foot yacht he uses as a retreat during the 100 days of the year when he isn't on the road. To make his dates he travels in a $75,000 customized bus (plastered, lately, with such patriotic slogans as I'M PROUD TO BE AN AMERICAN), and when he gets there he can choose from two dozen Western costumes and 15 pairs of boots. When he and Bonnie starting getting at each other's throats during the sweep through the Midwest and Canada—it isn't easy for a woman to share living quarters with nine men and a terrier on a 24-day tour—Merle stopped in Columbus to kick tires on a $100,000 second bus for himself, Bonnie, Fuzzy and a driver.

Yet success has worked few personality changes on him so

far. There are too many reminders of where he has been: the tattooed initials PBS on his left wrist (for Preston Boys' School, a juvenile home), badly buckled fingernails stunted by chemicals in the San Quentin laundry and a record that cannot be erased. Indeed, it wasn't until a year or so ago that he would talk for print about his prison background ("I don't see why they have to keep bringing that up," says Mrs. Haggard, who once asked Merle if he wanted to change his name and is now titular president of his fan club). His marriage, thanks in large part to Bonnie ("He's an Aries, very restless, and I have to remember that"), seems more solid than most entertainers'. And his friends are the same friends he had through school, prison and the station-wagon days. He may give each of his band members a five-acre chunk of his land, "so when I'm too old to work the road and feel like having a jam session y'all can get there fast." There is, in short, little distinction between Haggard the man and Haggard the entertainer.

And that is why a lot of people in show business don't expect him to become as big as Cash did in the late 1960s. The very things that make him a folk hero may keep him from spectacular success, they feel. "Do you think Cash would have made it like he did," asks a respected mogul in Nashville, "if he'd had a good old boy like Fuzzy for his personal manager?" When Haggard goes home to Bakersfield he is likely to go fishing, no matter who wants to talk to him about what, and this has infuriated more than one show business executive ("Just about every session we've ever set up with him has been postponed at least once," says Capitol's Ken Nelson). One fall he walked out on an Ed Sullivan special which called for him to sing a couple of songs from *Oklahoma:* "I was rehearsing 'Surry With the Fringe on Top' when about 30 fags came running out saying, 'No-no-no, *Mer*-rul,' and when they started telling me I was supposed to do my hands up and down while I sang—you know, that choreography—I told 'em to shove it and went back home."

And if he refuses to remake himself for Hollywood, so does he refuse to be gobbled up by the Middle America he is said to represent. Haggard and the Strangers have modishly long hair ("I think it's all right, long as there ain't nothin' growin' in it"), and when they come to the line in "Okie," "We don't let our hair grow long and shaggy," Haggard usually does a double-take over his shoulder at mop-headed guitarist Bobby Wayne. That night in Dayton, however, a heckler got the jump on them. Haggard was poised for another song when a voice bellowed from the darkened audience, "Get a haircut!" Haggard stiffened when he heard it, and for a matter of seconds the place was like a tomb. He went ahead and did the number, but when he finished he leaned into the mike and jabbed his finger toward the heckler and said, in a firm, measured, irritated voice: "And sir, just for you, we'll get haircuts first thing in the morning."

I must admit to some prejudice toward Haggard, for after interviewing more than a hundred country musicians for a book on the subject, I deduced that he was about the only honest one left. Country music has become an industry now, an industry worth some $100 million a year to Nashville alone, and the modernization has all but killed the basic earthiness that once made the music alive and real. This is an era when Jeannie C. Riley of Anson, Texas, studies elocution and choreography before opening in Las Vegas; when Bill Anderson considers installing a mobile phone in his bus so he can place public relations calls to disc jockeys while whizzing through Indianapolis; when Ray Price sings in front of a dozen violins (not fiddles, please); and when plans are announced for an antiseptic new air-conditioned Grand Ole Opry House amid a hokey Disneyland-type complex called Opryland, U.S.A. While all of this is taking place, however, Merle Haggard is walking out on Ed Sullivan, turning down notions of a network show of his own "if I've got to have those same old Hollywood writers doing it,"

135

ducking fans and disc jockeys because they keep him away from his guitar and his boat and his friends, and getting violent at Capitol for not letting him record a song he wrote about an interracial love affair ("They said it would've been bad for my image").

But I am fascinated most of all because of the transformation he is making in his thinking since "Okie" and "Fightin' Side." It is always hazardous, of course, to accept seriously any pronouncements on the issues made by entertainers because they are, after all, entertainers rather than statesmen; but I believe that Haggard is honestly trying to understand what is going on around him. As the son of an Okie family, and an ex-convict, he knows what discrimination is. As one who dropped out and ran away in an attempt to find himself, he is beginning to understand his kinship with today's kids. As a refugee from the lower working class, he clearly understands who runs wars and who gets killed in them. Any other country singer would have capitalized on the two patriotic hits with a string of others, but I don't expect Haggard to do that because he seems to feel embarrassed now by those songs.

Perhaps the best example of the changes that have come over him is an incident that took place one crisp Sunday afternoon in Akron. The band had retired to the Holiday Inn between the matinee and the evening show, and he and Fuzzy were sitting at a table in the dining room waiting for hamburgers to be brought. Fuzzy pulled his head out of the Sunday newspaper and sucked his teeth.

"Well, one thing's for sure," said Fuzzy, a veteran of the Korean War who fervently believes every word of "Okie" and "Fightin' Side." "If we don't hurry up and stop 'em over there, pretty soon we're gonna be fighting 'em in Bakersfield. Right there at the Kern Canyon, by God."

"Fightin' who?" said Haggard, straight-faced.

"The damn Communists, that's who."

"They interested in Bakersfield?"

"Aw, you know what I mean, Merle."

"Ain't no rice there."

Fuzzy's sap was rising. "Naw, it's that 'domino theory' thing. If we don't stop 'em in Vietnam, they'll take the rest of Asia. Then they'll take Australia, Hawaii, the whole damn world."

"Where'd you read that at?" said Haggard.

"I didn't *have* to read it. By God, I *know*."

"Fella here"—nodding toward somebody at the table— "says he's got about 30 books on Vietnam, and he's been there, and says all that stuff might not be right."

"Well, what do *you* think?"

"Tell you the truth, Fuzz, I don't know."

"You don't know?" Fuzzy had come unglued. "I swear, Merle, you're getting just like those damned hippies. Hell, you're just like 'em. Can't make up your mind about nothing."

10·WELCOME TO THE DEATH HILTON

> Show me the manner in which a nation or a community cares for its dead, and I will measure with mathematical exactness the tender sympathies of its people, their respect for the laws of the land and their loyalty to high ideals.
>
> —Gladstone

"Wife found that quote somewhere, typed it up and gave it to me. Been carrying it around ever since. Believe in it. Ray Ligon's motto, don't you see." Reverently rereading it to himself, H. Raymond Ligon smiles at the card through black horn-rimmed glasses, stuffs the bulging billfold back into his hip pocket, swings his dusty cowboy-booted feet onto the disheveled desk and sways back deeply in a swivel chair. Everything is right on this soft summer morning at the Woodlawn Cross Mausoleum and Funeral Home, Inc., on the edge of downtown Nashville. Grieving families sit quietly in several of the ten "repose rooms," waiting for services to begin. Somber music drones through the carpeted hallways. Ligon's army of funeral directors and embalmers and secretaries and janitors goes about its business inside, while outside two dozen laborers preen the grassy undulating 192 acres representing the final resting place for some 100,000 souls. But the true center of activity is behind the main building, where dozens of hard-hatted construction workers swarm over a hulking square concrete-and-steel edifice, now rising five stories out of the ground like one of the Pyramids, soon to be the third tallest building in Nashville. Ray Ligon's dream. A twenty-story mausoleum, cold storage for 129,500 bodies.

"Yes, sir," he is saying, "Ray Ligon is one of the most fortunate people in the funeral business, and I'll tell you why." It is only nine o'clock, but already he has been at work for nearly three hours, and the construction on the mausoleum is going so well that he is in an ebullient mood, his bright yellow shirt and gaudy boots and dyed black hair and leathery sunburned face belying his 70 years. "Hard work, and treating people right. I remember one time this lady called and said she'd had a vision that her husband was buried at my place with his head downhill. Said she couldn't sleep for thinking about it. I told her to come on out, and I got two lawn chairs and we sat there under a tree while the workers dug. When they put a level on the coffin, the bubble was straight up. She appreciated what Ray Ligon did for her, don't you see. Every human being is entitled to our love and respect, and to a decent farewell."

Ligon's chief engineer on the mausoleum project opens the door to the cluttered paneled office. He is wearing a bright yellow hardhat, and holding a bill of lading in one hand. "Got a load we need you to sign for, Mr. Ligon."

"What we got here?"

"One load of marble."

"Stuff from Italy?"

"Yes, sir."

"Fine. You know what to do with it." Ligon scrawls his signature on the bill. "Keep 'em rolling."

That business done ("Sent my engineer all the way to Italy just to find the right marble for the crypts"), Ligon sways back again and races off on another monologue about himself and his plans. While he talks, a 76-year-old retired newspaperman named Sewall B. Jackson—reedy, chain-smoking, ruined voice, pencil-thin mustache, mod high-heeled shoes and tacky checkered suit—takes shorthand notes for the book be will write on Ligon's life. "If it's never been done before, I thrive," Ligon is saying. "Night funerals. Funeral home and cemetery combined. Mausoleum. Ray Ligon likes to do sensible things that've never been done before. I tell 'em everything else in this world has changed, why not the funeral business. Know what I'm thinking about doing next?" Sewall Jackson's pen poises. He looks up at Ligon with an expectant conspiratorial grin. "Helicopters. Here's a loved one at the airport. Died in Chicago, wanted to be buried here. Put the remains on a helicopter, fly over here and land on top of the mausoleum, bring him down on the elevator to the repose room. Save time, save money. I can get a helicopter for $18,000, as cheap as a fancy hearse. Got to keep thinking all the time, don't you see . . ."

For the time being, before he goes airborne, Raymond Ligon's latest scheme will suffice in solidifying his claim as the most innovative, if not controversial, funeral director in America. The largest mausoleum in the country had been one of four floors at California's Forest Lawn, but when Ligon announced his audacious design for the Woodlawn Cross Mausoleum he left quite a target for any other entrepreneur who might care to shoot for the record. At a cost of $12 million, the mausoleum will provide, Ligon boasts, "a burial as fine as the Taj Mahal." The name Cross Mausoleum comes from the shape of the building, its four wings converging in the center, the foundation and immediate grounds consuming only seven of the 300 acres held by Ligon. Each floor will have bright carpet, air conditioning, elevators, piped music, cushy sofas and seven tiers of crypts beginning at floor level with the most expensive (the "Westminster" for couples buried side by side) and ending at the ceiling with the least expensive vault (the "Heaven Level"). There will be nighttime funerals ("working folks can't make it in the daytime"), visiting at all hours, and lounging downstairs in the Garden of Jesus: a natural underground spring spilling water into a corner rock pile, a clear fiberglass roof allowing natural sunlight to feed the flowers, and a "tomb of Jesus" made of rocks brought over from Jerusalem.

The reaction to Ligon's plans ranged from utter disbelief to jollity. "This is one time I'm sort of glad I can't see," said a blind Nashville singer named Ronie Milsap. Joked Johnny Carson on his television talk show: "How would you like to be the elevator operator on duty about three in the morning, and you're sitting on the sixth floor, and you hear somebody say, '*Down*?'" One magazine referred to it as "the Death Hilton," and a Nashville newsman no longer surprised by anything Ligon does guessed that "as soon as he finishes this one he'll go out and build a chain of the damned things across the country." Buyers of space in the mausoleum were hard to find at first, Southerners being more traditional about such matters as death and religion than most, but an aggressive sales campaign ("Keeping up with kings, queens and presidents costs less than you think," read one brochure) soon brought into the coffers some $2 million in "Pre-need" sales—the backbone of the burial business—so Ligon could begin construction. When the first five floors were topped out and put into service this fall (for the ribbon cutting, a state official landed atop the building in a helicopter), there remained some skeptics, one of them a disgruntled former Ligon business associate: "I don't see any necessity for a 20-story mausoleum, except that it'll get Raymond a lot of publicity. He contends that land in America is going to run out. I disagree. You can go three miles outside Nashville, on an old farm, and find plenty of land for plenty of cemeteries."

To Ligon, though, the availability and price of land in

America today make the argument for mausoleum burial overpowering. "We just can't afford to keep on burying folks on these shady little hillsides," he says, pointing out that he will bury the same number in a mausoleum covering seven acres that he has buried on the 192 developed acres of his cemetery. "I know what they say about the cemetery business, that you buy by the acre and sell by the inch, but you can't even make any money that way these days. Some of the land I paid $700 an acre for in the 1930s is worth $35,000 today, and some adjoining property just brought $55,000 an acre. We're sitting right next to the busiest intersection in Nashville now. I'm just not going to develop another acre. It's mausoleums from now on. Ground burial is going to go out." Armed with the arguments, Ligon can go on and on about the desirability—for himself and for the client family—of mausoleum burial: it is dryer, less expensive (no need for a tombstone, vault or elaborate coffin), offers lower maintenance costs (two people will be able to take care of the mausoleum, while 28 are required for the cemetery grounds), and "if there was a strike, why me and the preacher could get on the elevator and do the burying ourselves." Ligon does not mention that 130,000 crypts sold at an average of $2,000 would turn his $12 million investment into $260 million, and that air space comes free.

"Let's go across the road for a minute and see the old place, Mr. Jackson." Clapping his own personal yellow hardhat on his head, Ligon strides through a maze of corridors until he bursts out into the bright morning sun, quickly slipping behind the wheel of the luxury pickup truck he prefers to drive. Gliding over the smooth paved lane leading to the main entrance, he points straight ahead across busy Thompson Lane to a squat two-story concrete building with the word MAUSOLEUM discreetly printed on a green awning which shades the entrance. It was his first mausoleum—and probably the first of any size in the South—and today, seven years later, its 3,500 crypts are just about taken up. "I told 'em I wanted it soft and beautiful like a living room, not harsh and cold," Ligon says as he steps into the air conditioning and waves a hand over the bright carpeting and the deep sofas. A woman is vacuuming, her machine drowning out the soft music, and Ligon asks her to stop when he sees that several people—most of them old—are sitting around, apparently visiting family crypts.

"Mr. Ligon." Coming Ligon's way, his eyes red and bloated, is a retired Army colonel who has lost his entire family during the past 18 months, the last a son killed in a skyjacking. The man says, "I just wanted to thank you."

"What for, Colonel Giffe?"

"For this place you got here."

"Everything's all right, then."

"It's wonderful. Just wonderful. Well, you know what I mean. My wife, she sat right there on that divan. She knew she was going. But she wasn't horrified by this place. No, sir. Another thing, I can come visit with her even if it's snowing."

Ligon nods to some of the others and makes a quick tour. "Here's my first wife," he says, pointing to a crypt. The place is cool and quiet and eerie, in spite of the flashy colors and deep carpet. Here and there against the walls are small tables adorned with plastic flowers. On one of the tables is a stack of index cards and a note inviting visitors to "leave word so we can acknowledge your visit." One card has already been used. "Dear Lela," says a laborious scrawl. "Ethel and Norma came by to see you. We miss you so much." Beside the note is a tiny framed picture of the dead woman.

The burial business has changed very little in the decade since the publication of Jessica Mitford's scathing book *The American Way of Death*, still regarded as the definitive work on the subject. (Who, for that matter, can forget the grotesqueries in the movie made of Evelyn Waugh's *The*

Loved One?) Mitford gets to the point on the very second page of the opening chapter: "Gradually, almost imperceptibly, over the years the funeral men have constructed their own grotesque cloud-cuckooland where the trappings of Gracious Living are transformed, as in a nightmare, into the trappings of Gracious Dying." About 1 percent of America dies each year, leaving the disposal of some 2 million bodies to 22,000 "funeral directors" (not "undertakers," please) who do a gross of $1.8 billion each year. The competition is mean and often bitchy, the object of the hunt usually a grieving widow suddenly forced to make her first major financial decision within hours, and this fall the Federal Trade Commission announced an investigation into 76 District of Columbia funeral homes—tantamount to a national study—following numerous complaints about inflated prices and the selling of unneeded services. In the burial business today, as strongly as ever, "cremation" is a dirty word (35 percent of the dead in England are cremated, only some 60,000 a year in the United States). Indeed, semantics is important in the business: "grief therapy" and "memory pictures" and "slumber room" are the ABCs of the burial salesman's language. Talk about everything but death. A hole in the ground is a hole in the ground. *It's the last chance you will have to do something for your loved one . . . Now here is a nice casket, fit for a man of his stature . . . Oh, by all means, you'll want fresh flowers . . . For the memory picture, I would suggest a dark wool suit and a bowtie . . . It's going to be a nice funeral, I'm sure of that . . .*

Sales, then, is the most important aspect of the business. "They say Ray Ligon is a great salesman," says Ligon, "but he knows anybody can sell a couple if they love each other." The head of Woodlawn's 15-man sales force is Ligon's 34-year-old stepson, John Spivey, a handsome favorite at the Tennessee statehouse, who recently received a six-year appointment to the state's Youth Advisory Commission. When he dies, he says, somebody will simply pull out a file in the business office at Woodlawn and it will all be there: choice of casket, names of pallbearers, number of the crypt in the mausoleum, and so forth. "I remember this young guy whose wife had died," says Spivey. "Just before they closed the lid on her, he picked up his four-year-old daughter and leaned her over and said, 'Kiss your mother good-by.' A lot of people go hysterical at a funeral. You have all kinds. I don't see any reason why that should happen; any reason why it should be a hot, agonizing ordeal. It should be planned, together, in advance."

This "pre-need" selling is Spivey's responsibility, and he wraps his arguments around the low-key, sensible, pragmatic trappings of, say, a life insurance agent. "The funeral director doesn't have to put pressure on a couple, the family does that," he says. "A funeral is the third largest investment you make in your life, behind a car and a house. You going to let your brother-in-law do it? It's all a process of education, like my juvenile job. I just tell them the straight true story and put it in an honest, believable, attractive package." At Woodlawn, one price covers all: coffin, hearse, police escort, flowers, "open-and-close" grave charges, and so forth. The price can vary greatly, depending on such choices as gravesite and coffin, but Spivey says an average burial in the ground there runs around $2,500. In the new mausoleum, however, he says he "can do one" for $1,600. Woodlawn will also sell you the coffin, more than a dozen styles of them being on display in a sales room at the funeral home, and for the mausoleum there is a $495 Ligon-designed bier called the "cross repose," which is the cheapest way of all to go. "We don't back the hearse up to the door," says Spivey, "we just tell them the facts. Pre-need is the way you stop the high cost of dying." Ray Ligon, his stepson says with reverence, "is the greatest teacher who ever lived."

The funeral business is all Herschel Raymond Ligon has known since his birth in 1903 to the owner of the local funeral home in Lebanon, one of those lovely little middle Tennessee towns about 30 miles east of Nashville. When he graduated from high school ("All I've got is that diploma and a Dale Carnegie course"), he became a partner in Ligon & Sons Funeral Home, doing everything from embalming to directing services. "The first service I ever held, I was 24 years old," he recalls. "A logger had been killed on the job and he was so poor they were having to bury him out back of the house in the garden, don't you see. We fixed him up nice and took him over there, but there wasn't a preacher or any music. An old lady pulled me aside and said, 'I'll sing a song if you'll read some scripture.' The next day my father got a preacher to teach me how to lead a service, and I was in business."

Ligon was too adventurous to stick around Lebanon forever, and his chance at much bigger things came during the Depression when a large holding company in Nashville went into bankruptcy. In addition to insurance, real estate and a false-teeth factory, the group held a 40-acre cemetery in Nashville. One of the attorneys representing the creditors had been a high school classmate of Ligon's, so Ligon was hired as a trustee at $35 a week ("That's when folks felt lucky to make a dollar a day") and charged with disposing of the cemetery to pay off a $110,000 tax bill. He soon became an expert on the cemetery business in America—visiting the major ones like Forest Lawn in Hollywood on fact-finding excursions—and when it came time to put the cemetery up on bids, Ligon decided *he* wanted it. His bid for $90,000 was the only one submitted, so he took over Memorial Park and prefixed Woodlawn to its name and began building an empire.

Accustomed to checking into the office at daylight, Ligon quickly became a national figure in the funeral industry and a financial power to be reckoned with in Nashville. Bit by bit he bought up surrounding land, some of it for as little as $700 an acre, ultimately acquiring a package of 300 acres.

Stressing "pre-need" sales to a growing sales force, he was able to get his hands on money and put it to his own use long before it was needed to service his clients. With the funds he began acquiring other cemeteries in the Nashville area and claiming endless "firsts" in the region: the first crematorium, the first funeral home-and-cemetery operation under one roof, the first night funeral services, the first weddings in the funeral home chapel, the first previously all-white cemetery opened to blacks. That Ray Ligon knows how to come up with cash when necessary is never questioned around Nashville. "One time I needed some capital," he says, "so I announced plans for a white 25-foot 'Tower of Memories' across the road. I got 450 people to put up $10 each in exchange for their name on a bronze plaque. Me and two Negroes built it in no time." Finally, seven years ago, he raised his first mausoleum.

Today Ligon lives an active life. At one time or another in the past he has had his hands in many pies—a bronze works, a concrete vault factory, a half-dozen cemeteries, a finance company, a downtown office building—but has divested himself of most of these so he can concentrate on his dream mausoleum. His two sons are well-set now—one operates the Mount Olivet cemetery in Nashville, the other a bank in Lebanon and a tourist attraction in Gatlinburg called Christus Gardens—leaving Ligon and his second wife (a high-powered cemetery entrepreneur in her own right before they married) alone in a roomy white brick ranch house, set on a wooded knoll across from the rising mausoleum, of a simplicity belying his estimated net worth of some $10 million. Except when he is on brief visits to central Florida, overseeing a real estate development there, he starts his day with a 6:30 A.M. meeting with construction engineers and spends the rest of it swinging deals or hanging around the construction site. "He comes up with the ideas," says the current Mrs. Ligon, "and we what you call 'implement' them." Says Ligon of his standing in the community: "You know who criticizes me? Other funeral directors. You think there might be a little jealousy there?"

The man on the street in Nashville may hold little more than passing awe for a man audacious enough to build a skyscraper cemetery, but there is a tight corps of others whose emotions toward Ligon run from begrudging respect to outright hostility. "He can easily differentiate between the person who needs the services of a pious Bible-quoter and the one who needs a drink," says Nat Caldwell, a veteran reporter for the *Nashville Tennessean*. Says a young ex-banker who once wrote a 30-page report on Ligon's financial empire: "It was so complex, if there was any hanky-panky going on you couldn't find it." Says an embittered former associate who claims he once lost $15,000 in a cemetery development scheme engineered by Ligon: "Every time I get to thinking about the bastard, my angina starts acting up. I wouldn't speak to him if I saw him on the street." Even his enemies, however, respect his drive. "If Raymond Ligon stayed straight," says one, "he'd be the hottest thing in America."

The nearest Ligon has been to serious trouble was in the early 1960s when he became involved in the National Cemetery Development Corporation, which eventually sued him and his sons for $240,000 in damages on the charge that "transactions . . . resulted in diversion of funds to the Ligons." NCDC was organized in 1958 by a dozen or so Nashville businessmen, with plans to develop cemeteries and allied businesses all over the nation. As soon as its formation was announced, Ligon offered his services as an expert in the field and was promptly named president. More than $1 million was raised in a public stock sale during the first four months, the major partners kicking in as much as $30,000 each, and in the beginning all was happiness and light. "People bought because of what they knew about Woodlawn, because Ligon was obviously successful," says one of the original partners, Jim Bulleit, now a candy manufacturer in Nashville. "We finally got around to going to Raymond Ligon to find out who he was." Over the first three years the corporation lost some $300,000, bringing about Ligon's "resignation" as president. Finally, in 1963, claiming that Ligon and his sons were raking money off the top for themselves and doing little else for the corporation, the NCDC filed suit. The NCDC lies dormant today, the suit still tabled somewhere in court, and the embittered partners seem to have little heart to continue fighting. "Hell," says one, "our attorney moved off to Florida and won't even return my calls." The publicity did little good for Ligon, for when he tried to give a farm to his Church of Christ the church gave it right back on the grounds that it didn't want to get involved. "But the man has good lawyers," says reporter Caldwell, "and he always protects his flanks." Indeed, when the Securities Exchange Commission showed an interest in Ligon and the NCDC it was shut out of any investigation because Ligon had seen to it that only Tennesseans bought stock in the group.

Late in the afternoon, curious to see what sort of progress the engineers have made during the day, Ligon invites a visitor to ride with him to the top of the mausoleum and check out the work. The dark elevator groans and clangs as it rises from the wet and musty ground floor before finally bursting into the sparkling summer sunlight. Looking like one of the construction workers himself, hardhat and all, Ligon waves a hand at the two dozen men and asks the foreman to call the men together. Off in the distance can be seen Ligon's rambling house, sitting serenely in the cluster of shade trees beyond the grassy acres of his cemetery. The spread is dotted with tiny oases Ligon calls his "Biblical Gardens," each featuring a statue of a character from the Bible standing amid a garden of flowers. "Boys," Ligon is saying, flopping his hardhat back and forth on his head,

149

"this gentleman here is writing a story on us. *New York Times*. About the biggest newspaper in the world. Wants to find out how excited you are about having a part in this, don't you see. Y'all talk to him, now." It was an awkward moment. The young ones suppressed giggles. The foreman babbled something he thought Ligon wanted to hear. "Let's go downstairs and relax," says Ligon, getting back onto the elevator and going down a couple of floors.

He also has a conference room, which he hopes to entice various civic and business groups to use for their meetings. "Want to get 'em used to coming out to Woodlawn," he says. On the walls are pictures of Ligon with beasts he once shot on safari, and one of a group of middle-aged women he once threw a party for on a whim. "Bought every one of 'em, 15 of 'em, a $165 dress," he is saying. "Silly. But they had fun."

"You hunt?" he is asked.

"Used to, all the time. Quit now. Got to where I didn't want to kill anything anymore."

For several minutes, he rambled on about life and death and his own machinations. You see one cremation, he says, you'll never believe in it ("Reminds you of Hitler and the Jews"). He may lease out the rest of his land, he says, and go mausoleum all the way ("Government's going to get 30 percent of the price if I sell the land, anyway"). On the first floor of the mausoleum, he says, "we are already burying beautifully." People make jokes, he says, about funeral directors ("Call me the white Southern planter"), but you have to laugh with them and forget it. What would he be, he is asked, if he had it to do over?

"Evangelist," he says. "I never got to be what you'd call religious until I was about 15 or 16. Just went to church and slept up until then. Now I give 10 percent a year to the church. Believe in it now. But I got to thinking about these evangelists, and me. Got the same things in common. Trying to console people, don't you see. *Help* people. And here I

got this way with people, know how to talk 'em into things."
He bends over in his chair to knock some mud off his cowboy
boots. "Yes, sir, an evangelist is what I'd want to be. Instead
of working with their bodies, work with their souls, don't you
see."

11·HOME MOVIES FOR THE FOLKS

SNEAKY—Sir, we are United States government Secret Service men, and we're here to make you a serious proposition. Have you ever thought of becoming a secret agent?

BEAUREGARD—No, sir, can't say that I have, but I'd do anything for the U.S. guver-mint.

SNEAKY (*Confidentially*)—We happen to know there's a cave on your place which contains a machine which, with our materials and your water, will make the best darn missile fuel in the country.

BEAU (*Bewildered*)—Missile fuel? You mean to make them big rockets blast off? Criminentlies! There *is* a cave on the place, come to think. I've heard tell somebody had a moonshine still around here, too, and I haven't had the chance to get around and hunt for it so's I could smash it up. That's one thing we don't hold with, likker and drankin'. Tools of the devil. We is good church-goin' folks.

SNEAKY—That's exactly why you're our man. Your government needs a good, clean, loyal, upstanding American boy for this job.

(BEAUREGARD *overcome with emotion*)

SNEAKY—Now we're going to need the stuff as fast as you can get it to us. Jake here will show you how to make the mash—I mean the fuel derivatives. We'll supply you with the raw materials. You supply us with the fuel, and we'll pay you by the gallon. Now how does that sound to you?

BEAU—I think that's mightly generous of y'all.

JAKE (*Some moments later*)—Is this guy for real?

—Excerpts from *There's a Still on the Hill*, a full-length feature movie filmed at Clayton, Georgia

On a Thursday in August, just as the sun was crouching behind the cool green hills in the far northeast corner of Georgia, few occupants of the town of Clayton had noticed the sleek Atlanta car as it slipped off Highway 441 North and stopped in the large asphalt parking area of the new Heart of Rabun Motel. Every day, about dusk, the out-of-town cars begin peeling off into the motels dotting the road that crawls into the Blue Ridge Mountains. Most of them carry tourists on their way to the higher hills of North Carolina.

This time it was different. There were two men in this car, each wearing a coat and tie and looking as businesslike as possible. One of them was Frank Winecoff, a tight-lipped Atlanta investor whose family owned the Winecoff Hotel when it burned 20 years ago. The other, a large man with baleful eyes and a bald spot on top of his head and long, curly locks falling over the ears, was an Atlanta television personality whose name is George Ellis but who is better known as Bestoink Dooley. The two men immediately went into conference with perhaps a dozen of the most substantial citizens of Rabun County and environs, and by 11 o'clock at night

153

a cloud of cigarette and cigar smoke clung to the ceiling of the second-floor motel room. Only six men remained, and the liquor and Ellis' patience were running frightfully low.

"Well, it does look like a pretty good script, all right," said one of the boys from Clayton. He had pulled a huge roll of greenbacks from his khaki cotton trousers and was snapping the rubber band which held the roll together.

"It's a *helluva* script," Ellis said.

"You say ol' Slim Pickens is gonna be in it, George?"

"Look, I've explained that 40 times already. We're hoping for Slim to be in it. We can't say for sure until we raise the money."

"Well, George, then how about Boone? Just how 'bout ol' Randy Boone?"

"Same thing. We're 90 percent sure he'll direct it for us."

"It don't make sense to me, George."

"What do you mean?"

"I mean, I ain't gonna put my money up 'til you're sure about them boys. If I'm gonna buy a heifer, I get to see the heifer first."

"Dammit," said Ellis, "that isn't the way it works. This is the movies. There won't be any movie until there's money, and there won't be any Boone and Pickens until there's a movie."

"Tell you what, George. How about this. Suppose we just call ol' Slim and ask him to come down here—come right down here to Clayton—and promise us he'll be in the movie when we raise the money? How's that sound?"

"That's ridiculous."

"Huh?"

"Slim and Randy are busy making a living. They couldn't care less about Clayton. You pay them, they'll come."

One of the men said, "Sounds like a poker game to me."

"That's exactly what moviemaking is," said Ellis. "A big poker game, except the stakes are more like $100,000."

"Hell, George, I'd just as well lose my money playing

poker. At least I've got a night out with the boys to show for it."

"Shit," said Ellis.

The tentative title of the tentative film was *Moon Runners,* all about moonshine whiskey and stock-car racing. It was written by Guy Waldron, an Atlanta television director, and would be produced, hopefully, by Frank Winecoff. It would be filmed on location, in and around Clayton, for a budget of $100,000 or so, to be shown at neighborhood and drive-in theaters where only a moonshine and stock-car film could make it big at the box office. Winecoff and Ellis were not fooling anyone. They were having trouble raising the cash in Atlanta, so much trouble they were trying to squeeze it out of people who won't gamble unless the odds are something like 10:1 their way, plus an option to get out. That evening on the second floor of Tommy Ramey's motel said a lot about the present status of moviemaking in Georgia.

Yet Georgia ranked fourth in the country during the 1960s, in the number of full-length feature movies being produced within the state. There were only four turned out in Georgia during 1965, but by the end of the next summer six had already been put in the can, with five more scheduled for the rest of the year. Hollywood, of course, is still the leader, followed by New York. Miami has come on strong lately, particularly with "beach flicks," and is in third place. Nashville and Atlanta are bunched closely together behind those three. There are several reasons why the production of movies has begun to take a turn away from Hollywood and New York, almost all of them revolving around money. It is less expensive to produce a movie in Georgia by Georgians because (1) there are no unions, so far, (2) there is no competition, and (3) the "sets"—the Georgia mountains, beaches and swamps—are already there, waiting, virtually rent-free. ("We can film one here in 12 days at a cost of $100,000 or less. In Hollywood the same product would take $500,000 and six months, and they'd spend 12 days deciding when the next meeting would be.")

Most of the Georgia products have followed a sure-fire formula. Except for one, a "skin flick" called *Bad Girls for the Boys,* they have been syrupy with country music, stock-car racing, moonshine and a city-slicker-gets-done-in-by-good-old-country-boy plot, if you can call it a plot. Witness the titles: *Legend of Blood Mountain, Gold Guitar, There's a Still on the Hill* and, tentatively, *Moon Runners* and *The Speed Lovers.* They are usually budgeted at $100,000 or less; country music stars are hired and bolstered by local talent; filming is accomplished on location in Atlanta or in the north Georgia mountains in less than two weeks; and the product—in surprisingly good color and wide screen— is rushed to small-town theaters all over the South. "All you have to have is something about moonshine, stock cars or country music and the people will buy it," says an Atlanta producer. "Look, if a guy will pay 98 cents for a Roy Drusky record, he'll pay a dollar to see and hear Roy sing two songs, plus get a movie."

The returns have not yet been conclusive on most of the Georgia pictures. There is one, *Legend of Blood Mountain,* that none of the participants likes to talk about. *Blood Mountain* came out in the fall of 1965, with George Ellis starring. Because shooting took six weeks instead of two, the budget far exceeded the original $50,000, and now, a year later, the film has suffered a most embarrassing fate: It is being leased out to whoever will take it, for a flat fee of $25. One Nashville film, *Forty-Acre Feud* (backed by Georgians, but filmed in Nashville), stars Ferlin Husky and Minnie Pearl and Del Reeves and has already returned more than $250,000 on its original $100,000 investment. It is still draw-ing crowds, not only in the country-music South but in the Midwest. What Georgia investors regard as their ace in the hole is the possibility of showing the films in Europe. "This stuff is pure Americana," says one.

There is mixed opinion on the future of moviemaking in Georgia. Bill Packham, a former Atlanta radio and television man who backed *Gold Guitar* (and filled in as a credible cab driver in a scene at the Atlanta airport) says, "Atlanta's a perfect center. We've got mountains in the north, swamps in the south, beaches, a big city, and we're only about 300 miles from Nashville, where the country music stars and the studios are." Bob Moscow, owner of the Central Theater in Atlanta, has backed several films made in and out of Georgia and is less optimistic: "Most of it, so far, has been hobby business. Until somebody makes it big at the box office, it'll stay that way." A free-lance Atlanta publicist who had pumped some money into several films: "It stands to reason we're becoming more experienced, learning more about making movies every day. It has been proved you can make money off them. We can't go anywhere but up." And director Hunter Todd: "We're slowly building a real nucleus of good people here, but in a way we will create our own monster. When we reach the point where a man can make a living by working all year on movies, the unions will come. I say the unions will form in two years, doubling production costs. We'll just have to wait and see what that does to us."

If you want to churn out a feature film in Georgia, the man you turn to is Todd—J. Hunter Todd III—a precocious William and Mary graduate who has had his hand in almost every feature movie produced in the state since the push began. In his 27 years, beginning when he was barely out of short pants, Todd has directed 94 films of all descriptions, from documentaries and television commercials to featurettes and full-length features. *Still on a Hill*, completed in August, was his third feature film of 1966, and by the end of the year he expected to have completed seven.

Todd is a most memorable character in his own right. You would not expect to find one of his age directing full-length movies, but he does, with much flourish and little noticeable sweat. He is a slight man who drives a Lancia Flaminia import, wears expensive English linen shirts and silk ascots and an occasional pith helmet when on location, regally dates his Girl Friday—a Julie London-ish dish by the name of Marlene Spivey—and relishes every moment of being a very big frog in a small pond.

He produced a color-and-sound documentary on the Woodstock, Vermont, fire department while in prep school, bought his own equipment at the age of 18, formed Todd Films International, "started getting flunky jobs" with television networks and movie companies, spent his Army time filming for the government at Cape Canaveral and Redstone Arsenal (winning three international awards), worked on several beach-party movies in Hawaii, and, finally, was named to head Governor Carl Sanders' new State Department of Education Motion Picture Department. The state job is where the money comes from. But for Todd, the big break and the big money are in the feature-film business. And to him there is no better place to start than somewhere —anywhere—outside Hollywood.

"You can make films here, that's why I'm better off here than in Hollywood," he says. "Hollywood is full of good directors, and most of them are car-hopping or doing whatever they can to eat. I wouldn't turn down an offer from Hollywood, certainly, but there is a wonderful amount of experience available here for a new director, and with no competition. Of course, I don't want to be branded as a director of hillbilly movies. I'm hoping to go in other directions, more challenging and more creative."

The same goes for George Ellis, but for Ellis the stakes are higher because the fame is in the second half. Ellis is 47 years old now and best known to most people around the state as "Bestoink Dooley," the garishly outfitted satirically somber emcee for WAGA-TV's late-night *Big Movie Shocker* for the past few years. Ellis has a large popular following anywhere he goes in Georgia, because of the television exposure and constant personal appearances at drive-ins and shopping centers; this is why he receives good billing and is sure to become more and more an integral part of future movies produced in the state. He is also a good actor, better than he has had an opportunity to show so far in his career. But the hour is late, and while he is doing well enough on these hillbilly productions and with his artsy Festival Cinema on Atlanta's Spring Street to drive a Lincoln Continental, he is hopeful something better will come from it all. "The approach with me has always been, 'Look, George, your name's not big enough yet.' It'll get better for me. If I could make money every day of the year like I do during the two weeks I work on one of these films, I'd be doing all right. I could go to Hollywood right now and do bit parts, I think, but I've got no desire to leave the South, and I don't think I'd have the opportunity in Hollywood that I have here. If I were in Hollywood I'd be doing bit parts, but I'd be working menial jobs to support myself. Look at me here: *Gold Guitar, Still on a Hill, and* two other films in a six-month period. This is better than a screen test and a job in a hamburger joint."

And so, once again, they all came together late this summer in Clayton, a comfortable mountain town nestled in the most distant corner of northeast Georgia. Clayton had seen movie people before, most notably in the late 1950s when Walt Disney invaded Rabun County to film *The Great Locomotive Chase.* This time the townsfolk were to be infiltrated by George Ellis and J. Hunter Todd and a host of crewmen who would spend two weeks on location, in the hills and on the streets, filming a mountain drama entitled *There's a Still on the Hill.*

Still on the Hill was typical. No one wanted to talk about where the $100,000 backing originated, specifically. By scheduling it for small-town theaters, beginning with the South, the film would reap, hopefully, a three-to-one return on the investment. The writer and producer-in-name was Atlanta film distributor Gordon Craddock, who wrote the script at night in motel rooms while on the road. In the story, Beauregard Dooley (Ellis) is duped into turning out moonshine for a pair of big-city dandies and gets nabbed by the Feds, but in the end Beauregard is acclaimed as an undercover agent and a hero, and everybody lives happily ever after. There would be 13 country songs—by Dottie West, Del Reeves, Tommy Cash (brother of Johnny), Joyce Paul, Ellis—and, if the deal could be swung at the last minute, the popular comic team of Homer and Jethro. Producer-writer Craddock's seven children also would have substantial parts. Using $30,000 worth of equipment (leased, however, at $2,000 for the two weeks on location), the film would be in color and wide screen. Todd, of course, was the director.

Todd is an investor's dream. His nonfans say he has no creative ability, which is debatable on the strength of some of his more serious work, but if they want it in the can in 12 days then he will, by Todd, have it in the can in 12 days. Craddock, during the weeks preceding the beginning of shooting, had thoroughly scouted out the territory. He had located just the right country store (Alley's Grocery, several miles out on a back road), just the right log house (at Tiger, Georgia, 120 years old and occupied by a 70-year-old widow, Mrs. Dora Smith), just the right garage (Duvall Ford), just the right spot for a still (a slave-built railroad tunnel out Warwoman Road, never completed because of the Civil War), and just the right experts to construct the still (they requested no credits). Except for a few shots back in Atlanta, the bulk of the 365 scenes would be filmed and air-expressed to the lab in New York within 12 days or less. So by the end of July when Todd and his crew of 25, plus the talent, moved into Clayton, they plunged into a back-breaking schedule which would begin at 8 A.M. and sometimes end very close to midnight.

The first week had gone beautifully, with well over half the filming out of the way. Dottie West had come down from Nashville and handled her first acting part "surprisingly well." Some of the acting was poor, as could be expected, but Ellis' strong slapsticking would cover it up somewhat, at least. Craddock's kids had never acted before and were inclined to argue with the director but it was not serious. And the weather had held up, bringing dozens of curious townspeople out to check on the progress being made.

But the eighth day, a Saturday, stumbled out of bed. To begin with, the lab people in New York had reported that a great deal of footage had come out much too "thin," or underexposed. This prompted a bitter 8 A.M. meeting at which Todd, 27, ripped into cinematographer Jack Steely and lighting man John Murray—the only Californians on the crew, with 38 years in Hollywood between them. Then dark clouds began to boil, threatening the shooting schedule. And if that had not been enough, a Clayton laundry had ruined two perfectly smashing J. Hunter Todd English linen shirts.

Later that morning, Todd sat on a wooden bench on the porch of Miss Dora's creaking log house in Tiger, up to his ascot in worry as the rain pelted down. They had finished shooting inside the house, and now they could do nothing until the weather broke—but not too clearly, because some of the sequences had already been shot in an overcast.

"Would you believe we're waiting for the sun not to come out?" Todd said.

"How much of the film do they think is bad?" asked Ellis, sharing the bench with Todd.

"Not too much. I don't think so, anyway. If it's some of the scenes Dottie [West] was in, we're in trouble. She's already gone somewhere."

One of the children yelled from the end of the porch, "Hey, I'm hungry. Let's go eat while it's raining."

"Wonderful idea," Todd mumbled.

"I was just thinking, Hunter," Ellis said.

"What's that?"

"Oh, how if we were shooting this in Hollywood we wouldn't have to worry about rain or anything."

"You're right about that."

"And you could have two Lincolns instead of just one," somebody told Ellis.

Todd said, "And I'd have a whole flock of people just to pamper me."

"But I don't want that and neither do you, Hunter."

"Oh? I don't?"

"'Course not. Jes thank how nice it is. Jes-a-sittin' here, a-watchin' th' boxwoods grow."

"Get out of here."

The clouds broke just enough, and the crew scrambled for positions in the yard. J. Hunter Todd sat in his director's chair, one of those cheap aluminum-and-nylon lawn chairs, beneath the camera with Marlene Spivey, leaning over his shoulder and keeping her eyes on the script. Ellis sat on the edge of Miss Dora's porch as five of the Craddock children gathered around him for a song. A crew member in bermuda shorts sat downporch, out of camera range, to accompany Ellis on a song which would be lip-synched in a studio later. Mrs. Craddock and her husband stood behind Todd, arms around each other's waist, beaming at their kids.

"Roll audio," Todd ordered.

"Speed," came the answer.

"Camera."

"Slate."

"Scene 124, Take One."

"Action."

On the second take, George Ellis and the Craddock kids did "You Get a Line and I'll Get a Pole" letter-perfect. Everything went uphill the rest of the day. They finished shooting at Alley's Grocery at 9:50 P.M., and by the time everybody was digging into the steaks at the motel the news had spread that there had been a misunderstanding, and the film had turned out well, after all. There were a lot of bad heads the next morning. Bad heads, but happy hearts. And plans for *Moon Runners*.

12·GOD, MIKE GILCHRIST, AND THE NEW EVANGELISM

When the harsh morning sun broke between the parted drapes of his room at the Ramada Inn in Baytown, Texas, a scruffy oil town on the outskirts of Houston, The Evangelist conquered the impulse to burrow beneath the covers and bolted upright in bed, jerking his head and rubbing the sleep from his eyes, letting his better instincts take charge. "Morning, Lord," he said aloud, as he has done obediently every dawn for the past 25 years, "Mike Gilchrist reporting for duty." Looking a bit like Mel Torme or a sawed-off Richard Widmark, with a lean five-foot-ten frame and a toothy theatrical grin and a shock of swept-back silver hair, he went about the business of preparing for another day and night on the road: showering, shaving, kneeling at his bed for a morning prayer, reading from one of his six Bibles stacked on the night table, finally sitting down to the portable Olivetti to catch up on his correspondence and to mail off a brochure to the church in Orlando, Florida, where he would conduct another revival two weeks hence. Selecting a white suit and ribbed black turtleneck sweater and two-tone suede high-buttoned shoes from an impressive wardrobe in the closet, he briskly stepped off to breakfast in the motel coffee shop.

They were waiting for him, as though he were unlocking the door to officially begin office hours for the day. There was a flabby young girl Peggy, the motel barmaid, who stood puffing a Winston and wanted to know how to handle her new husband's abrupt decision to become a Baptist preacher ("Was it Jesus talking to him, honey, or just a nightmare?"). There was a Houston travel agent, dropping by to talk him into throwing his Holy Land tour business his way ("Fellow I've got now is a New York Jew; think you can top that?"). There were endless phone calls, from his wife in Lake Charles and from a pastor in Fort Worth and from a variety of people wanting advice ("Bet there won't be any phones in Heaven"), and finally breakfast with Ronnie and Linda Marshall, the attractive young couple who owned the motel. The Marshalls were in trouble. They had just been taken for $100,000 by the previous manager of the motel and now had eight days to come up with a plan to pay off their debts. Gilchrist talked practicalities with them for nearly an hour, then held their hands and began praying right there in the coffee shop as groggy traveling salesmen looked on in bewilderment ("Lord, these are good people and the devil has no right to take this business . . ."). Finally Mike Gilchrist got a chance to eat, signed his check and started to walk out.

"You a preacher?" one of the waitresses called out.

"Yes'm," he said.

"Sure don't look like one."

"What's a preacher supposed to look like?"

"You know. Bald, glasses, plain suit. Serious."

"Well," Gilchrist laughed, "I'm glad I don't look like one, then."

With that, he walked out the door and slid into his dusty unpretentious Buick and drove to the Memorial Baptist Church of Baytown to conduct the daily businessmen's luncheon where, after a hot lunch of meat loaf and mashed potatoes and homemade biscuits and a rendition of "How Great Thou Art" by a revivalist singer hauled in from Atlanta for the week, he delivered a quickie sermon. It was entitled, "Nine Steps to Financial Freedom," the general point being that it's hard to do God's work when you're broke.

There was a time—a very long time, beginning with the so-called Great Awakening of the early 1700s and running to the late 1940s—when the impassioned pleas of the fundamental evangelist were as pervasive over the South as the sweet summer smell of honeysuckle. In the beginning, most historians agree, there was a Georgian named George Whitefield, who once rode 800 miles to preach 175 sermons in 75 days. "His voice, unaided by amplifying devices, could carry in the open air to 20,000 people," writes Samuel Eliot Morison in *The Oxford History of the American People.* "He made violent gestures, danced about the pulpit, roared and ranted, to the huge delight of the yokels who were tired of gentlemanly, highbrow ministers from Harvard and Yale. Congregations, mad with religious ecstasy, shrieked, rolled on the floor, ran amok." The poor whites and blacks of the rural South were particularly susceptible to the sensuousness of heart-pounding old-time religion, there being little else to bring them hope in those days, and soon the circuit-riding Southern evangelist became a raw piece of Americana. Daddy Grace, Billy Sunday, Gypsy Smith, Mordecai Ham, Cyclone Mack. The movie *Elmer Gantry.* Something for everybody: snake handling, speaking in tongues, swallowing poison to test the faith, REPENT OR BURN IN HELL scrawled on barns, and the pitches over radio when it came. *And-ah the world-ah will not-ah be saved-ah until you drink-ah of his-ah precious blood-ah . . . That'll be $1.98, friends, for this precious vial of genuine water from the Red Sea . . . Write Jesus, that's J-E-S-U-S, for your magic prayer cloth.* There were thousands of them fanning out across the Southern outback, setting up their tents and gyrating and professing to heal broken legs and turning the people on. Some were good, some were evil; but none were dull.

The changes began after World War II, when a measure of "progress" came to the Deep South. People began moving into the cities from their farms, working at jobs paying more money than they had ever dreamed of. Now the Southerner, yesterday's "good old boy," had some respectability—a brick house, one or two automobiles, a good job, a beauty parlor for his wife to go to—and suddenly he was developing the notion that many of his old ways were, as we say, *tacky*. That went for the evangelists he had once fervently listened to. Now, sitting out back on his patio after waxing his new Chevy on a Saturday afternoon, he didn't want some *weirdo* coming around disturbing his reverie with these terrifying shouts of *JEE-zus*, talking about burning in hell and begging salvation, asking for his money, trying to sell him plastic Jesuses that light up in the dark. He'd had all of that, and now he didn't need it. What he needed was some *respectable* preacher—grandfatherly, pious, business suit, sedate and calm and not too pushy—to go with his new-found respectability.

This is not to say that evangelism as we once knew it in the South completely died out during the 1950s and early 1960s. It could still be found out there in the boondocks, still thriving out there where people stayed in the smallest towns and cussed Atlanta and listened to the radio and ordered everything through the Sears catalog, but the boondocks were shrinking. But religion at this time was striving for more respectability itself. The action was in the big downtown Protestant churches with their edifice complexes—impressive buildings, Baptist Training Union, Sunday school, nurseries for the kiddies on Sunday mornings, huge professional choirs, solemn pastors—and on television. Oral Roberts quit faith-healing and built his own university. Billy Graham counseled Presidents and staged massive international "crusades." Oh, sure, we would later find out about Marjoe Gortner when a documentary of his life was filmed (*Marjoe*), and just this year two men in a fundamentalist church out in the flat Delta stretches of west Tennessee died of strychnine poisoning while testing their faith, but they were exceptions. Religion was predominantly found in places like the First Baptist Church of Dallas, one of the richest churches in America: 18,000 members (including Billy Graham and H. L. Hunt), $4 million annual budget, 23 choirs, and an elementary school, 373 Sunday school classes, a 2,500-seat sanctuary and closed-circuit television for those who can't get inside it on Sunday morning.

And yet, as we moved into the 1970s, there were indications that the evangelists were coming alive again. Bored with the big bland downtown churches, which had become too comfortable, many Americans felt the urge to have their emotions juggled now and then. More than 350,000 people, consequently, turned out for a seven-day Graham crusade in Atlanta Stadium. The 200-odd periodicals under the Evangelistic Press Association experienced a growth of more than a million subscriptions during 1971. A black evangelist out of New York began doing so well on mail contributions that he was advertising his revivals in gaudy *New York Times* ads. A glamorous 50-year-old lady faith healer was packing them in at cities like Chicago and Pittsburgh, claiming to cure everything from cancer to arthritis. Many churches began inviting evangelists in for regular revivals, even advertising big in local newspapers, and bringing electrified gospel bands right inside the church to jazz up their Sunday services. Although it was quite another matter with religious leaders and evangelists, many people were fascinated and a bit saddened by the movie on Marjoe— saddened because they had to admit they sort of liked his magnetic personality, even if he did say he was being hypocritical.

Today, then, the evangelists are coming back. Like the various denominations across the country, they come in all shapes and sizes. Some are rich, some poor. Some are honest, some not so honest. Roughly, they could be separated and broken down into five distinct types:

• *The Heavies*—Billy Graham, Oral Roberts and Rex Humbard are three of the very biggest in the business, from the standpoints of following and wealth, and it was Graham who set the pattern. When he began his crusades in 1947 he was regarded as a religious sideshow rather than a legitimate preacher, but these days he receives some 8,000 invitations a year to hold crusades all over the world. Often criticized for his comfortable life style and his cow-towing with President Nixon, he claims to receive only his $30,000 annual salary as compensation. He recently defended wealth in one of his syndicated columns: "At the death of Christ it was a rich man who bought the burial spices and assisted in the final preparation of His body for the tomb." Roberts has gone legitimate after a stormy career as a faith healer. He has a weekly color television show syndicated to more than 200 stations and a glossy college named Oral Roberts University, and he gets more mail than any institution in Tulsa (including the Shell Oil Company's international credit-card operation). Like Graham and the other heavies, his evangelism is over television and at broadly publicized week-long crusades in major cities. Humbard also runs a college, on Mackinac Island in Michigan, and has a syndicated television show, and the roof over his multimillion dollar empire is called the Cathedral of Tomorrow. The empire includes the Realform Girdle Company in Brooklyn, purchase of which led Congress to pass legislation requiring churches to pay taxes on property not related to religion. Many of the heavies are under constant surveillance for dodging taxes.

• *The Politicians*—These may have started out as earnest

THE GOOD OLD BOYS

preachers of the Gospel, but they took an ultraconservative political turn around the time of Sen. Joseph McCarthy's "Commie" purge in the 1950s and are now, for the most part, more political than religious. The big names are Carl McIntyre, Billy James Hargis and Garner Ted Armstrong, all of them reaching wide audiences with syndicated radio shows popular in politically conservative areas of America. Like many of the "heavies," they stay in hot water with Washington over taxes—trying to claim exemption on the basis of being in charge of "religious organizations." McIntyre employs 16 secretaries at his headquarters across the river from Philadelphia in southern New Jersey, their primary responsibility being merely to *open* the mail. A postal truck rolls up each day to deliver bags of letters containing money to aid the conservative cause. Hargis runs Christian Echoes National Ministry, Inc., out of Tulsa, has a college and museum and various publications and a $175,000 private plane, is forever involved in disputes over tax exemption. "They don't understand our ministry or our religious philosophy," he said of an appeals court which had pointed out in 1967 that Hargis spoke more of civil rights legislation and the nuclear test ban treaty and firearms control than of God. Armstrong is a highly persuasive radio commentator who now and then gets around to religion.

• *The Circuit-Riders*—These are the last of the old-fashioned evangelists, ranging from the blatantly crooked *Elmer Gantry* types to the poor-but-honest Church of God lay preachers. This is where you still may find a Marjoe—sleek sequined suit, silvery oration, fancy car, women, phony faith healing—but will more likely find a fellow who believes everybody ought to share his God with him, pitches his own tent, stays at a local pastor's house, rides around in a dusty station wagon, earns what the people feel like putting in the collection plate. They play the outback, like the south Georgia swamps and the Big Thicket of East Texas,

170

and there aren't many left. The Church of God, based in Cleveland, Tennessee, has a 25-man "evangelistic team" in most states, most of them young men who get a supplement from the Church of God and a percentage of the collection taken at revivals. One of them is Jimmy Swain, 30, of Brunswick, Georgia, who has been at it for less than a year. "It isn't easy for my family," he says, "but it's something I just had to do. It was a calling. God talked to me and told me to quit my job and start preaching, so I did."

• *The Blacks*—The current superstar here is "Reverend Ike," an elegant strapping New Yorker whose real full name is Frederick J. Eikerenkoetter II. Born in South Carolina 38 years ago, Reverend Ike started as an Air Force chaplain and now heads the United Church of the Science of Living Institute in New York. His appeal is to urban blacks, and it is simple: don't wait around for Heaven, enjoy life *now*. It is made simple by his "Blessing Plan," whereby pledges can be paid off by $10 a month, $5 every two weeks, or $2.50 a week, Reverend Ike's magazine imploring constituents to put the pledge payments ahead of routine bills such as power and gas. Resplendent in high-buttoned shoes and diamond rings and mod suits, Reverend Ike defends his techniques: "I'm no harder sell than Billy Graham. He's been sending out blank checks for years." What happens if one reneges on the monthly pledge? God reneges on *His* blessings.

• *The Faith Healers*—Many people inside the church believe that faith healing can possibly work in cases where the illness is psychosomatic—what the "healer" does is simply talk the patient out of believing he is ill—but there have been so many tragic results that faith healing is on the decline. Typical was a case in Natchez, Mississippi, where a healer and a mother were arrested on manslaughter charges when they allowed her diabetic 11-year-old daughter to be withdrawn from insulin and the girl died three days later. Although the faith healers still in business tend to be

171

deep in the provinces, in the land of snake handlers and rural blacks and voodoo, Kathryn Kuhlman works Pittsburgh and Los Angeles and other major urban areas with success. A handsome woman who has been preaching and healing for 25 years, she restricts advertising and has respect from those who ordinarily question faith healing—including a Johns Hopkins cancer researcher who often shows up at her services to testify to healings he says he has investigated and found genuine. Then there are those like R. L. Stiles of Akron, Ohio, who go about selling bottled "miracle blessed waters" and the "blessed oil of gladness." They, too, are shrinking in number because of radio stations' reluctance to accept their spots.

Somewhere in the middle, in a category that has not yet been clearly defined but could be called "the new evangelists," are the Mike Gilchrists. In some ways they represent an homogenization of all the others—they are generally honest, vaguely aspire to be as big and powerful as Graham, do some television and radio, work on the road for weeks at a time, tend to be theatrical as was Marjoe and acknowledge the possibility of curing psychosomatic illnesses with what amounts to emotional shock—and they appear to be the wave of the future. If they have an "organization," it is likely to be a secretary back home taking calls and dictation. If they have any income other than what they receive from the host church after revivals, it is likely to be from a modest regionally syndicated radio show. They usually start out with small churches of their own, become disenchanted with the political and business savvy necessary to keep a congregation happy, then simply chuck it and hit the road on a circuit that takes in most of the medium- and large-sized cities in America—particularly in the South, where religion is still taken more seriously than in any other geographical area in America.

It all began for Mike Gilchrist in 1946 when he was 17

years old. He had been born in Nacogdoches, Texas, moving to the Cajun swampland of southern Louisiana when his hard-drinking father decided to work the offshore old rigs out of Houma. "I wasn't what you'd call a bad kid," he says, "just nervous and unhappy. I was going to school and working on the side, doing what most teenagers did, but there was something missing." His mother was a "fairly good Baptist," he recalls, and when a new young preacher came to town he and Mike's mother started concentrating on Mike, "praying me into a corner." He vividly remembers his conversion: "I was in this field cutting grass when something snapped inside of me. I threw the blade away and ran home, like I was in a trance or something, went to my room and locked the door, and I dropped to my knees at my bed. 'I want to know you, God,' I said, 'I don't know what it is, but I'm unhappy and I want you to help me. I'm putting my life in your hands. I belong to you now.' I never went back to cutting grass in that field. I was like a new man. All of a sudden I was smiling and happy. All of that happened on July 15, 1946, at 10 o'clock, on a Monday morning." He cracks a broad grin at the memory. "I guess I was an evangelist from the start. You know how the old gun-slingers in the West used to put a notch in the handle every time they got another man? Well, I had this New Testament I started carrying around in my pocket that same morning, and every time I figured I'd converted somebody I'd make a little mark on the fly leaf of that book. Another notch on my 'gun.' I put three marks on the fly leaf that first week: for my two best buddies, and for a fellow I met on a bus."

He graduated from Louisiana College in Pineville, a Bible college, and took a series of small churches in that part of the country before deciding in 1958 to hit the road as a full-time evangelist for the sprawling Southern Baptist Convention (next to Catholicism, the second largest denomination in the United States). That is where he has

173

been ever since, working an average of 30-odd week-long revivals at Baptist churches across the South. He has no staff (his wife, at home in Lake Charles, Louisiana, takes calls for him), no radio or television show, no political interests ("I'm a member of God's party"), and gets paid about $1,000 plus expenses for each revival, the money coming to him from the church once the special offering for that purpose is counted out. He says he gets no money in the mail, and his only other possible source of income are the Holy Land tours he has recently begun to lead, getting free passage for himself and his wife for acting as a guide for two dozen people or so ("I'll take 'em to where Jesus walked on the water and read from the scripture while they look at it; it's pretty good"). The Gilchrists have five children, not a one fortunate enough to have his traveling father present at birth, and they live comfortably but unpretentiously on the lake their city was named after ("Airline connections out of Lake Charles are terrible, but I kind of like that old buggy swampland over there").

He is convinced of the good a forceful, positive, earnest evangelist can do. "In a way, we are supposed to come to town and shake 'em up a little—get them to thinking about God again—and leave it so the pastor can follow up on the new interest we've revived," he says. "That's what 'revival' means, isn't it?" There are those, he knows, who still look down on evangelists: "I tell you who they are, too. They're making $40,000 a year, they've got fancy cars, they're 40 years old and they're bored. Maybe they slip out of town with their secretary now and then. I come to town, and they don't want me to upset their world. They'd prefer some old preacher up there talking on Sunday morning so they could sleep through the service." He tries to prepare at least one new sermon each week, he says, "so I can stay fresh," but if you hang around him long enough you see that he does nearly as much evangelizing outside of church—on planes, in the street, at coffee shops—as he does inside. "The other day," he says, "I was sitting in a restaurant and this big Texas oil man walks over and looks me up and down and says, 'I bet you're in the oil business, aren't you?' I said, 'Well, yes, my father is, anyway,' and he said he could spot an oil man a mile away and asked if he could join me. I started leading him on. Pretty soon I'd told him my father had extensive holdings in everything—oil, land, cattle, everything—and then he asked me who my father was. That's when I pulled out this Bible and quoted a passage about the Lord owning all the silver and cattle and all. Sometimes I can see it in their eyes, whether they're ready to talk, and this man was. He stayed for two hours."

The first week of April was fairly typical of how Mike Gilchrist operates during his 30 or so revivals each year. This one was to be held at the 1,700-member Memorial Baptist Church in Baytown, a drab town of 45,000 sitting 20 miles east of Houston on old U.S. 90. The big downtown church in an area dotted with a dozen oil refineries affording comfortable jobs, Memorial Baptist wasn't exactly your live-wire church and needed some reviving. "Frankly," said one prominent citizen, "it's a dead church with too many middle- and upper-class members in it." Gilchrist began communicating with the pastor, a stooped and lumbering man named Ed Thiele, several weeks in advance, sending along a brochure completely outlining the recommended timetable for the week, including businessmen's luncheons and nightly "rap" groups preceding the regular services. On a Sunday afternoon he made the short drive over from Lake Charles, checked in at the Ramada and opened the revival that night. He was joined by a full-time revival singer from Atlanta, Felix Snipes, who was also charged with putting the choir in shape.

By Thursday of the week, Gilchrist was puzzled. The opening night crowd had been good, as it usually is, but attendance at night wasn't what he thought it should be.

"Christians shouldn't be in*hibit*ed," he grumbled, "they ought to be in*habit*ed, with love for God." After holding forth at the Ramada Inn coffee shop that morning, he gave the "Nine Steps to Financial Freedom" pep talk at the noon businessmen's luncheon in an upstairs cafeteria at the church, and at dusk was back—this time down front in the sanctuary, with about 50 church members, young and old, listening—to give what amounted to a 30-minute lecture about the generation gap. Afterward a middle-aged man with a crewcut and khaki work pants and a deeply worried look on his face came down to talk privately with Gilchrist about his errant teenaged son ("Now, look, right off let's forget about the hair because that's not what's important; what's important is that boy's soul"), and then Gilchrist excused himself for a drink of water before the night's services began.

If Mike Gilchrist is no Marjoe, running around and jumping up on pews, neither is he a ponderous stuffy big-church pastor. Although he has never had formal training at it, he has mastered the tricks of holding an audience's attention: the gyrations, the pauses, the inflections, the changes of pace. For some reason the audience had almost doubled on this night in the finely furnished mahogany-and-white sanctuary, the crowd drawn by a marquee announcing the "team: Gilchrist & Snipes" ("It sounds like a vaudeville act, doesn't it?" said Gilchrist). Felix Snipes, in a form-fitting powder blue stretch suit and yellow shirt and white shoes, warmed up the crowd of some 1,000. Ed Thiele dogmatically rambled on with such business as "pew chairmen" and revival attendance. The collection plates were passed, "so these two fine men may continue their work as evangelists." Snipes was up again, going it alone on "His Eye Is on the Sparrow." And then it was Mike Gilchrist's turn.

To a cloistered teenaged girl or a tired businessman in a

place like Baytown, Texas, Mike Gilchrist must bring a touch of Hollywood—of excitement, of an outside world unexplored, of dazzling people and breath-taking places—as he whirls to the podium in a white suit and black shirt and tight buckled boots, a Lavalliere microphone strapped around his neck, his silver hair shining in the lights beneath a banner reading MAKE THE DISCOVERY, flashing a Bible with one hand and waving the other clear up to God in making his points. They reacted that way on that night, from the moment he came on. He began talking about the crucifixion, nimbly flipping the pages of the black Bible, theatrically pacing back and forth: "The world's a wonderful place. One time God sent His son here and they killed him, didn't they? They would do it again if— Wait a minute, did I say *they* did it? Is that what I said? No. *You* did it and *I* did it. *We* did it . . ." Off to one side, a teenaged boy was interpreting for some three dozen deaf visitors. "It's all in this book, and if you read everything in this book it'll give you the greatest case of lockjaw you ever saw . . ." For nearly half an hour Gilchrist went on, reading scriptures and pausing and letting the imagery pour out, and when he stopped there was not a sound. He went to one knee beside the podium, on the deep red carpet, asked for some low organ music, and began to pray. "We're talking about something so much bigger than church membership, Lord. This is a fine church, but we're talking about something else. We're talking about giving our lives to you, Lord." Five young people drifted down the aisle, then eight more, then a couple of rough-handed men who looked as though they had been working in the fields all day. Soon there was little room in front of the altar. "Leila Woods wants to share her testimony," said Reverend Thiele, amazed at the response. The girl started telling about her conversion and began to weep. When it was done, nearly 100 people had gone down front to join the church or announce their conversion or merely reconfirm their faith. Halting bass voices and wavering sopranos boomed, "Roll, Jordan, Roll," as Mike Gilchrist, a toothy grin splitting his face, sank back in a deep velvet chair and observed his handiwork.

13·GOD BLESS LESTER, HE MEANS WELL

Although it now seems like something that didn't really happen—whatever became of the early '60s anyway?—our first meeting took place only six years ago, when it was as easy to ridicule him as it was to belch. A lot of people were doing both in the same breath back then. This was, after all, a time for reasonable men in America, a brief moment of measured and calm social growth in our country, and Lester Maddox seemed like a pathetic clown when set beside the patient black preachers and pragmatic white businessmen who were trying to negotiate the matter of equality as though it were a real-estate deal.

Lester was a 10th-grade dropout, a refugee from the white slums on the fringe of Atlanta. Lester was a teetotaling, hell-fire southern Baptist, residing in that curious hysterical world of Carl McIntyre and Billy James Hargis. Lester was owner and operator of the Pickrick, a fried chicken emporium popular with truckers and route salesmen and service station flunkies. Lester, most of all, seemed possessed by a demonic fear—*à la* Chicken Little—that the non-WASPs of the world would eventually cause the sky to fall. And he had gone on to greater things in July

1964, the day after Lyndon Johnson signed the civil rights bill into law, when he showed up on network television as a fanatical little pinch-faced racist brandishing a pistol at three blacks trying to integrate his place, his teenage son at his side flailing a varnished pick handle, then announcing he would close up rather than give in to "the un-Godly Communists and race mixers who want to destroy my business."

But even to that majority in Georgia who shared his opinion about blacks, Lester remained something of an embarrassment; maybe he had his heart in the right place, but old Lester was, as we say, *tacky*. Perhaps the worst indictment of all came from the segregationist comic Brother Dave Gardner—the one who had been kicked off the Jack Paar show once for saying he wasn't for segregation, he was for slavery. "God bless Lester," Brother Dave would say to a thigh-slapping crowd of rednecks during his night club act, "he *means* well."

At any rate, Lester and I finally met at his cafeteria on a crisp blue-bright afternoon in February 1965, and the occasion was, like almost anything else he touches, a bit unreal. Beside the building was a 20-foot tall white frame tower he was calling his "Monument to the Death of Free Enterprise," which held a black pine coffin and numerous signs and symbols attacking the Supreme Court and other of his enemies. The sign in front of the cafeteria was now covered with a black plastic bag with a legend in white letters reading, "This Light Turned Out by L.B.J."

Inside, standing beside a long table laden with souvenir items such as Confederate-flag automobile tags and Pickrick Drumsticks (the new, commercial name for those varnished pick handles), Maddox jabbered on in his rushed whining nasal voice—he always sounds like a quiz-show contestant trying to beat the buzzer—about how "the Communists in Washington" had taken his rights away from him. Two businessmen in dark suits were impatiently waiting to speak to him, but he wasn't in the mood to talk business. He pulled a piano roll from a sack on the floor and inserted it into the old player piano in the middle of the cafeteria, then began to furiously pump the pedals and whistle along just like he used to do every Sunday when the place was filled with customers. ("Well, that's one more thing they've taken away from me.") And finally, after a short tour of the Monument to the Death of Free Enterprise, he went back inside and stood over a table heaving with piles of mail.

"Where'd all that come from?"

"Everywhere. *Yisseh*"—nobody can write "yessir" the way he says it—"everywhere."

"Since when?"

"Since they struck me down last July."

"All of that for you?"

"*Yisseh*. Must be 12,000 letters here. One of 'em didn't even have an address on it. Just a picture of me from the paper and 'Atlanta, Georgia.' *Yisseh*."

"They for you, or against you?"

"*For* me. *Yisseh*. Only 2 percent against."

"It's going to make a hell of a fire," I told him.

"Oh, *nosseh*. Answering every one of 'em. Been keeping records on little index cards of everybody that writes. Got addresses. *Yisseh*."

Had I not been so fascinated with the outward buffoonery of Lester Maddox at the time, as nearly everybody else in Georgia was, I might have been smarter and taken the cue. Those little index cards helped form one of the damnedest political bases in the history of American politics. And that is exactly what they were. While the old politicians were on the phone lining up sheriffs and party bosses and bank presidents, Maddox was looking up the people listed on those index cards. While the "fat cats" were stuffing their campaign coffers with big contributions from big interests, Maddox was borrowing on his house and his life insurance policies and begging for $1–$5 contributions from "the little people." While the pros were hiring ad agencies to create glossy television and newspaper campaigns, Lester and a driver were covering every inch of Georgia in his personal station wagon: stopping to nail white posters reading THIS IS MADDOX COUNTRY high in trees, getting out to walk around courthouse squares and shake hands with people who remembered him from his most famous television appearance. It was populism in its most basic sense. "How's the campaign coming, Lester?" a newsman would ask Maddox, scurrying around the crowded halls of the state Capitol while the legislature was in session. "Nobody wants me but the people," he would yelp, sending gales of laughter through the hall. But then everybody woke up one morning in January 1967 to find that Lester Garfield Maddox was the new governor of Georgia.

Before you can understand the phenomenon of Lester Maddox you must understand Georgia, because I have a firm conviction that no other state—with the possible exception of Mississippi—would have let something like this happen. Most of the other Southern states have had their share of goons in the state Capitol, but Georgia seems to work at it harder. Georgians seem to have a higher tolerance for mediocrity in state government than most other states I know about. It was Marvin Griffin who said, as recently as 1952, that the way to handle blacks was to "cut down a blackjack sapling and brain a few of 'em." It was Gene Talmadge, ol' suspender-snapping Gene, who boasted that he'd never be caught campaigning "anywhere they've got streetcar tracks" and grazed a cow on the lawn of the governor's mansion while he lived there. One time we even had three governors at once: Gene Talmadge was elected, but died before being sworn in; Herman, his son, claimed his few hundred write-in votes entitled him to the office; others said the lieutenant governor-elect should get it; the incumbent, Ellis Arnall, changed the locks at the Capitol and stayed on another year before it was settled. They say progress has just about wiped out that peculiar Southern phenomenon known as the good old boy, which is generally true. But Georgia is still a state with an ample supply of people who go for style over substance—recently a nationwide study ranked its legislature 45th in the nation in competence, and it would take a book to tell you some of the terrific gags those boys have pulled off over the years—so Lester was perfect.

Few have ever had such a poor background for the governor's office. Lester was one of seven kids born to fiercely religious Flonnie Maddox and hard-drinking Dean Maddox, a machinist who worked in various factories around Atlanta. Lester had it tough most of his young life, carrying newspapers and at one point selling soft drinks and candy out of a sidewalk stand made from a pigeon house, and in 1933 he quit school in the 11th grade because he simply didn't like school and because the family needed help. He scrambled his way through the next decade or so, and it finally began to pay off in 1947 when he stockpiled enough money from smart real-estate deals to begin building the Pickrick.

Politics simply grew on Maddox as he began to make it financially, and the fuel he moved on was the racial issue. All along he had been running paid advertisements in the Atlanta newspapers under the heading "Pickrick Says," and about the time of the 1954 Supreme Court decision on school desegregation he began to roll up his sleeves. Interspersed in his chatter about Pickrick fried chicken there were occasional ravings about "integrationists" and the state of the city, state and nation in general. He ran a patchwork campaign against Mayor William B. Hartsfield, a liberal in his time, in 1957, and a resounding defeat really turned him loose. Sample, in a reply to a liberal: "I do hope you'll get your integration wishes—a stomach full of race-mixing, and a lap full of mulatto grandchildren, so you can run your fingers through their hair." When he ran again for mayor in 1961 he was wiped out by liberal businessman Ivan Allen, Jr.—Maddox polled 237 of the 22,000 black votes cast—and only a few months later he lost his third political race trying for the lieutenant governor's spot. By the time the 1966 gubernatorial campaign came around, though, he had clearly identified himself as a good old boy and a populist and determined segregationist—no matter how tacky he might have been.

In many ways, his victory that year was a fluke. He had an incredible chain of circumstances going for him: race riots in the big cities and the resulting polarization, cross-voting in the Democratic primary by Republicans who thought Lester would be a pushover for their man, and a last-minute write-in campaign in the runoff by disgruntled Democrats which tended to take votes away from Maddox's opponent—a bland, velvet-glove segregationist-conservative named Howard (Bo) Callaway, of the textile Callaways. Maddox squeezed into a runoff in the primary (there was a memorable scene that night in the Dixie Ballroom of the Henry Grady Hotel in Atlanta, perennial lodging house for Georgia redneck politicians over the years, when four fat matrons in tight shiny green dresses broke into "God Bless *Ah-murr-i-cer*" while the back-slapping guests sipped punch and nibbled pound cake under American flags), and the vote in the finale against Callaway was so close—Maddox still didn't get a majority—that it was thrown into the lap of the legislature. Mostly Democrat, mostly small-town, mostly good old boy and mostly segregationist, they gave it to Lester in a walk.

"Georgia was the most progressive Southern state," said Barry Goldwater, "and all of a sudden they have a fellow that belongs back in the Stone Age . . ." Crackled Ivan Allen, then the Atlanta mayor, "The seal of the great state of Georgia lies tarnished. The wisdom, justice and moderation espoused by our founding fathers must not be surrendered to the rabble of prejudice, extremism, buffoonery and incompetency." Charles Weltner, the liberal and bright young Democratic U.S. representative from Atlanta, quit his job rather than be in a party headed by Maddox. Guys were sitting around in bars saying they were moving to another state. The end, it appeared, was at hand.

Actually, it was a lot of laughs. Lester outdid even Gene Talmadge and Marvin Griffin for burlesque. A born publicity hound, he saw that a day never passed when he didn't make the newspapers and television one way or another. "Lester sort of grows on you," said one aide, clearly enjoying himself. Every week there was Little People's Day, when the governor's office was opened to endless lines of folks who came to Lester with problems like drunk husbands and leaking faucets (he always passed the problem on to an aide after lending a sympathetic ear). He rode a bicycle backward at the mansion with a group of neighboring kids once, making all of the wire services. At an open house at the mansion one Sunday, four escaped convicts turned themselves in to him personally. At a press conference he said the federal government could "ram it," but came back with a clarification when people got mad: "I didn't tell 'em *where* they could ram it, did I?" He walked out on the Dick Cavett show when Cavett, Jim Brown and Truman Capote bugged him, and came back home with a stunning limp-wristed impersonation of Capote. He almost broke his neck when he rode on the hood of a car for a tape breaking at an interstate-highway opening and the tape proved to be extremely strong. He passed out Pickrick Drumsticks at the Senate cafeteria in Washington. He threw up his hands over state prison problems and opined, "What we need is a better class of prisoner." He preached in tiny rural churches every other Sunday for four years. He ran for President of the U.S. for at least a week. He ripped the

Washington Hot Line phone out of his wall one day when he got mad at the feds, claiming the wire was tapped. Cruising through Macon one night, he jumped out of his car and ran down two kids who had broken into a store. He proclaimed the day of the Muhammad Ali–Jerry Quarry fight in Atlanta a day of mourning because Ali had refused to go into the Army. Where do you stop? At first we were horrified—worried about our image, worried about not getting any more industry, worried about the state collapsing—but after a while it became a sport. What's Lester going to do next?

In retrospect, and in seriousness, it is being agreed now that Lester really didn't make much difference one way or another. We were lucky in the fact that he came along not in the first part of the 1960s, when there was genuine crisis and a need for calm decisions, but in the second half, when Georgia and Atlanta were going on the momentum generated earlier. Lester talks about how much industry he brought to Georgia and about hiring a record number of blacks for state jobs, but that is the sort of thing that had already been set into motion when he got there.

"There isn't much a governor can do, either way, on a day-to-day basis," says one top Capitol reporter, "except in a time of crisis; and Maddox never really had any crises like in the early 1960s." Maddox's poor qualifications, in fact, were a boom to the state, says former Atlanta Mayor Allen: "He probably wanted to be anti-Atlanta, but he just didn't know how to hurt us." Maddox has also boasted about his prison reforms, and he did go far toward eliminating the state's notorious prison work camps, but as one longtime lawyer put it, "It would take $100,000,000 to rehabilitate that system, and don't tell me one man is going to pull it off."

There are the strong detractors, of course, led by Reg Murphy, the young editor of the liberal *Atlanta Constitution:* "The people who say Lester Maddox didn't do any harm overlook the fact that a governor must do more than that. Leading a state doesn't mean talking at the Baptist church on Sunday morning. He let the momentum grind to a halt. Every time something got complex he'd just say 'Phooey.' All he did was create all of those animosities. He got the 'little people' involved in rhetoric, and that's about all." In spite of the critical judgments, Murphy agrees, with some cynicism, that Lester Maddox held a great mystical spell over the masses and may continue to do so for quite a while. "He made more people feel they had a voice in Atlanta," he says, "even if they didn't."

To the newsmen who regularly covered the Maddox administration, it was a dizzy sleigh ride. Lester is an impetuous man, hard to predict and just as hard to keep up with, but his relationships with the press have been generally good—if for no other reason than the fact he loves to see his name in print. "Just spell the name right," says one Capitol correspondent. One of the best to cover Maddox was Steve Ball, then political editor of *The Atlanta Journal*. "Nothing he ever says reads as good as it sounds," says Ball. "He's got a pretty good mind, not philosophical or deep but quick. The trouble is, you can't get him to stay still for more than three minutes before he's off on tangents and talking the code and quoting statistics. At the press conference he just keeps going, giving 'em new stuff if they want it, until he thinks everybody has a story, even if they're different stories. That's how he came up saying the federal government could 'ram it' on school segregation; it was his third or fourth press conference of the day and he wanted to give the boys something new." Bob Cohn, who was Capitol correspondent for a string of medium-sized Georgia dailies, forgives Lester for his sins: "Only this country can afford a Lester. We need him for levity. The longer you look at him the funnier it is. It's funny that he got elected, and it's funny the state didn't crumble."

Some Georgians are getting tired of laughing. Unable to succeed himself as governor, by state law, Lester ran for the obscure but influential job of lieutenant governor and won without a runoff—the first clear-cut political victory of his career—to become a poor man's Spiro Agnew to the new governor, a moderate Plains, Georgia, peanut farmer named Jimmy Carter. On his last day as governor, Lester gave us an idea of what we had ahead of us by protesting the fact that the lieutenant governor wasn't afforded a state automobile (it worked; he got one). The smart money in Georgia was saying Lester had it all ahead of him. *Senator* Maddox. Think about it, and laugh if you wish, but remember how everybody was laughing one time at the riddle making the rounds: "How does Lester resemble a monkey climbing a pole?" it went. "The higher he climbs," was the answer, "the more he shows his ass."

14·THE NEW HILLBILLY

He really doesn't give a flip what they think about him, just so they listen to his songs. Good thing. Because right now, shortly after the annual Country Music Association awards show—emceed by trusty Tennessee Ernie Ford and sponsored on network television by the wonderful folks from Kraft—the establishment on Nashville's Music Row is still seething. "I mean, hell, he didn't even wear a tux," one of them is saying. When it was announced that his "Sunday Mornin' Comin' Down" was the Song of the Year, you could sense Tex Ritter and Roy Acuff and all the rest hunkering down in their seats as Kris Kristofferson floated to the stage of the Grand Ole Opry House to accept the award: suede bell-bottoms, shoulder-length hair, strange deep-set Jack Palance eyes; weaving back and forth with his back to the audience for nearly 10 seconds like a cowboy who had lost his way, finally leaning on the podium and mumbling a few words about Johnny Cash, then stumbling away to cool applause and a lifted eyebrow—the old Jack Benny treatment—from Tennessee Ernie. I mean, Sonny James won't even sing in a place that serves alcohol, and here's this *weirdo* up there, God knows what he's been smoking, and, well, *hell*, a hippie or something.

> *Homer Lee Hunnicutt was nothin'*
>   *but a hippie*
> *Walkin' through this world without*
>   *a care,*
> *Then one day six strapping brave*
>   *policemen*
> *Held down Homer Lee and cut his*
>   *hair;*
> *'Cause the law is for protection*
>   *of the people*
> *Rules are rules and any fool can*
>   *see.*
> *We don't need no hairy-headed*
>   *hippies*
> *Scarin' decent folks like you and*
>   *me.*

"Yeah, well, you know how it goes, man." It is late at night and he has dropped by the makeshift studio in the rear of his publisher's office on Music Row to put down a couple of new songs, and while he peels down to a washed-out T-shirt and sips from a can of Budweiser it is all he can do to keep from laughing. "Like, man, this is the *truth* I'm telling you. Two beers. We were layin' some stuff down for an album and I didn't even want to go to the show. Bob [Beckham, his publisher] said the least I could do since I was nominated was go, and, while he changed into his tux right here we drank a couple of beers to cool off and . . ."

"No smokes?"

"Bull Durham count?"

"Grass. You were sailing."

"Hell, man. I was *scared.* I was rappin' with [Merle] Haggard about 'Okie from Muskogee' and when I heard 'em call my name I slammed my head back against the pew. I didn't know where I was at. I don't even remember

190

going up there to get the award. Like, those cats can believe what they want to, but I'm puttin' it to you straight. Two beers. I coulda *used* some grass."

They'll never believe it, of course, because Nashville isn't quite ready for Kris Kristofferson. Music City, U.S.A., has always been the most staid and pious of our music centers, regardless of its surface image as a command post for hell-raising good old boys. The $100-million-a-year music industry thriving here today owes its very foundations to the rigid back-country white gospel thwanging of such performers as the Carter Family, and the Opry House itself ("Mother Church of Country Music") started out as a tabernacle for a Bible-pounding soul-saving evangelist. Country music traditionally has been a mixed bag of basic themes covering Mother, Home and Flag; and lately, as the Silent Majority has begun to be heard, it has become even more fashionable in Nashville to be conservative, patriotic and, well, American. There is nothing mystical about the fact that Haggard's "Okie from Muskogee" was the most memorable country recording of 1970: "We don't smoke marijuana in Muskogee, and we don't take our trips on LSD; and we don't burn our draft cards down on Main Street, but we like living right and being free."

How, then, can you expect them to accept overnight somebody like Kris Kristofferson? He was once a Rhodes Scholar and has read extensively: Salinger, Shakespeare, Hemingway, Thoreau. He has long hair and two basic changes of clothes, both of them suede cowboy outfits, one brown and one black, bought in Peru while he worked on a movie with Dennis Hopper. He openly smokes pot, has been known to walk around with a flask of booze jammed in his boot (in a town that only three years ago allowed liquor to be served by the drink), uses "cat" and "man" and "chick" as others employ basic pronouns, travels with the likes of

Joan Baez and Bob Dylan, and writes bluntly sensual protest songs that are sometimes only a shade away from underground.

But the fact remains that Nashville, ready or not, is going to have to learn to live with Kris Kristofferson simply because at present he is the hottest country songwriter going. The term "country" is used advisedly, of course, bearing in mind that we are in the midst of a period when the distinctions separating all types of popular music are being blurred. Still, you can call Kristofferson's best stuff country, using the term loosely, because the thing that makes it go is a basic simplicity and a tight, simple story line aimed straight to the gut. In addition to "Sunday Mornin'," he has written "Me and Bobby McGee" and "For the Good Times" and perhaps a dozen others that will probably become better known in time, and the CMA award was the first official recognition that he is on his way.

He is the leading protégé of Cash, who wrote the liner notes for his recently released first album. Hopper, pleased with his score and acting in "The Last Movie," will base a movie on "Bobby McGee." A producer spotted him at Janis Joplin's funeral and signed him on the spot for the lead in a movie about a luckless musician-turned-junkie. He was a smash when he debuted as a performer at the Troubadour in Los Angeles and at the Bitter End in New York. He took in something like $200,000 for 1970, and the royalties hadn't really started rolling in. After five incredible years of moving around and scrambling to find himself, Kristofferson had been thrust upon us like the troubled, enigmatic, latent genius of one of his songs, "The Pilgrim: Chapter 33," a song that is about as autobiographical as a song can get:

> See him wasted on the sidewalk
> in his jacket and his jeans,
> Wearing yesterday's misfortunes
> like a smile;

Once he had a future
  full of money, love and dreams,
Which he spent like they was
  going out of style;
And he keeps right on a-changing,
  for the better or the worse,
And searching for a shrine
  he never found;
Never knowing if believing
  is a blessing or a curse,
Or if the going up
  is worth the coming down . . .

If the emergence of Kris Kristofferson had come in more stable times—say, 15 years ago—his biography would read like fiction. "I got a great future behind me," he is fond of saying, which is his way of summing up as succinctly as possible the agonizing transformation he has put himself through. But it doesn't sound so fictional today, or so shocking, because the very same thing is happening every day in almost every comfortable Middle America town in the country: bright middle-class kids with the game plan already worked out for them, suddenly deciding they don't want the ball, breaking out of the mold their parents have made. Except it took Kristofferson 30 years before he made the break. Once the word gets around, he could become a hero to these hordes of kids trying to find their own truths because his story is a classic.

Kristofferson's horizons first began to shift while he was a Rhodes Scholar, studying English literature at Oxford, in the late 1950s. Up to that point, everything had been programed. He had grown up in Brownsville, Texas, and San Mateo, California, the son of a retired major general who later became manager of air operations for Aramco in Arabia. He had been a model student in high

193

school and college: at Pomona College he starred in football, boxed Golden Gloves, wrote sports for the student newspaper, commanded the ROTC battalions, dug songwriter Hank Williams and started writing a novel.

Although his family "told me in so many words that we had had this background in the military and I was expected to excel," he wanted to be a writer and toward the end of his college career he was buoyed when he won four of the *Atlantic Monthly's* 20 prizes in the national collegiate short-story contest and was then awarded a Rhodes Scholarship. At Oxford, he began writing another novel—"which I really got into"—but he also started doodling around with songwriting. (He had first written a song when he was 11 years old, "nothin' but a copy of Hank Williams.") This sidetracked him into show business, and he was signed by Tommy Steele's promoter and became Kris Carson. When *Time* wrote about him as a rising young pop-singing idol and he mentioned his two unfinished novels, two publishers asked to look at the manuscripts. "I thought, 'This is it, I'm going to be a published novelist.'" But curt rejections followed and, as he puts it, "I lost my guts."

The bottom fell out after that. So deflating was the experience of being rejected that within two months he bailed out of Oxford, married his childhood sweetheart and joined the Army. "I never intended to stay in, but I decided I should get out of it all I could," so he went through Jump school, Ranger school and flight school and was assigned to Germany as a helicopter pilot. He extended for an extra three years so he could bring his bride overseas at government expense.

The Army didn't seem to be the answer, either. "I dug flying, but I hated the Army. It's not, like, being antiwar especially, but the Army per se. I hated being supply officer, filling out forms, all that kind of shit. It seemed like so much crap, like having any kind of government job is. I

194

mean, I don't dig politics, either, for the same reason." He was into the bottle and he totaled two automobiles and had four motorcycle accidents. "I got to feeling bad about not writing, not doing anything, so about the fourth year I started traveling with this group and playing EM and NCO clubs. I started writing some songs again, and another helicopter pilot had this relative in Nashville, and she told him to tell me to send her some of my stuff on tape. Right before I split Europe, we got a letter saying I oughta drop by Nashville while I was on leave."

His next assignment was to teach English literature at West Point, but he had two weeks to report. He sent his wife and baby home to California, and he headed straight for Nashville. He had intended to stay there a couple of days and find out what his buddy's relative, songwriter-publisher Marijon Wilkin, thought of his chances; but he wound up staying nearly two weeks. He sat around at late-night jam sessions, shook hands with Cash backstage at the Opry ("They had to tell me who he was") and was so smitten with the spirit that he wrote seven songs.

"All of a sudden I felt like this was where it's at. I figured if I didn't write songs maybe I'd try another novel, because I could see stories all over the place. One night I called Marijon and said I was going to bust out of the Army and come to Nashville, and she didn't offer me any encouragement. I think it scared the hell out of her, knowing how tough it is to make it. She said, like, 'Don't do it, man,' but I'd made up my mind." He went straight to the Pentagon and managed to have his orders changed, springing himself from the service of his country. "And then I went back home and, like, told the people."

The people, of course, didn't go for it. "It was, like, instant bastard; they thought I was insane." He went on to Nashville and had one of his songs picked up right off the bat ("Vietnam Blues"), but then began to discover why Marijon Wilkin hadn't wanted to take responsibility for him. Between 1965 and 1969, it became a struggle just to stay alive and write. He dug ditches as a part-time common laborer. He tended bar in a tavern on Music Row. He commuted to Morgan City, Louisiana, where he piloted helicopters flying men and equipment out to the offshore oil rigs. "I turned down an offer to run a publishing company, and some other jobs that would've paid good bread, because they wouldn't leave me enough time to write."

He finally took a $58-a-week job cleaning ash trays and carrying things around at Columbia Studios ("The beauty of that one was, I didn't have to think"), which gave him an opportunity to get closer to people like Cash and push his songs. He was moving further away from his roots and getting deeper into a new life every day. It was in this period that he wrote some of his best songs, including "Sunday Mornin' Comin' Down," and that one more than any tells of the lonely flight he was going through: "On the Sunday mornin' sidewalks, wishin' Lord that I was stoned; 'cause there's somethin' in a Sunday, makes a body feel alone . . ." After two separations, his wife had finally packed up their two kids and left for good. So he wrote "For the Good Times," about the reluctant but inevitable breakdown of a marriage: ". . . and make believe you love me one more time, for the good times."

In the great folk tradition he slaved away over his songs in a rundown $25-a-month rooming house on Music Row, making the best of his adversity. "For a while there," says Red O'Donnell, a columnist for *The Nashville Banner*, "We were spelling his name 'Christopher' and 'Kristofson'; every way but the right way. I think the problem was, a lot of his stuff was over everybody's head." Indeed, Kristofferson's first break didn't come until mid-1969, when Roger Miller recorded "Me and Bobby McGee," a bouncy and partly autobiographical tune about a young couple hitchhiking around the country together:

> *Freedom's just another word*
> *for nothin' left to lose,*
> *Nothin' ain't worth nothin'*
> *but it's free;*
> *Feelin' good was easy, Lord,*
> *when Bobby sang the blues;*
> *Feelin' good was good enough for me,*
> *good enough for me and Bobby McGee . . .*

It is fitting that Miller would be the first to pick up on Kristofferson because he is the one who opened the doors five years ago for the growing underground of folk-country writers in Nashville, a "new breed" of which Kristofferson became the spiritual leader. It was around 1965 when Miller broke away from the usual fare of beer-drinking and heart-breaking Nashville songs with "King of the Road" and a dozen tunes featuring upbeat, near-pop melodies and clever fresh lyrics. He stood Nashville on its ear for some three years, and was quickly followed by John Hartford ("Gentle on My Mind") and Bobby Russell ("Little Green Apples"). Those three and the others who joined them had grown up in the South and had been raised on country music, but they had not shut their ears to other types of music and they weren't content to spend their lives turning out pure country hits, playing the Opry and hitting the road on back-breaking one-night tours. The songs they began writing, then, showed more sophistication but still retained the blunt simplicity that is the common denominator of most country songs. Miller, of course, has been gone from the Nashville scene for some time now, working television and Las Vegas, singing other people's songs. Hartford, too, has cut out for the West Coast. (In Nashville, they like to sit around in their offices

THE GOOD OLD BOYS

on Music Row and tick off the names of writers who quit writing once they went off to greener pastures.) In their places are fewer than a dozen members of the "new breed," all but Kristofferson unknown to much of the rest of the country: Mickey Newbury, Chris Gantry, Dennis Linde, Steve Davis, Tony Joe White. They do not work the Opry or country road shows. There is a lot of hair. There are no flashy clothes and Cadillacs and painted ladies. They are intelligent, in their 20s, liberal and oriented more toward Dylan than Ernest Tubb. "These people aren't basically songwriters," says writer-publisher Bub Tubert, who is close to the group, "they're poets." And their records generally don't sell enough to write home about, primarily because they cannot be easily tagged "country" or "pop" or "folk."

One influence on the group is Bob Beckham, a former pop singer who came to Nashville in 1960 to go on tour with the Brenda Lee road show and who, as a part-owner of Combine Music, holds the publishing rights on most of Kristofferson's material. "I don't know why, exactly, but there aren't many hours of the day when some of 'em aren't hanging around here, talking or writing or jamming," said Beckham, who had decided to get with it by growing a beard. "I guess they thought they saw somebody who'd listen. I've always thought Nashville could be much broader than country music. This town was based on simple, strong lyrics. There's no limitation on Nashville's expanding into all fields. The limitation, if you ask me, was self-imposed."

But probably the biggest influence of all is Johnny Cash, by his mere presence. In Cash, writers like Gantry, Newbury and Kristofferson found an artist who wanted fresh material and would stop to listen. "When Dylan was starting and nobody was listening, John wrote to tell him he dug him," says Newbury, who, along with the others, is a regular guest at Cash's rustic mansion on Old Hickory Lake for late-night jam sessions. "He's sympathetic. It means a whole hell of a lot to know he cares for you. Cash showed people from out of town that there's a lot more going on here than beer-drinking songs." And Kristofferson recalls a time when he was still emptying trash at the Columbia Studios, and almost got fired when some friends of his tried to push some songs on Cash in the middle of a recording session: "He came all the way down to the basement the next night, where I was working on some tapes, and after he bummed a cigarette he said, 'Understand you got into some trouble.' Man, I was shaking like a leaf. I said, 'I want you to understand I didn't have nothin' to do with that,' and he said he knew I didn't. Then he asked me to come up for the session and when I said they told me I couldn't he said, 'You might as well come on up, because I ain't gonna cut the session without you.' Can you imagine that, a guy as busy as he is, foolin' around with some nobody like me? It was a horrible experience, sitting there on the floor and getting those cold stares from the control booth, but it showed me what kind of man John is."

Kristofferson resembles Cash, and quite a lot of other folk country musicians from the past such as Woody Guthrie, in a remarkable number of ways. He tortured himself for so long that he didn't really start to make it until he was 33. He is a poet rather than a musician, more concerned with interpretation than with quality of voice. He is at once blunt and mystical, above petty prejudices, strongly appealing to the campus and intellectual sets. He is an important link between country, pop and underground music. Like Cash, he possesses a raw masculine mystique, hinting of unbridled physical excesses and senseless odd-hours scrapes with the authorities, and when he ambles onstage ("Ladies and gentlemen, Kris Kristofferson" is the extent of his fanfare) he is a road-weary troubadour come to tell about what he's just been through: no patter; wiry, 5-foot-11 frame hunched over a 12-string guitar, deep blue eyes trying to remember exactly how it was, raspy voice half-talking and half-singing the lyrics; yellowed fingers reaching for a beer and another Bull Durham (three packs a day) during instrumental breaks. When he debuted as a performer last summer at the Troubadour in Los Angeles, he stole the show from headliner Linda Ronstadt—who came out in bare feet and a supermini for her electrified country-rock spectacular— hypnotizing the crowd with nothing more than his hoarse voice, one guitar and one bass. "You could have heard a pin drop," says Bob Beckham. "Whatever that thing is, he's got it."

Although a career as a performer has quickly opened up for him—the lead in Jerry Ayres' *Dealing* opposite Karen (*Five Easy Pieces*) Black, a series of college concerts for next year, an album that sold a respectable 60,000 copies after only three months—Kristofferson would prefer to be known as a songwriter. He didn't want to cut his album ("I sing like a goddamned frog") but was convinced by Monument's Fred Foster that it would be the quickest way to pitch his songs. He shouldn't be mistaken for a formally trained writer capable of putting down intricate scores or writing songs to order for certain artists, though Beckham swears he "could probably do anything he made up his mind to do." He doesn't have the background for it, having done little more than play at songwriting until he began to point himself toward Nashville five years ago, at the age of 29.

The last week of October brought Kristofferson back to Nashville, two weeks after the CMA awards show, to tape another Johnny Cash show for ABC-TV. He lives in a modest hotel in Los Angeles catering to musicians, artists and writers (and still rents the $25-a-month room next to Combine Music in Nashville, where he wrote "Sunday Mornin'"), shuttling back and forth to record, read scripts, rap with friends and write songs. He would tape the show that night, then fly back to the Coast in the morning so he could start filming *Dealing*.

He kicked off his boots, poured a shot of Scotch into a motel tumbler, lit another cigarette and stretched his frame over a bed as the late afternoon sun shimmered through the drapes. His sister is married to an Army officer who teaches at West Point, he said, "a great cat I introduced her to," and has a happy life. His brother is a Navy jet pilot. His parents are retired now, living in California near his former wife and his children. As he talked about these things, about his "bailing out" for a new life, his drawling, husky voice sagged and he went off on a stumbling monologue:

"Not many cats I knew bailed out like I did. When I made the break I didn't realize how much I was shocking the folks because I always thought they knew I was going to be a writer, but I think they thought a writer was a guy in tweeds with a pipe. And I quit and didn't hear from 'em for a while. They were over in Arabia for about nine years. And they came through Nashville for a day, when I was workin' labor jobs, and they left the next morning. It was a very uncomfortable scene. And then they sent a letter just flat saying, you know, don't visit any of our relatives, you're an embarrassment to us. Worse than that, but I ain't going into it."

He went quiet for a minute or so, and then started talking again. "You know, like, 'You've given us moments of occasional pride but it'll never measure up to the tremendous disappointment you've been to us.' They couldn't tell their friends at the bridge club that their Rhodes Scholar son was digging ditches in Hicktown, U.S.A., which is what they considered Nashville . . . For a while I was really eaten up by this. I could have answered with an angry letter, you know. But you can either let it eat you up or you can cut it off, which is what I wound up doing." He cleared his throat. Therapy. "About a year ago they said they were sorry they wrote that letter. They still can't understand me, like they can't stand to look at me on TV with long hair. My old man finally said, 'We're really with you, even though we can't say it.' That really broke me up. It was the first nice thing that cat ever really said to me. But I really think he realizes. He beat his head against the wall all of his life, and he was really a success as far as the old terms go. But what's he got now, you know? He really kinda lost and, ah, after I'd split with my wife I was out there and he said, 'It really is important to do what you're doing, what you feel you have to do, because you only go around one time' . . . They try to understand me, but they just can't."

"You don't second-guess yourself, then."

"What, about all that shit I put myself through?"

"Right."

He was up now, booted again, looking around for his guitar case. "I remember talking to this guy one time at a bullfight in Spain, when I was hitching around. I told him I didn't like the picadors. You know, all that jabbing and bleeding. He explained the whole ritual and said it may be an ugly part but it's part of the whole picture. I wouldn't want to go through it again, but it's part of what I am . . ."

He may have put it better in a song called "To Beat the Devil," which he dedicates, in his album, to Johnny Cash and June Carter. A destitute songwriter wanders into a tavern and runs into the devil, who tells him it is hopeless, that nobody is going to listen to his songs anyway. It is a song for late nights and boozy heads and cigarette tongues, a song for anybody who ever tried to go against the grain:

> *You still can hear me singin'*
> *to the people who don't listen*
> *to the things that I am sayin',*
> *prayin' someone's gonna hear;*
> *An' I guess I'll die explainin'*

how the things that they complain about
are the things they could be changin',
hopin' someone's gonna care;
An' if I never have a nickel
I won't ever die ashamed,
'Cause I don't believe that no one wants to know . . .

PART FOUR

Eat–Gas–Motel

15·ON THE ROAD, 1969

Dayton is a northern city. It says so on the map. Cincinnati is 50 miles to the south, Columbus 70 miles east, and in only three hours you can drive to Lake Erie. The city is the sixth-largest in Ohio (pop. 280,000), a sprawling place with wide streets and bleak old buildings, one of this country's major industrial towns. Hubert Humphrey got more votes out of Montgomery County than Richard Nixon did in 1968. The accent you hear is Midwestern. The weather, in the winter, can be bitter. The talk you hear, this time of year, is about Woody Hayes and the Ohio State Buckeyes. A Southerner, accustomed to smaller towns and warmer weather and a slower pace, wouldn't care much for Dayton.

But they come, anyway, and they have made Dayton "upper Appalachia," as some Daytonians bitterly put it. It began in the 1930s, when poor whites from Kentucky, Tennessee and West Virginia streamed out of the hills, coming north by every means imaginable on U.S. Highway 25 (officially called the "Dixie Highway") to take jobs with the Crosley Corporation (radios, cars, refrigerators) in Cincinnati. When the jobs there were filled, they continued north on the same road to Dayton and Toledo and Detroit. There were plenty of jobs for the uneducated and untrained,

207

good union jobs with health plans and retirement, and they kept coming because back home the mines were dry and the babies were sick. And still they come, and the Southern Baptist Church experienced a membership growth of 385.3 percent in Ohio between 1953 and 1963 and George Wallace knew enough' to bring his campaign here to Dayton twice a year (getting 13 percent of the county's votes).

And what you have, in Dayton today, is a not-always-peaceful coexistence between the natives and the "briars," as the Appalachian migrants are called. They seldom participate in local politics, except to vote "no" on almost anything. They live together, drink together, fight together, wind up on the police blotter together and go back home on weekends together. Every weekend there are legendary traffic jams where the interstate highway bottlenecks near old Crosley Field in Cincinnati, and a lot of the trouble is caused by carloads of Southerners going home on Friday and coming back to work on Sunday.

The major area for Appalachians here is East Dayton, a cluttered old neighborhood of corner taverns and narrow streets and second-hand furniture stores and laundromats. East Dayton used to be a German settlement, but now it is made up of 38,000 people—23 percent of them born in the South. The people there work in factories such as National Cash Register (employing 15,000 workers) and Frigidaire and Delco and various General Motors plants. "I'll tell you one thing, buddy-boy," says a Manhattan-born newspaper reporter named Bernie Wullkotte, "you better have a Southern accent or keep your goddamned mouth shut when you go down into East Dayton at night. Hell, I've heard third-generation Southerners in this town say they're from 'Dayuh-ton.'"

A young social worker named Don Wollmeier, a Dayton native who quit his family's hardware business eight months ago to take over a program called East Dayton Community Council, thinks the influx will continue but feels optimistic about the future. "What happens is, a fellow comes up and maybe a church loans him $20 while he looks for a job, and he goes back for his wife and kids, and pretty soon a cousin or a brother or a friend comes up, too. As long as there are jobs up here and nothing back home, they'll keep coming. It's hard for them to adjust, particularly since a lot of them were having a hard enough time adjusting in the South. But I sense a slight change in attitude here. Dayton is beginning to realize there are people coming in with different situations who need help. You still hear plenty of jokes about 'briars,' but not as often."

You get the feeling, though, that it will take a long time before the Appalachian migrants are absorbed into cities like Dayton and Detroit and Akron. Maybe they don't *want* to be absorbed. It is as clear as a glass of beer, for example, when you hit any of the three dozen honky-tonks in Dayton that feature live country music on weekends.

At noon Saturday, a joint called Jo De Bri Cafe on East Third Street in East Dayton was already jumping. There was a four-foot wide Confederate flag on the wall behind the bar, and a pool table and pinball machines and a jukebox, and a sign behind the bandstand saying "The Country Four, Fri. & Sat. Nite." A red-faced mountain boy had dumped a handful of quarters in the jukebox and was playing Ernest Tubb records over and over again. He pretended to dance with the jukebox, a wrinkled shirt spilling out of his shiny black cotton trousers, and then he said, to nobody in particular, "Boy, I sure love to hear ol' Ernest sing."

CRUM, WEST VIRGINIA

The impact is greatest if you approach it from the north, over the smooth plains of south-central Ohio. This is Middle America, as well-scrubbed as a Miss America contestant. This is sweeping valleys of tall corn and fat cattle and full trees and amber waves of grain. It is orderly small towns and white two-story houses and front-porch swings and thick green lawns and dependable Buicks in driveways. It is Old Glory, Eisenhower-Nixon, quiet streets, Rotary, apple pie, *Reader's Digest* and the garden club. You don't think of hungry people or Harlem or Eldridge Cleaver or Vietnam when you drive southeast through towns like Washington Court House and Frankfort and Richmond Dale. You think pleasant thoughts, of the order of things, and you smile from deep inside because everything is right.

Abruptly, the changes come when you reach a hill town called Jackson. This town is rough and dirty and disjointed. Teenaged boys hang around drive-in hamburger stands, leaning on tight-springed and unkempt '64 Chevys. Many of the houses and most of the downtown buildings need repairing and painting. And it is all uphill after Jackson, as you turn directly south for the 50-mile run to the high bluffs overlooking the Ohio River. Now, in stark contrast to the serenity that had come before, you fight over twisting roads past unpainted shacks and depleted coal mines and abandoned automobiles and sharp rock ledges. CHEW MAIL POUCH TOBACCO, say the flaking billboards, and JESUS IS COMING. And suddenly you come to a silver bridge that crosses the muddy Ohio, and tall smokestacks are belching black smoke and the buildings of Huntington are of dirty red brick and the mountains ahead are like a jagged wall, and the sign over the bridge welcomes you to "The Switzerland of America," West Virginia.

And you find that you are not prepared for West Virginia, especially after the pleasant drive on a Sunday afternoon through that part of America they were dreaming about when the country was established. You have seen the horrible deprivation on television and read Harry Caudill's *Night Comes to the Cumberlands* and know all about the Hatfields and the McCoys, but you are not ready for West Virginia. "Actually," wrote Caudill, a former Kentucky legislator, in a beautiful study of what has happened to the Appalachians, "much of the Cumberland Plateau can best serve the nation by being submerged." Cruel, when taken out of context like that, but sensible. Damming and flooding huge portions of Kentucky and West Virginia might be the only way to save these strong-willed and isolated people from themselves.

The land in southwestern West Virginia, as you take meandering U.S. Highway 52 south out of Huntington, is so harsh and ragged and crude that it is beautiful. It takes at least two hours to drive the 78 miles from Huntington to Williamson over a winding road that snakes along the narrow valleys like a great running back poking for openings in a defensive line. The fog has already closed in at dusk, which comes early. Four abandoned automobiles lie in a ditch in front of an unpainted shack, stripped to support one that is still running. The young are at the Dew Drop Inn, the old are at the Church of God, the middle-aged are staring blankly at the jagged hill across the road from their front porch. No motels, no billboards, no gardens, no Buicks, no jobs, no Rotary, no American flags flying. Only West Virginia.

The only place to stop, on a fogged-in Sunday night, had been the Mt. Laurel Motel. It sits across the road from the Mt. Laurel Coffee Shop, which has a bar and pool tables and gas pumps and pinball machines and a sign on the wall that says, "I'd Like to Drown My Troubles, But My Wife Won't Go Near Water." A young guy had run across the road without a shirt and closed the deal on a room for the night, for $6.18, and hurriedly dashed back to the cafe so he wouldn't miss any more of *Hee Haw* on the color television set behind the bar. Their only other motel customer was a truck driver headed to Huntington to pick up a house trailer for Pennsylvania. The phones were out.

"That young man last night, was he your brother?" Callie Wright was asked the next morning. It was 8:30 and an old mountaineer was sitting at the bar with a quart of beer. A Pabst sign on the wall in front of him, in Gay '90s lettering said, "Next Time Bring Your Wife." Callie Wright is 49, a frail woman with a pathetic ponytail and deep lines around her eyes.

"That was my husband," she said.

"But he's so young."

"He's 25. We been married two years now."

"You were married before, I guess."

"Thirty years," she said. "But I'd been leavin' him for 30 years. He drank a lot and threw his money away. Miners are like that. When they're working, they work. When the mines dry up, they go crazy. Hey, if you're goin' down to Crum, you've got to stop and see my sister. Addie Mae Burnett." Her sister is postmistress at Crum, she said, and won an award for keeping the neatest post office in the state. Callie Wright was very proud.

SARAH ANN, WEST VIRGINIA

The trouble began nearly a century ago in these same dark hills and eerie valleys, and because this land has changed so little it is easy to imagine guns flashing at each other across the hillsides at dusk. The brood of William Anderson (Devil Anse) Hatfield lived on the West Virginia side of the Tug Valley, and Randolph McCoy's people were no more than 10 miles away in Kentucky. The first signs of bad blood had come during the Civil War, when the Hatfields fought for the Confederacy and the McCoys for the Union. Both clans were well stocked with free-living young men who could drink hard and shoot straight and hate long, and the first time they fired on each other was as marauding bands of irregular troops in the war.

The feud grew out of a series of events, some real and some imagined. A McCoy was found dead during the war in a cave near the Hatfield spread. A Hatfield and a McCoy who had married sisters got into a bitter argument over a razorback hog. A Hatfield boy fell in love with a McCoy girl, neither family would allow the marriage, so he impregnated her. If there was a single event that brought the Hatfields and the McCoys together in mortal combat, it came on an election day in 1882 when a drunken argument left a Hatfield dead and three McCoys paid for it; all three of them were found the next night, tied to pawpaw bushes in the hills, riddled with gunshot wounds.

So that is how the famous feud between the Hatfields and the McCoys began, and during a period of 25 years more than 100 Hatfields and McCoys and their allies—not to mention a considerable number of reasonably innocent bystanders—were killed. Although many were eventually thrown in jail, the law tended to stand back in awe and watch from the sidelines. When the McCoys began kidnapping Hatfields and carrying them back to Kentucky to stand trial, they set off a fight over state's rights that went all the way to the U.S. Supreme Court. The feud had attracted newspapers from all over the country, awakening the nation to the existence of these strong, independent, fierce men who had populated the Appalachian hill country.

The feud began to die out around 1900. The law began to tame the hills. Schools came and took the children's minds off revenge. The coal mines came and brought with them new people. The Hatfield and McCoy families began to lose their clannishness. Devil Anse became a prosperous farmer and in 1911, after two of his sons were killed by an Italian liquor peddler, he was baptized and began to lead the pure life. In succeeding years, Hatfields and McCoys became doctors and lawyers and sheriffs and politicians (one, Henry D. Hatfield, was elected governor of West Virginia in 1921 and later became a U.S. senator).

Today, in the hills where Kentucky and West Virginia come together, the two family names are prominent. In the slim Williamson, West Virginia, phone book there are 172 Hatfields and 91 McCoys. Almost everybody else can claim some Hatfield or McCoy blood, somewhere. Chambers of Commerce in the area are laying plans to capitalize on the famous feud to snare tourists.

The only one of Devil Anse's nine sons still living is Willis Wilson Hatfield 82, now hospitalized in Charleston with yellow jaundice. The others are buried on a rocky hill here, between the towns of Logan and Williamson, arranged around a near-lifesize marble statue of Devil Anse himself. At the bottom of the steep hill, on the highway next to a white-frame Crystalblock Freewill Baptist Church, is a white cast-iron historical marker telling about the feud. Late in the afternoon one day last week, as a cool breeze wandered through the narrow valley, two carloads of Ohio tourists in Bermuda shorts clambered over the gravestones and fired away with Instamatic cameras.

Henry Hatfield said people are always stopping. He is a pleasant, slow-moving, bespectacled man, 44, a grandson of Devil Anse. He lives in a Jim Walter home that hangs from a cliff perhaps 100 yards from the family cemetery. He runs the Hatfield Monument Company, serving five counties with gravestones.

"Lots of McCoys stop, too," he was saying.

"Is there any bad feeling left?"

"Naahhh. Been so much intermarriage and everything. Besides, that's been 90 years now. We died laughing the other night when we were watching TV and they were interviewing one of the McCoys. He's 92, I think they said, and when he started talking about the feud he got to crying. I swear. Crying, right on TV. He wasn't even born when what he was talking about happened."

Hatfield said he ran for constable in the last election and his wife ran for committeewoman, but both were defeated. "The machine beat us," he said.

CELINA, TENNESSEE

As the highway rises up from Nashville for the run into the jagged Appalachians, the hills begin to blip across the horizon as though a child had scrawled them with a crayon. The people call it Upper Middle Tennessee or "foothills of the Cumberland," this land some 100 miles northeast of the state capital, and as you approach it at dusk over a rutted winding road you are touched by something mystical. Gray fog rises off the meandering Cumberland River. Rabbits dart across the road. Smoke curls from chimneys. Stark rock ledges, stacked like pancakes, hang precariously from the sharp cliffs. Ominous Black Angus cattle graze in the narrow valley meadows. Quail flee from clumps of dark bushes. Snakes wriggle. Crows call. Things go bump in the night.

And yet, people are leaving Clay County. WELCOME TO CELINA, WHERE SPORTSMEN MEET, says a rusting sign at the city limits of the county seat. But sportsmen come up for a weekend, bring their own motels and restaurants with them, catch a few trout, then leave. The true population is dying. In 1940 there were nearly 11,000 people living there, but now there are barely more than 7,000. The day after a kid graduates from Celina High School he follows the road that has always taken kids to Indianapolis or Anderson, Indiana, or Detroit. Last year the county judge was smart enough to actively campaign in a certain neighborhood of Indianapolis. Last year the county's only funeral home made a dozen trips to Indiana to bring expatriates back home for the last time.

They are leaving Clay County because there are no jobs. There are no jobs in Clay County because no industries dare settle there. No industries will settle there because, ironically, of the same reasons that give the area its mysticism: isolation, independence and rugged beauty. Natural beauty is fine, but it scares the hell out of a company president who has to worry about how he's going to get his product out of

215

the hills. Clay County can't, in other words, have its cake and eat it too.

"I don't guess I can blame the young people or the manufacturers," says Clyde King, 46, who has lived in Celina all his life and is now cashier of the bank of Celina. "Our biggest problems are inaccessibility and lack of housing, and that's enough to scare off a small industry. We don't have a movie house or a golf course. About the only entertainment we've got in the whole county is fishing and slow-pitch softball. I can't say I'd blame a teenager for wanting to leave, the way it is now."

Clay County may be the epitome of the isolated Southern border area that has always lost its finest to the lure of the better-developed North. Farming won't cut it anymore. Indianapolis is less than 300 miles away, with its factory jobs and union scale. So the young ones go away to make a decent living. They swarm over Celina on holidays and weekends, and they even buy vacation or retirement homes in Clay County, but on Monday they are back on the job in Indianapolis or Detroit or wherever.

One of the few young ones to remain is Jimmy Hay, director of Upton Funeral Home in Celina. Jimmy Hay was born here, went to Middle Tennessee State University for a while, married a Celina girl and ignored the temptation to leave. He is 25 years old. Last year, in a town of 1,200 people, he conducted 86 funerals.

"We brought 10 of 'em back from Indiana," he was saying. "So far this year, there's been, let's see, four we had to go and get. It's all right to go up there and work, if that's what they've got to do, but they don't want to be buried up there and they don't want to stay up there on the weekend. Just last Saturday I bought a boat down here for my brother-in-law, so he can come down from Indiana every weekend and use it."

"How many graduated with you?" he was asked.

"Sixty-nine," he said. "Exactly 69."

216

"How many would you say have stayed here?"

"Fifteen. Naw, probably not that many."

"But you stayed on."

Jimmy Hay considered that for a minute. "Yeah, but I had to work at it," he said. "I studied every way I could to stay. I don't want to go up there if there's any way to keep from it. So look what I had to do. Funeral director."

CHEROKEE, NORTH CAROLINA

In the beginning, the Southern Appalachians belonged to the Cherokee Indians. They had been here for several centuries when De Soto spotted them in the mid-16th century. Even after the white man began to move into the mountains to cut trees and kill game, the Cherokee nation prospered in the Carolinas, Virginia, Tennessee, Georgia and Alabama. The Cherokees then, the history books tell us, were proud and industrious people who hunted and fished and farmed and would later be the only American Indian tribe to invent their own writing system without the help of the white man. But the white man had come to these lush green hills, more sophisticated and better educated and in large numbers, and bad things had to happen.

The 18th century meant tragedy for the Cherokee. White settlers came in droves during the early 1700s. Smallpox killed half the tribe around 1740. For the rest of the century there was warfare between Indians and whites. The last straw came in 1828, when gold was discovered on the edge of the newly founded Cherokee Nation, in Georgia. By 1830, removal of the Cherokees had become national policy.

There followed, then, the westward migration of what had once been the most civilized and powerful tribe in the Southeast: over the "Trail of Tears." The Cherokees, some 16,000 of them, were herded like animals to Oklahoma, about 4,000 of them dying along the way. But 1,000 of them stayed in these Southern mountains running from the white man, hiding in the narrow valleys, escaping the federal troops, hunted and hated people on land that had been theirs.

Liberals and conservatives bleed for the Indian, and Johnny Cash (part Indian, like many Southerners) even writes songs about him, but nothing tells his sad story like the hard statistics. There are 600,000 Indians living in America today, two-thirds of them on reservations or in big-city ghettos, almost all of them completely cut off from the mainstream of American life. The average life span of the Indian is 20 years shorter than that of a white American. Indian unemployment is 40 percent. Illiteracy is more than 30 percent. Median family income is around $1,500. The incidence of tuberculosis is seven times greater than the national average. Most nations defeated by Americans have been lifted up by their bootstraps afterward, but the Indians were not so fortunate. The irony, of course, is that they were the original Americans.

Of those 600,000 Indians remaining, some 6,000 of them occupy the mountainous 56,000-acre tract in western North Carolina called the Cherokee Indian Reservation. It is a terribly divided, poor, unstable, poorly educated community. There are the bitter, conservative, full-blooded "black Indians" who live deep in the reservation. There are the "white Indians" (sometimes called Uncle Tomahawks) who have gone to school and bent themselves to white culture and in some cases have become rich. And then there is a middle class, those who don't know whether to hate the white man or go along with him. There are, curiously, many who moonshine whiskey and are hard-shell Baptists as though they were white mountaineers.

Sadly, what most Southerners or tourists in the South know about the Indian is what they have learned by blowing through Cherokee, North Carolina. Cherokee sits on the edge of the reservation here, at the base of the Great Smoky Mountain National Park, like a junk roadside stand. It is here that white traders and "real Indians" peddle plastic Jesuses, "genuine Indian woodcraft" made in Japan, girlie postcards, cameras and film, cigarette lighters, *et al.* The strip runs for a mile, and more than 5 million tourists drop some $6 million there every year.

Business reaches a crescendo on the Labor Day weekend, of course, and last week the cars were jammed bumper-to-bumper along the main drag while Cherokee Indians in Sioux warbonnets (more colorful) peddled their wares and posed for pictures under the crisp late-summer sun. One of them stood in front of a novelty shop, decked out in bonnet and moccasins and feathers and buckskin, beneath a poster that said a picture would cost $1.25 ("25 cents with your own camera"). He was old, with deep creases on his bronze face like a relief map of the Grand Canyon, and he was talking to a young white mother whose little boy clung to her skirt.

"And you've always lived here?" she was saying.

"Yes," he told her.

"How *fascinating*."

Without any emotion, the "chief" looked at his watch and saw it was almost noon. He left his post and came back in a minute, wearing a wool hat and blue jeans, and he went down the street for a hamburger at the Dairy Queen.

SANFORD, NORTH CAROLINA

Sanford is a town of about 13,000 people, a drab collection of old one- and two-story buildings in Lee (for Robert E.) County in the so-called Sandhills section of North Carolina, where the land begins to flatten out and glide monotonously past stunted piney woods and on into the sea. This used to be a big farming area, but now the farms are small and a lot of the people have moved to town for jobs in the brick-and-tile and textile-machinery plants. This town's boosters like

219

to boast about the good climate and the solid nonunion industries and what they say is an extremely low rate of unemployment.

They also like to brag about Sanford's amicable race relations. About one-third of the population is black, and in years past the Ku Klux Klan was strong and the Negroes *yassuhed* and everybody lived more or less happily together in that state of seething coexistence native to most rural Southern towns. The Negroes, in other words, stayed in their place.

But all of this changed in midsummer. One night at a drive-in hamburger joint on the edge of town a white boy from a nearby town beat up on a black kid from Sanford. The town, after all of these quiet years of anonymity, started making the headlines. Black civil rights leaders began paying attention to Sanford. Black citizens were huddling together in the humid night air and saying they'd had enough, and white citizens were saying "the nigger" started it. Since then there have been other racial incidents, and the long-dormant Klan has come back to life, and you can't find out the truth anymore about Sanford's race relations because passion and anger have taken over.

So this is the agony that has come to Sanford and many of the other towns like it over the South. Times have changed on them, and changed abruptly. Old systems are being toppled almost overnight. Where there used to be farming, there is now industrialization. Where there was velvet-glove segregation there is resistance from determined young militant blacks. Where there was serenity inside the white power structure, there is now self-righteousness and frustration and a dose of panic.

"I'm shocked and mad and a lot of things you couldn't print," Roy Stewart, the mayor of Sanford, was saying late one afternoon last week. He is a talkative man with thinning gray hair and a middle-aged spread, and he gulped coffee beneath a travel poster of Rome in the Farm House Restaurant at the end of a long day. For the past two nights there had been rock throwing and gunfire between police and Negroes, and that day's Sanford *Herald* had quoted an anonymous Klansman as saying that "patience has grown thin." During the day a half-dozen Klansmen had paraded through the mayor's office to tell him they were prepared to take the law into their own hands.

"The Klan must be strong here," somebody said.

"Not until now," said Stewart.

"They've rallied, then."

"Damn right they have. Hell, over in the county next door they used to have a sign at the city limits that said, 'The Ku Klux Klan Welcomes You to Lillington' or something like that. It never was that strong here. But now everybody on both sides is riled up and I don't know what's going to happen."

Mayor Stewart, who doubles as president of a paving company, says he has always thought of himself as a liberal. He says that the blacks in Sanford "have always been treated fairly" and that he has "a lot of friends who are black," and although this sounds like your basic Southern segregationist he does back up his image and Sanford's image with specifics. The police force was integrated "15 or 18 years ago," he says, and now there are "seven or eight" black cops ("including a captain who works with white policemen under him") on a force of 35 men. Negroes are well represented on city planning committees, he says. "Between federal housing and urban renewal," he adds, "we're spending $6 million in areas where the Negroes live." And, he says, there is "little trouble" in the lightly desegregated schools, and with Negroes who hold positions as foremen and secretaries.

Maybe so, the pretty young Negro girl who works at the Kentucky Fried Chicken place was saying, but maids are still making $20 a week in Sanford. It was dark now, and the anticipated crowd of militant black kids had not shown up at the Minit-Market across the street where there had been trouble nearly every night that week.

"Had you expected trouble in Sanford?" she was asked.

"No, I hadn't," she said. "I was surprised."

"How did you feel about it?"

She pursed her lips for a second and said, "Like it had to happen sometime." Then she finished packing a box full of fried chicken and started telling how her father was a country-club chef and she had gone to college, and she had "never known what prejudice meant" until now. Times, she said, had sure changed.

DAWSONVILLE, GEORGIA

There have always been two versions of the South, both wrong. On the one hand there is the *Gone With the Wind* South: bronze men in white linen suits, demure ladies with lace parasols, white-columned mansions framed by magnolias, courtly black butlers named Melvin, and gentlemen who make their own whiskey. On the other hand there is the *Tobacco Road* South: sawmill towns, pot-bellied sheriffs, hillbilly singers, Jackleg radio preachers, tin-roofed chicken houses, and gentlemen who make their own whiskey. So you can see that Margaret Mitchell and Erskine Caldwell didn't totally disagree.

Moonshining has been one of the few constant truths about the South for all of these years (90 percent of the nation's output comes from six Southeastern states), right up there with segregation and hard-shell religion. Rural Southerners always saw it as a God-given right, and took it personally when the feds started hounding them. In many of the Southern Appalachian counties, it was the biggest industry going. One guy made barrels for the still operators, another put strong springs in the drivers' cars, and a little old lady would initiate the early-warning system over a crank telephone when she saw agents sneaking into the woods.

The bootleggers, themselves, may have been the last of the true American folk heroes. It took a special breed of man to make moonshine or fly it over the treacherous backroads into Chattanooga and Atlanta with cops on his tail. Southern-style stock-car racing had as its early heroes old boys from the hills, uneducated and daring and in possession of damned good automobiles. They like to tell about the one in Dawsonville, Georgia, a runner during the week and a racing star on Sunday, who was fined $10 for speeding back home for another load but gave the cops two $10 bills. "I'll be back in an hour," he said, "and I'm payin' in advance."

All of this has been in the past tense, because moonshining and the way of life it represented are about to become as extinct as the buffalo. Good. Moonshine has done a lot of maiming and killing in its time, and the loss of tax revenue to the government is considerable. The woods where the stills used to be are being populated, the people have been alerted to the dangers of the stuff, and IRS agents have reached the point of scouting out the remaining stills with helicopters. The majority of the moonshine today is being brewed by big-time operators who can turn out more than 1,000 gallons a day (125 gallons was good work before the 1900s) and who make a better product. The little guy, the legendary Southern moonshiner who boiled his own, is as common now as the American Indian.

You've got to figure it's all over but the lying when you come here to the low hills about an hour north of Atlanta and pay a dollar to walk through Fred Goswick's Moonshine Museum. Dawson County was always a main supplier of homemade hooch to the black ghettos in Atlanta ("I bet you 99 percent of the people in the county had their hands in the moonshine business, one way or another," says an old-timer). And Fred Goswick was one of them: drove his first load into Atlanta when he was 15, abandoned many a car along U.S. Highway 19 when roadblocked by the feds, an expert on every kind of still. He says he quit fooling around with the stuff 15 years ago ("By the time you finish paying fines, you don't have anything left"), when he converted a chicken house·into a furniture store on a dirt road near the town square.

On a fourth of July, they held the formal opening of "The World's Only Moonshine Museum" in a false-front log cabin next to Goswick's Furniture Company. The main attraction is a dirt-floor room, exhibiting four types of stills, authentic to the point that the boilers and the wooden barrels came from working stills in the area ("Two carloads of revenuers came by one day to look at it and said there was a rumor I was making whiskey during the week in the stills"). Goswick, 33, a loose-jointed, open-faced, drawling mountain boy, thinks he has a big tourist attraction in the making. "Tell me what other way there is to see a real moonshine still," he says. "Ol' Carl over there, he ain't had a drink since the Fourth, he's so excited."

Ol' Carl is Carl Phillips, the guide at the museum. Carl Phillips is 63, toothless, born and raised in Dawson County, can't read or write, wears Levi overalls and a plaid flannel shirt and Hush Puppies, and in a 54-year career as a moonshiner spent a total of 69 months behind bars. "You might say it was kinda like payin' income tax," he was saying the other day. He was rolling a cigarette, shaking the tobacco out of a red tin of Prince Albert.

"When's the last time you were caught?" a tourist asked him.

"All I remember's, they give me prohibition," he said.

"You mean probation."

"Uh-huh. Prohibition."

"But you don't make the stuff anymore."

"Not to talk about," Carl Phillips said, suddenly finding

something to do up under the shade trees next to the museum.

GRANITEVILLE, SOUTH CAROLINA

It seems like ancient history, but it has been less than 150 years since the South went into the business of processing and finishing its own cotton. Early in the 19th century, when cotton was king, the South was getting the short end of the stick. Most of the nation's cotton was being grown here, but by the time the raw stuff had been processed in the East or in England and been sent back in the form of finished cotton products the man who had grown it in the first place wound up paying the most to use it. On top of that, some 50,000 poorer white Southerners were unemployed due to cheap slave labor. The obvious answer to both problems was the establishment of textile mills in the South, at the source of most of the raw material.

And so the mill village became a way of life in many parts of the rural, cotton-producing South. A company would build a mill and then put up a whole town around the mill. Droves of poor whites would descend on the new town, or mill village, and it was as though an umbilical cord attached them to "the company." The people lived in company houses, attended company-built churches, shopped at company stores, relaxed in company recreation areas and sent their children to company schools. The mill village became an inbred principality, a commune, an almost totally paternalistic system. "It is only necessary to build a manufacturing village of shanties in a healthy location in any part of the state," wrote one textile official in those early days, "to have crowds of poor people about you, seeking employment at half the compensation given to operatives in the North."

The man who wrote that was named William Gregg, an

ex-jeweler whom some call the father of the textile industry in the South. In 1845 Gregg was granted a charter to build a mill in the sandy western part of South Carolina between Columbia and Augusta near the Savannah River. Soon the Graniteville Company had a string of textile mills and mill villages in what is called Horse Creek Valley, and in spite of Gregg's brusque written feelings on running mill towns he became known as something of a social reformer. He eliminated child labor, insisted that all mill children attend school and everybody go to church, and was very much against strong drink. Through various depressions and wars the company thrived (it was the only mill in the South to stay open during the Civil War), and today its 11 plants employ 5,600 people, who turn out 150 million yards of cloth each year.

Horse Creek Valley today isn't as rowdy and desperate as it seemed to Erskine Caldwell when he wrote *God's Little Acre,* but neither is it Utopia. Some 20,000 people live in the 20-mile-long valley, which is an endless chain of unincorporated towns (Graniteville, Clearwater, Warrenville) and white frame houses (some built in 1850) and bars (Crow's Nest, The Gum Drop) and rambling red-brick or granite mills. The few Negroes huddle together in communities with names like Mixville and Boogers and Easy Street, and Klan membership is strong among whites. In most families, husband and wife work in the mills because starting pay is the minimum $1.76 an hour. Traditionally, their children have followed after them.

There are indications, however, that the days of the Southern mill towns are numbered. The enforcement of minimum wage laws some years ago cut into company profits. Although the industry is still strong (over the United States, 980,000 workers, in 7,000 plants earn more than $5 billion a year), synthetic fabrics are hurting. The threat of integration has prompted many textile companies to sell the old company houses to their inhabitants. In Horse Creek

Valley, regional planners not aligned with the textile mills are hitting hard at the necessity for bringing in new industry (and getting silence from the textile people). And, perhaps most telling, the young people are not staying on to work in the mills like they used to.

One of them who doesn't intend to stay is Wallace Greer, a senior and student-council president at Graniteville High School who is the son of a line foreman for a utility company serving the valley. By 3:15 Thursday afternoon, Wallace Greer and a buddy were already shooting pool in the rear of the Graniteville Cafe while three other teenagers hammered away on the pinball machines next to the pool table. Greer, a tall kid with long blond hair and striped mod trousers, said he has been saving money and will study electronic engineering at the University of Miami. He guessed that 15 of his 50 classmates will go to college and that half of the remainder will stay and work in the mills.

"What'd you do to save money?" somebody asked him.

"I've got a soul-rock band," he said. "Each one of us can make $100 a week on the side, just playing. You look at that and then look at $1.76 an hour, you don't want to stay." He swept back his hair and sank two balls on the break.

SUMTER, SOUTH CAROLINA

Stock-car racing is one of the phenomena that struck the South like a thunderclap when World War II ended, and it quickly became an underground culture native to the back-country regions of sawmills and turpentine and cotton fields and moonshine stills. You had all of these boys coming back from the war—"good old boys," we have come to know them—coming back home to places like Wilkesboro, North Carolina, and Mullins, South Carolina, and Welch, West Virginia, which is some kind of a letdown after Place Pigalle, and they had money and wheels and a lot of time on their hands. And so these little dirt tracks were scraped out of the piney woods of the Carolinas and carved in the high Appalachian valleys, and all of a sudden you had a new brand of American folk hero: the Southern stock-car driver.

For a while there, nobody seemed to know quite how to take it. It was, to a lot of people, so, you know, *crude*. Stock-car racing was an uninhibited world of moonshine runners, yellow bouffant hairdos, bourbon in Dixie cups, dusty oval tracks, pale lights, patched-up jalopies, tire-iron clubbings in the pits, Rebel yells, short-shorts, and prize money that would barely pay for the gas and tires. Sportswriters paid about as much attention to it as they did to professional wrestling. The Southern Snobs, sitting uptown in their latticework *Gone With the Wind* palaces, started cussing Erskine Caldwell again. But the boys kept pressing on, as inexorably as Junior Johnson riding Fireball Roberts' rear bumper for 83 laps, and it wasn't long before stock-car racing had replaced minor league baseball as the sport of the South's lower white classes.

Sad to report, stock-car racing has lost its innocence and jumped into the mainstream on us like almost everything else in the South. The sport got too big for its grease-stained britches. Detroit saw a gold mine and started taking these good old boys and giving them cars and tires and everything short of elocution lessons, and huge superspeedways started growing up in Daytona and Charlotte and Atlanta, and it soon became possible for an ex-chicken farmer to earn as much as $100,000 a year at racing fancy new high-powered automobiles. Just three weeks ago these boys hired themselves a New York lawyer and formed the Professional Drivers Association, and one of their first demands was for better seats for their wives during races. And it was just this Friday night, in Columbia, that a fancy testimonial dinner was held to honor a driver named LeeRoy Yarbrough, who set a record this season by winning $170,000 in prize money.

So you have to drive a lot of backroads these days to catch stock-car racing at its source, which is on a quarter-mile dirt track on the edge of a small town in the back country. One of the few of them left is Sumter Speedway, about four miles from the center of this town of 23,000, where on Friday night some 800 had paid $3.50 apiece to watch a 100-lap feature that offered $600 to the winner. Sumter Speedway is a classic. It squats among a cluster of scrubby, gnarled pines under the orange-mooned Carolina night, a caricature of splintered wooden bleachers and hard-packed sand and stagnant pools of water and pale yellow light bulbs on creosote telephone poles and no retaining walls whatsoever on the treacherous low-banked curves; and Clinnie Hyatt is going to do something about all of that.

Clinnie Hyatt is the promoter at Sumter Speedway, a dashing man in his late 30s who was born here and has steel-wool gray hair swept back like Hollywood and used to be a driver himself before he found out where the real money is. It was four o'clock Friday afternoon and Clinnie was leaving the Sumter Texaco station, which is his, with a roll of pale-red tickets he would sell at the track. "I hate to say it, but I don't think the dirt tracks will last more than about five more years," he was saying. "To me, they're the best. We'll have maybe a half-dozen guys go right over the bank, into that pasture, every night. The fans love the dirt tracks, and it's the biggest test for a driver. But the money now is on the big tracks." Before next season, as his bit toward the uplifting of stock-car racing, Clinnie Hyatt is going to put up some new bleachers.

It probably won't matter, anyway. The action is on the track. They had come from all over for this one, attracted by the big prize money: Lee Jackson from Pinewood, Sonny Ard from Florence, Arnold Hutto from Holly Hill, Lyn Hamm from Darlington. Warmups began at 7:30, and the racing ended at 12:30. Two cars flew off the track and into the swampy pasture beyond, the drivers unscathed, thanks to roll bars and shoulder straps. It was a delightful night of flying fenders, choking dust, clanging metal-on-metal, belching engines, yellow caution flags, swarming gnats, white bell-bottom rear-ends, Hush Puppies and—the essence—a driver, his car stalled on the first turn, ordered to the pits by the flagman, a tow truck backing up to him, four kids trying to get him started. "I ain't hooking up to that son-of-a-bitch," he yelled. "Give me a shove." The four kids heaved, and he started the engine, and he roared off into the inky Carolina night.

CHARLESTON, SOUTH CAROLINA

History clings to Charleston like moss hanging from a gnarled but beautiful swamp cypress. If you believe the travel folders, more things happened here "first" than in the Garden of Eden. The first shot of the Civil War was fired here, of course, against Fort Sumter in Charleston Harbor. The harbor was also where the first submarine was used in actual warfare, and where the first decisive victory of the American Revolution took place. Charlestonians keep up with their firsts so meticulously that they can tell you this is where the first artificial ice was made, the first book jackets and the first fireproof building. History is the name of the game here. This is *Gone With the Wind* country, pickled and preserved as though it were still the 17th century. "Charleston," those who haven't visited the place like to say, "it is a figment of the imagination."

Here she sits, though, like a proud old dowager, on a peninsula formed by two rivers that form Charleston Harbor, a musty collection of palm trees and narrow cobblestone streets and wrought-iron balconies and pink stucco-and-old-brick town houses and salt air and shuttered windows and ivy walls. It is paradise for connoisseurs of restoration, a town full of bronze plaques and historical markers paying homage to buildings that seem modern if they are less than 200 years old. It is a haven for writers and artists and actors and, in certain sections, homosexuals, who come here so they can do their things without any plastic trappings. It is a place where the Old South lives, oblivious to skyscrapers and smog and traffic jams and most of the other prices we are having to pay for, quote, Progress.

So the tourists come, at the rate of a half-million of them each year, to buy antiques and ride through the old section of town in horse-drawn surreys and visit Fort Sumter across the harbor and see the South the way it was at its elegant best. They don't drop a lot of money because it doesn't cost you much to look at old houses, but it is enough for the old-line Charlestonians that they come from all over just to marvel at the restorations. Besides, tourism is so, well, so *common*.

Which brings up the new Charleston. Another faction has come of age here, as in all of the other regions of the South. This new faction includes some sons and daughters of important old families, but mostly it is made up of young people who either came from somewhere else or never did their homework on Historic Charleston. These young ones think less about restorations and more about economic progress and unemployment and civic growth and, let us come out with it, racial equality. They can understand the historic significance of Charleston and they want to keep that part, but they can also see the folly in trying to live an 18th-century life in the 20th century.

This coming of a new Charleston is, in a sense, an inside job. It has happened even at the local Chamber of Commerce. Instead of some elegant old Southern gentleman with a thin gray mustache and a broad Carolina-cultured drawl and a family tree dating back to George Washington, you find a mod 30-year-old native of Augusta, Georgia, in charge of the chamber. Four years ago the chamber was a two-person operation, Curtis H. Carter was saying the other day, but now it is a platoon-sized 22 and only one of those 22 is a Charleston native and most of them are 30 years old or less.

"The old line is passing on, whether they like it or not," Carter said from his modern office overlooking the Ashley River. "Times ·have changed. People here are starting to realize we've got to keep up or we'll die. We've got to get new industry in here, and we've got to get some things like more motels and golf courses so we can build up our convention business. I mean, it's almost the 21st century." Charleston, he said, is no longer merely that elegant old section of town south of Broad Street on the tip of the peninsula. It is now suburbs across the rivers, and a 52 percent Negro population and a burgeoning middle class.

When this old Charleston falls, it will mark the passing of the last vestige of the South of *Gone With the Wind*. Up until now, Charleston's black people have been the obedient Southern butler types. But among the groups conventioning here recently was the Southern Christian Leadership Conference. The black hospital and sanitation workers have struck for a better shake. A spokesman for them said it all Monday after a meeting with the mayor. "We live here, too," she advised. So much for Olde Charleston.

JESUP, GEORGIA

The roads spill out of the big cities on the Eastern seaboard, beginning as high-speed interstate highways in Boston and Washington and Philadelphia and Baltimore, promising an easy trip all the way down, all of them headed south toward the sun. Through Richmond, Rocky Mount, Lumberton, Manning and Statesboro they come, blowing past the tobacco fields and sawmill towns and tenant shacks as though they weren't even there, everybody headed for

Florida, Land of Sunshine. Migratory birds, flying south for the winter.

So I told the wife here, Let's go.

Just sold everything and left, did you?

Yep. Kids gone and all, shoot, no reason to stay around and freeze again up home. Hey, when do we pick up the interstate again?

Soon the interstates begin to fade, and the worn old U.S. highways take over. U.S. 1, 301, 17 and 82. Tired roads that have seen millions of them come and go, oil-stained roads groaning under the load of buses and trucks and campers and station wagons and house trailers frantically fighting their way south toward the great funnel just north of the Florida line in piney-woods southeast Georgia. Heat and mosquitoes and pulp plants and black-water creeks and dust and sweat. Kids fighting in the back seat. Swarthy truck drivers down to their undershirts. Bloodshot eyes and aching kidneys and pink skin. Rolling on, heading south, into Paradise.

The first signs begin to appear in South Carolina, near the Georgia line. Palmetto and palm trees, swamps and moss and cypress, a faint odor of salt water in the air. And after that, the ugly man-made signs that Florida is near. Pecans, Pralines, Shake and Burger. Liquor, EATS, Live Alligators, Horne's, Stuckey's, Truckers Welcome, Rooms $5 Couple, Madame Zorra Palmist, Last Chance and See Silver Springs. Motels sprawled in the sand, jammed with cars by sundown and abandoned by 10 o'clock in the morning. Chenille bedspreads, oranges, billboards, free ice water, clean rest rooms, gas wars, Confederate-flag bedspreads, See Live Monkeys, Ride Glass-Bottom Boats.

There are 17 motels listed in the telephone book in Jesup, Georgia, population about 6,000. It is an old game, the only game in town. "Three million cars a year come through this intersection," says a newspaperman in a small South Georgia town. Industry? Tourists will do. Flying south for the winter, buying gas and sandwiches and beer and Cokes and oil and sunglasses and pecans and bedspreads and lodging. The bigger your sign out front, the more you catch. Get the speed limit down so we can catch their eyes. Summer rates, winter rates. Checkout time 10 A.M. Extra bed, $3. Drive Safely and Bring Them Back Alive.

A truck stop in lower South Carolina, 10 o'clock on a dusty late-summer morning, three big diesels parked in the gravel out front, three sweaty drivers sitting at the counter inside while a girl with a name like Myrtice empties the grounds from the stainless steel coffee urn. Postcards in a rack next to the door, cards that show a henpecked little guy writing a note home: "Having a wonderful time, wish you were *her*." Sign behind the counter: JUST A CUP OF COFFEE TO YOU, BUT A REPUTATION TO US. Another room with five pinball machines and a pool table. Showers and bunks in the back.

Hey, Myrtice, what happened to the other girl?

Ruth? Got married.

That right? Who to?

Fred. Guy that drives for Dixie-Ohio. More coffee?

Naw, hon, I gotta make time. You gonna wait for me?

Till hell freezes over, baby. You know that. See ya.

Yeah. Don't take any wooden ones.

I'm a lady. Don't you know that?

And outside, on the road, the race is on. The campers and cars and trailers and buses and trucks are swirling the dust beside the road, everybody headed south for a load of grapefruit or two weeks of sun or a whole new life. Headed toward the sun, to Paradise, to downstate New York.

MIAMI, FLORIDA

One thing about working in a meat market, the temperature on the sidewalk is somebody else's problem. Faustinio Menendez had spent most of the morning in the freezers at La Casa Sierra, a combination grocery store and meat wholesaler in Miami's Cuban section, and when he came out it was noon and waves of heat were shivering up from the white concrete on Eighth Street SW and beating against the rows of neat one- and two-story buildings that line the busy, wide boulevard. The Cubans themselves refer to Eighth Street as "Little Havana," with reason. What used to be a dying inner-core neighborhood has become a replica of what Miami's 250,000 Cuban refugees know as home: narrow coffee shops, fruit markets, Latin music on the jukeboxes, Spanish on all the plate glass windows, an occasional notice that says WE SPEAK ENGLISH.

Menendez wore a long white coat and a white plastic helmet that protects workers from the meathooks hanging from the ceiling in the freezer. He took another swig from a canned soft drink called Matevan and smiled and said, in good English, "Even this is the same. In Cuba, it is called Mate."

"Is anything different here?"

"Not much," he said. "For some, Miami is better."

"Do you plan to go back to Cuba?"

"Maybe. If Castro leaves. Maybe."

"You belong to a Cuban association, I guess."

A toothy smile spread across the face of Faustinio Menendez, who left Cuba 18 months ago. "You kidding?" he said. "I'm too busy working to go to meetings."

They started coming 10 years ago, of course, the very moment Fidel Castro took over their country. There was a period when they were captives and had to get out the best way they could, but for nearly four years now they have

235

been able to come to America on regular airlifts and today there are some 340,000 refugees from Cuba in the United States. The Cuban Refugee Center in Miami likes to point out that the refugees have been "resettled" in all 50 of the states, that there are 63,000 of them in New York and 6,500 in Massachusetts and even 1,800 in Georgia. But the fact is, the minute they are able to put together, say, $3,000, they resettle once more in Miami because Miami has become the closest second to Havana in the world. In 1959 there was a cluster of 22,000 Cubans in Greater Miami, but today Cubans make up nearly one-fourth of the population.

The larger point to be made about the Cubans in America, however, is the type of citizens they have become. There have been screams, particularly from the conservatives, that the refugees are draining the welfare budgets. A recent statistical survey, in contrast, shows that we ought to have more people like the Cubans come to visit us now and then. Last year, for instance, a taxable $317 million was generated in Miami by the Cuban community. It is generally agreed here that the cost of processing Cuban refugees has been repaid at least four times by taxes on Cuban-generated business. Only 20,000 of them are on welfare, an estimated 90 percent of those being over 60 or disabled. The average Cuban refugee has been a middle-class worker or businessman who left everything he owned in Cuba and is quickly making it back here through hard work.

Faustinio Menendez, for example, is not too far from the "average" Cuban refugee in spite of two years' education at Florida Southern in Lakeland. This same survey showed that 56 percent of the male heads-of-household were high school graduates or better. In Cuba, Menendez owned grocery and meat businesses with his father and his brother. They were doing well, but Faustinio didn't care for the Castro system and he got his family—a wife and two small children—out of Cuba a year and a half ago. He was lucky, he says. He got a job right off the bat working for Roy

Sierra, who had worked for *him* before leaving Cuba 10 years ago.

"I would have left earlier, too, but at first I thought the [Castro] regime was not going to last," Menendez was saying the other day. "I made definite plans to leave when President Johnson said anybody was welcome." That was the beginning of the twice-daily airlifts that bring 180 refugees a day, five days a week, to Miami.

"What if Castro were to fall?" he was asked.

"I think most Cubans want to go back," he said, "but it would depend. The young ones, they don't know anything about Cuba and are happy here. The carpenters and the plumbers had a hard time in Cuba, but here they have color television and cars and air conditioning. The owners, maybe the owners don't want to start all over again for the third time. I don't know what would happen. We are happy in Miami. It is very much like Cuba." In the papers, as Faustinio Menendez went back to work in the freezers, there was a story quoting Fidel Castro as saying he was glad to get rid of the Cubans who had chosen America.

MOBILE, ALABAMA

The place is in a musty old two-story brick building on a narrow one-way street, Conti Street, stuck between an aging resident hotel and a place that sells carpets and drapes, and the only identification is a flaking white sign hanging over the sidewalk with red lettering that says Littleton's Gymnasium. It has been there for at least 40 years and it has changed very little. On the first floor there are metal lockers and massage tables and an exercise bike, and upstairs there is a steam box and a large room full of punching bags and barbells and mirrors. You could walk in there blindfolded and take one whiff and you would know where you were, because nothing smells quite like an old gymnasium.

At noon, Tommie Littleton had it all to himself. The businessmen would not be in until midafternoon for their massages and steam baths and light workouts, and the only customer was a muscled-up weightlifter, who sat on one of the tables upstairs and ran a hand through his greasy black hair while he read a comic book. Tommie Littleton dropped a dime in the pay phone and dialed a number and then waited, scratching his chest through a white T-Shirt imprinted on the front with UNIVERSITY MILITARY SCHOOL in washed-out maroon letters.

"Hello," he was saying. "I want to talk to Tillman . . . Tillman, the one's brother's a fighter . . . Yeah, that's him . . . Oh. Tomorrow? . . . No, I'll call back tomorrow . . ."

Littleton hung up and said, "He's off today."

"His brother's pretty good, you say."

"Good kid. Good puncher. Only about 20."

"Are there any other fighters in town?"

"You kidding?" he said. "Nobody fights anymore."

Mobile used to be a good fight town, 30 or 40 years ago, when boxing had some respectability as a sport. For one thing it was a tough shipping town, meaning there were always a lot of seamen around who would pay good money to watch a fight. For another, there were enough Negro kids and poor whites and sailors hungry enough to fight for a buck. So Mobile, in the 1920s and 1930s, had a lot of gyms around and they were busy every day with young fighters who would work out during the week and then ride to New Orleans or even Tampa to fight on the weekends. Or they would stay and fight right here. Tommie Littleton remembers when 1,000 people would crowd into the upstairs room at his gym to watch the fights.

Littleton was a part of it then. He was born on the west side of New York City, in a tough neighborhood where "you had to fight to stay even," and he fought his first professional fight when he was 14. He wound up in Mobile in the late 1920s, when he was about 35 years old, and he fought in towns all over the South. He ran the gym and fought and was boxing coach at Spring Hill College, and his last fight was when he was 40 years old and Jack Dempsey brought a stable of boxers into town for a show. Since there was nobody else around to fight Dempsey's light-heavy-weight, Tommie Littleton volunteered and decked the heavier and younger man in the sixth round. "We were trying to get me a fight with Young Stribling in Macon," he remembers, "but I guess he figured he had everything to lose by fighting me and that was it."

Those days will never come back, of course. Boxing is dead here and everywhere else. Gamblers and television helped kill it, and nobody wants to fight for a living anymore because it isn't worth it. There are fights in New Orleans on Monday nights that draw up to 2,000 fans, but that's it for the Gulf Coast. Now and then there will be fights in an armory in Mobile, but they don't amount to much. About the only fighter left in Mobile is a 20-year-old kid named Jack Tillman, whose father was a good one in Mobile until boxing died and he had to take a job on a garbage truck. Jack Tillman works out at the fire station where his brother works, and he has won 17 of his first 18 fights. Beyond that, there is nothing.

"Amateur boxing, that's what you've gotta have first," said Tommie Littleton. He was leaning on a parking meter in front of his place now, soaking up the bright noon sun, well preserved at 75 with only a trace of cauliflower ear to show for the years of fighting. "You gotta start with amateurs and bring 'em along before you can have professionals. It's a nucleus."

"What're the chances?" he was asked.

"Of what?"

"Getting amateurs going."

"Nothing," he said. "The gamblers ruined it. Them, and the way things changed. Nobody'll fight anymore. You get some hungry kid to fight, soon as he gets the wrinkles out of his stomach he quits. Nobody's hungry anymore. Maybe that's good." Then Tommie Littleton wandered back inside to tidy up his place. He does a pretty good business, he said, with businessmen who come around every afternoon to keep their bodies in shape.

There is little in the history of Greene County that would set it apart from the other counties of west Alabama or of Mississippi, which lies sprawled in the heat only 30 miles from the county seat of Eutaw. This area was first settled around 1820 by people who were running from the more populous areas of east Alabama and Georgia and Tennessee, and the softly rolling, lush, almost tropical land was quickly planted in cotton and cleared for grazing. This part of the country came to be known as the black belt, a land of rich black soil and huge cotton crops and fat cattle and large plantations, and black belt did not refer only to the color of the soil. It also referred to Negroes. Black people made up well over half of the population, and they were bound in the strictest system of slavery known to the South.

Today, because it is so isolated and cut off from the mainstream, Greene County still seems to be a pastoral scene from the past. The steadily dwindling population is down to some 13,000, 81 percent of the people being black. The only town in the county of any size is Eutaw (pop. 2,784), which presents the usual Deep South small-town image: stately old white-owned homes, ramshackled Negro shacks, white-painted courthouse in a trim square, one movie house, sleepy hotel, white cops cruising aimlessly around the dull and dusty streets, most of the people on their farms feeding cattle or looking after crops. There is really only one major difference between the Greene County of today and of yesterday, but it is a whopper. The Negroes, these sons of yesterday's slaves, are in charge.

On August 11, 1969, with *Gone With the Wind* playing at the Eutaw theater, the people of Greene County went to the polls in a special election ordered by the U.S. Supreme Court. Fifteen years ago there would have been only three Negroes registered to vote, but this time there were 4,000— two times the number of white voters—and the results were predictable. Black citizens gained a 4–1 majority on the county commission and a 3–2 edge on the school board. The day of the inauguration brought a parade, picnic, swearing-in and inaugural ball. A lot of whites stayed home that day. But the blacks and civil rights workers who had been guiding them for many months celebrated into the night and then started worrying about how they were going to raise the Greene County per capita income from its current level of $865, which is one-fourth the national average and nearly one-third the average for the Southeast.

Greene County is a monument to all of those people, all of those years, all of those events, all of the sweat and the bloodshed and the sacrifice that took place in the South in the late 1950s and the early 1960s. Once the spotlight swung to Birmingham and Little Rock and Selma, it was inevitable that one day the majority who live in a county were going to govern that county. The voter registrars came, and the whites who had always controlled the lives of 80 percent of the people must have known what was coming when young Greene County Negroes began peacefully demonstrating in 1965. And it is only the beginning, in the black belt. Sumter County, to the southwest, is almost certain to fall in the next election.

One of the four black men elected to the county commission last month is Harry Means, who is 45 and has a wife and four kids and owns or controls 800 acres six miles south of Eutaw on the road to Demopolis. Means is by no means a typical Greene County resident, black or white, because he studied agriculture for three years in college at Tuskegee and earns about $15,000 from hay and soybeans and 200 head of cattle. But his thinking is representative of the new Negro thinking in the black belt.

"I guess I started thinking about running when everybody started registering in '65," he was saying Saturday night in the den of his wide brick home. He had attended a commission meeting at the courthouse that morning and then spent the afternoon in the fields. "I started thinking about all those years of slavery, and how every time an appointed job opened up it went to a white man, so I just did it."

"You never thought of leaving, did you?" he was asked.

"Leaving?" he said.

"Going somewhere else to live, or work."

He looked incredulous. "I was born and raised here. We had a little property. Lot of the other ones left, but they didn't have no property. If we can get some industry in here, won't nobody have to go off."

"Your kids want to stay?"

"Sure," Harry Means said. "They got a chance now. Everybody got a chance, including poor white folks. This is a new day we've got here now."

LAFAYETTE, LOUISIANA

Longfellow's "Evangeline" did for the Acadians what Steinbeck's *The Grapes of Wrath* did for the Okies. Each story told about the wholesale migration of a dispossessed people, and any school kid who read Longfellow's long poem knows the general history of the Acadians, or Cajuns, as they call themselves. The Acadians were French peasants living in what is now called Nova Scotia, and because of their rebelliousness and their language differences they were driven out in 1755 by the ruling British. Some 1,500 of them eventually wound up in the bayou country of lower Louisiana, and by 1785 that part of the country was firmly held by perhaps 5,000 of these people who were totally distinct from any other group in North America.

The Cajuns had a reputation for being prolific, and their numbers grew rapidly over the years. Holed up in their own hard-to-reach corner of the world, all of the effects of isolation set in. The French language, Catholicism, spicy foods, hard drinking, *joie de vivre* and intramarriage ruled. The Cajuns were poor and uneducated trappers and shrimpers, but they had style. When the English language crept into the area, the Cajuns joyfully took it on and created a *patois* that brought a bushel of Cajun jokes. The Cajun would sign a letter "wit' deep infection" and say "aromatic shootgun" for automatic shotgun and talk about a "police petroleum car wit' de syringe on how-you-call fool blast, mon, I gawr-on-tee you, me, yeah." The Cajun was, according to one who is now a New Orleans newspaperman, "the hillbilly of the bayou country."

About the only place you will find this uneducated, garrulous specimen today is in the repertoire of a night-club comedian (one is a Slidell, Louisiana, automobile salesman named Bud Fletcher, alias Cyprien Robespierre, who has recorded more than a half-dozen party albums). There are an estimated one million Cajuns now, one-fourth of them concentrated around Lafayette, Abbeville and Crowley, halfway between Beaumont and New Orleans in swampy scrub land that is rich in rice, oil, cotton and sugar cane. Transportation, television, public schools and military service have brought the Cajun out of the bayous. French and *patois* are still spoken in the smaller towns, but mostly by the older people. The young ones are in miniskirts and bell-bottoms, swinging at the University of Southwestern Louisiana (called the "Cajun college") in Lafayette.

"Me, I was born in one of the small towns and when I went into the first grade all I could speak was French," Ken

Blanc, manager of a Lafayette motel, was saying the other day. "I still speak French when I want to. A lot of Cajuns won't do that anymore because they're ashamed to be Cajun. Some of these politicians, the only time they'll speak French is when they're running for office. Television, that changed a lot of things. Even in the small towns, kids are dressing and talking like kids anywhere. Some of the things that have happened are good, but I hate to see Cajuns get like everybody else."

This is not to say that this part of the country has flattened out and become just another piece of modern America. Not by a long shot. When you drive through the small towns and communities like Breaux Bridge and Indian Bayou and St. Martinville, there is a feeling of being in southern France. Many radio and television stations carry Cajun music and French-language programs (a Lafayette TV station once ran *Gunsmoke* with French subtitles). The big churches are Catholic, the small ones Baptist. In the Lafayette (pop. 70,000) telephone directory there are 640 Broussards and 380 Heberts, only 230 Smiths and 100 Joneses. You go into a restaurant, they wait to see what language you use before they commit themselves.

Saturday, one of the big events of the year was held in Crowley, a small town some 20 miles west of here. Parkerson Avenue, the main drag, had been roped off and thousands of natives had come to town for the 33rd annual International Rice Festival. Swarms of people moved up and down the street, taking in the carnival rides and games-of-chance, drinking beer, eating spicy Cajun food, observing a rice-eating championship, arguing the merits of the 29 dark-skinned beauty contestants and throwing softballs at a Jaycee who would be dumped into a barrel of water if you hit the yellow target.

"No Broussard can hit me," said the Jaycee.

"Dot make me mod, mon you bet," yelled the laughing Cajun in a straw cowboy hat, who wound up and cut loose with the softball and dunked the Jaycee. The Cajun went into a little dance on the spot, and then everybody moved up the street to watch the beauty contest. It was won by Deborah Elizabeth Jones.

NEW ORLEANS, LOUISIANA

They stood in front of the heavy old black wrought-iron gate on St. Peter Street, shuffling their feet on the buckled and worn sidewalk beneath a trombone case with the words PRESERVATION HALL on it in tarnished bronze letters, and they could hear the noise drifting through the carriageway from Bourbon Street. There were three of them, three of these beautiful old black men with sad faces and gnarled hands and gold-capped teeth, and while they waited for somebody to come and open the gate they stood there in the chalky glare of a streetlight and they talked about Clarence Hall.

"It was a nice funeral," one of them said.

"The band play?" he was asked.

"Oh, sho. Three songs. Marched eight blocks."

"How old was he?"

"Don't know. I played with him 40 years, though."

Another of the men, a member of Alvin Alcorn's band, the band that would work Preservation Hall that night, crushed a cigarette on the sidewalk and said, "We're startin' to conk out now. Ain't many of us left no more. That's three died right here in the last two weeks." Then the man with the key came out of the shadows and opened the huge gate, and the last of the old New Orleans jazzmen shuffled into the musty little hall. The sounds of their battered horn cases hitting the oily board floor came back at them from the peeling plaster ceiling, and it was all like visiting a museum in the middle of the night.

At the turn of the century, when there was a jazz joint on

nearly every corner in this town, there were literally thousands of musicians to play them. For the most part they were black kids, born to poverty, kids whose only chance was music. They would learn how to blow a horn from their father or an uncle or a grandfather, and by the time they were 15 they were playing the dives in Storyville or working the pleasure boats on Pontchartrain or playing one-nighters on the road. Now and then a Louis Armstrong made it big, but most of them were known only to an exclusive circle of jazz buffs. They played their kind of music, more for themselves than for anybody else, and out of it came the only kind of music that this country can call its own.

But now, finally, time is catching up with them. Israel Gorman died four years ago. He has been joined by Kid Howard and Creole George Guesnon and Papa John Joseph, and now Clarence Hall. There are no more than 200 of the old New Orleans jazzmen still living, most of them beset with things like arthritis and bad hearts and failing eyesight. You spend a lifetime sleeping all day, playing all night, working the road, smoking too much and eating too little, bad things are going to happen to you. The only thing that had kept a lot of them going was their music, and it is not irrational to assume that fewer of them would still be alive today if not for Preservation Hall.

Preservation Hall is dedicated to keeping pure New Orleans jazz alive. The place itself is purposely unwashed. The front panel of the piano is out and the windows are caked with dirt and there is no air conditioning or heat. The musicians sit in straight-backed wooden chairs and the customers (about three dozen at a time) pay a minimum of $1 to sit on backless benches to hear the real thing. It is in stark contrast with the rest of the French Quarter, which rings with the sounds of rock 'n' roll and commercial Dixieland and the raucous pitches of strip-joint barkers now. Preservation Hall is so ugly it is beautiful.

The important thing, though, is what it has done for people like Earl Humphrey. He is 67 now, and it has been a long haul. He was born in New Orleans, learned to play the trombone when he was 10, went on the road when he was 17, but had to take a job as a janitor at the University of Virginia during the Depression. For 25 years Earl Humphrey was a janitor, and for the last 15 of those years he never played his horn. So in 1962, when his wife died, he was alone and out of his element and drawing a pension and ready to die.

"This place kinda saved me," he was saying Thursday night. The band was taking a break, and he had slipped into a back room and was sipping bourbon from a paper cup. "If I couldn't play here a couple of times a week, I don't know."

"You don't have any children, any family?"

"All I got," Earl Humphrey said, "is my horn."

HOUSTON, TEXAS

One time Bob Hope said the place is furnished in Early Farouk, and Hope wasn't kidding. This is where the action is, the combat operations center for Astrodomain, and if you're going to play around with dollars in increments of millions at a time you might as well do it with a little style. The boomerang-shaped desk sits in a field of lush carpet and is flanked by dappled mirrors and ancient Chinese wood carvings and six-foot-tall Thai dragons, and on one wall is a particularly impressive painting of the Astrodome.

The man who occupies all of this has a Faroukian look and air about him, too, which is only fitting and proper. Now the Judge is showing the spread to a visitor, and he is like a kid showing a pal what he got for Christmas. The Judge, Roy Hofheinz, is waddling toward the painting with a sly grin behind his horn-rimmed glasses and a mound of a stomach jiggling behind a tent-sized pair of chartreuse slacks and a short-sleeved white sport shirt, and he is saying the painting was done by a bright local artist.

"It's a nice painting," he is told.

"It moves, too," he says.

"How's that?"

"Watch." The Judge flips the side of the frame and, lo, the frame is on runners. When the frame is slid out of the way, the wall is found to be hollow. Behold, there stands a room-sized bar. "Some of my friends," the Judge says, "get tired of art after a while."

Roy Hofheinz may not be the richest millionaire in Texas today (his $15 million would be walking-around money for H. L. Hunt), but he'll do for a prototype. The son of a Beaumont laundry-truck driver, he has all of those flamboyant ways we like to see in our millionaires. There is the rags-to-riches element, naturally: first job was selling newspapers ("I never gave away my 'extras,' I sold 'em on the corners"), flunked out of Rice University in his freshman year, was a member of the Texas Legislature at the age of 22, made his first million and "retired" before he was 40. Now, as king of the Astrodomain, as they call the complex taking in the world's first domed stadium and an amusement park called Astroworld and other holdings, he lives his life to the hilt. Smoking nearly two dozen cigars a day and sipping on a strange concoction of Jack Daniels bourbon and Diet Dr. Pepper, he spends up to 16 hours a day holed up inside the Astrodome making calls on a gold telephone all over the country.

The Astrodome, of course, has been his *pièce de résistance*. You have to see this place to believe it. They could put the 18-story Shamrock Hilton Hotel in the center and there would be room at the top of the 208-foot dome, a dome that blips out of the brown Texas prairie like a giant gray toadstool. The Astrodome is a city unto itself, a place where everything from Houston Astros baseball games to political rallies are held. And inside, in the labyrinth of tunnels, there are such accouterments as a Presidential Suite and VIP boxes that go for $15,000 a baseball season on a five-year-lease basis. Billy Graham is supposed to have called it the "eighth wonder of the world," to give you an idea.

But, alas, Judge Hofheinz (he was a county judge for several years) is not universally loved. Most of his unpopularity in certain circles can be traced to his years in politics, particularly to his two terms as mayor of Houston. Another thing has been the Astrodome. "I don't know what it is," he was saying Thursday, "except that people look at something like this as a way to make money for a promoter. They say, 'He's using our money to make himself a fortune.' Well, hell, this is the last self-amortizing stadium in the country. This whole town is making money off this place. I took all the risks and did all of the work, and when the last penny is made I'll make it."

It was slightly past noon, and the judge and his pretty bride (she was his long-time secretary and they married after his first wife died) were looking out on the floor of the Astrodome, lined off for football now, from his special box high above the gaily colored stands. In front of him was a copy of the Buffalo paper, with a streamer announcing that city's plans for a domed stadium. Hofheinz is helping out.

"The Judge can't stop working," his wife said.

"Tried once," he said.

"He was in his 30s and he'd made what they call his first million, but after three months of retirement he came back."

"I don't even like to remember that," Hofheinz said, suddenly remembering a call he had to make (he never writes letters). He snapped up the gold phone at his fingertips and was barking into the phone to somebody, long-distance, and his wife suggested a tour of the place. "It's a nice house," she smiled.

The pale yellow lights hung in the hot Texas night like bare lightbulbs in an incubator. Now and then a sudden wisp of cool air would whip through the slats in the skeletal grandstand and raise small whirlpools of brown dust off the churned-up floor of the rodeo ring. The show wouldn't start for another hour, but several hundred people had already taken seats in the stands and were silently squinting toward the chutes where two dozen men were calming the bulls and the steers and the frightened young calves. In the distance, beyond the black silhouettes of the exposition buildings on the fairgrounds, the people who were sitting high enough could see a ferris wheel spinning against the blue-velvet sky.

The cowboys were hanging around the chutes, looking over the stock and joking with each other and grinning at the perky young girls in tight cowgirl pants, but Bubba Goudeau sat on the second row, in beige denims and pearl-buttoned Western shirt and gray 10-gallon hat and scruffy cream-colored boots, and the wiry kid next to him was about to cry.

"Damn, Bubba. I told 'em you wanted to go out *tomorrow* night," the kid said. "Damn."

"Look, it's all right," Goudeau said.

"Makin' you come down here and everything. Damn."

"Don't matter. Rather be here, anyway."

And then the parade around the ring began, with pretty cowgirls riding prancing horses and carrying the American flag, and Bubba Goudeau knew it was right. The rodeo is where he belongs. He stood when the flag came by. The scars the bulls have given him stood out like etchings when he raised his face toward the lights.

Bubba Goudeau is a cowboy. He uses the term proudly, like other men do when they call themselves a Marine or a senator or a doctor. He never lived on a ranch and never roped cows for a living. This is a different kind of cowboy, a rodeo cowboy. "You put a rodeo cowboy on a gentle horse and tell him to go out and rope a cow, he wouldn't know what to do," he says. When he was 13 he saw a rodeo and decided he wanted to try it and now he is 26 and the only important thing he has ever done is ride bulls. From January to the end of October he stays on the road and rides bulls at rodeos in places like Boulder, Colorado, and Odessa, Texas, and Deadwood, South Dakota, and then he comes back home to Alvin, which is between Galveston and Houston in the flat brown prairieland of southeast Texas, to lick his wounds. He earned around $12,000 this year in prize money.

It is not an easy way to make a living. Four months ago, in this same rodeo ring in Angleton, a cowboy was trampled to death by a bull. That doesn't happen very often, that a man is killed in the ring, but Bubba Goudeau's scars and plastic surgery show you the dangers. Even so, the real danger comes from traveling the interminable Rodeo Cowboys Association circuit, which took a half-dozen lives this season in highway accidents. But for the 600 or 700 professional cowboys in the RCA, it can be profitable. The best cowboy going today is a 24-year-old from Oregon, Larry Mahan, who competes in five events and travels in his own plane and has just set an all-time record by taking $53,000 in prize money.

This week they were holding the 27th annual Brezoria County Fair, the largest county fair in the state of Texas, and some 200 cowboys had come into Angleton, a county-seat town with a population of 9,000, to compete in the rodeo. It would run three straight nights, and when they totaled up the points at the end the winner of the bull-riding event would walk off with $350 for his eight-second ride astride a 1,500-pound wild bull. The investment was a $15 entry fee, and risking your neck. Provided he could win, that would be a lot better than Bubba Goudeau could do with the honky-tonks he runs in Alvin and Huntsville.

"Those things are real good investments, though," he was saying as they finished the bucking-horse competition and moved on to the calf roping. "I figure I can ride bulls for six or seven more years, and then maybe I'll have me some more clubs. Only time I ever worked for a living was when I worked for the government for three and a half years. I was married then."

There is a great similarity between rodeo cowboys and the stock-car drivers who run small-town dirt tracks in the Southeast. They may represent the last of the American folk heroes. The lives of these cowboys are made up of the odor of leather and horses, the sounds of thrashing wild animals and wounded men, the feel of muscle and hard ground. "You know what we call a bad accident?" Bubba Goudeau said. "A hand injury. When something fixes it so you can't hold on to that rope and ride the next bull. I don't mind the face, the leg, anything. Just so he don't get my hand, I don't mind."

LONGVIEW, TEXAS

It is Saturday night in East Texas, and the natives are restless. At the Reo Palm Isle Ballroom, Inc., on the outskirts of Longview, more than 1,000 farmers and ranchers and oil-field hands are launching into their weekly orgiastic ritual of boozing and dancing with their ladies at the biggest dance hall in East Texas. Out in the asphalt parking lot, which is bigger than two football fields, the cars and the pickup trucks are jammed together like a herd of motionless cattle in the blustery Texas night. Inside is a blur. Cartons of opened Cokes, Sprites and Seven-Ups sit on top of the bar so the waitresses can serve setups without breaking stride. The band sits beneath a Schlitz clock and plays "San Antonio Rose." At the tables, which are draped with red linen tablecloths, men in white short-sleeve dress shirts and snap-on ties sit in straight-back wooden chairs and pour bourbon from bottles they have brought through the door in brown paper sacks.

And the owner, a hulking man named Glynn Keeling, is standing on the edge of the hardwood dance floor with a big smile on his face. He is counting the empty tables, and there aren't many of them left. "It's not even 10 o'clock," he is saying.

"Is it always like this?" somebody asks.

"Ought to see it on Nigger Night."

"What's that?"

"Sundays. We bring in a nigger band. You can't move."

But tonight, Saturday night, is the big one. Country music for the all-white over-30 set. Admission $1.50 and you get your hand stamped at the door. Red-sequined dresses and Levis and gold slippers. Grandma is trying the bugaloo, and it is a lot like watching your own mother headline a strip show.

East Texas always has been in a league of its own. This is not the Texas of sprawling cattle ranches and Neiman-Marcus and cowboys and NASA and the Astrodome and filthy-rich oilmen. This is the Texas that was settled after the Civil War by people who would be damned if they would put up with Reconstruction in Tennessee, Georgia, Alabama and Mississippi. This is the Texas of small dirt farms and truck stops and high school football and moonshine whiskey and hardshell Baptists and George Wallace; a dreary, monotonous, slowly rolling scrubland that makes a place like the Reo Palm Isle Ballroom look like an oasis.

The dance halls dot the landscape like blinking oil derricks. Danceland, Roundup Club, Horseshoe Lounge, Ranch House, Al Perry's Country Club. They came in the 1930s, when a 40-mile-long oil field was discovered, and for the most part they were geared to the oil worker's tastes: inexpensive, less than elegant, big dance floor, plenty of booze, country music.

And they have been boot camps to 30 years' worth of country musicians. Perhaps half of the big stars working out of Nashville today came up out of the clubs in this part of the country: Ernest Tubb, Hank Thompson, Lefty Frizzell, Faron Young. Even Glen Campbell owes a debt to what he calls "fightin' and dancin' clubs" in the Southwest. "Some ol' drunk would throw a half-dollar at you and yell, 'Tumbling Tumbleweed,' and if you knew what was good for you you'd play 'Tumbling Tumbleweed,' " he says.

"Yeah," Jimmy Caldwell was saying, "but what's worse is when they throw a five-dollar bill at you and tell you to quit playing." Jimmy Caldwell ought to know. He is 29 years old and has spent most of his life playing places like the Reo Palm Isle. He spent eight years working out of Las Vegas with his own country band, Jimmy Caldwell and The Problems ("I got a lot of compliments for that name"), but came back home a year ago to Gilmer, a little town north of Longview. Now he works as a carpenter during the daytime and leads the band at Reo on Wednesday, Friday and Saturday nights, writing songs on the side and hoping to make it big someday in country music.

Saturday night at 10:30, during an intermission, he sat at a bar in a white pearl-buttoned Western shirt and Levis, an angular young man with bowed legs and slick black hair and wind-whipped skin. Cigarette smoke clung to the blue-lit ceiling like a low cloud, and there were lines at the rest rooms.

"I was making a dollar a minute in Vegas," he said.

"What'd you leave for?"

"Wasn't worth it. Wife got lonesome, me being gone like that. We're buying a place now, up at Gilmer. Figure I'll keep on playing and writing. I ain't got to go to Nashville, way I see it. Reckon they'll have to come to me one day."

Jimmy Caldwell inhaled the rest of his Coke and went

back to the bandstand. "Here's the old Ex-Lax song," he said into the microphone, "called, 'You Got Me Running.'" The tide swept back onto the dance floor while Jimmy Caldwell thumbed his electric bass guitar and wailed the words toward the bar across the room.